BURNOUT
AND HEALTH PROFESSIONALS

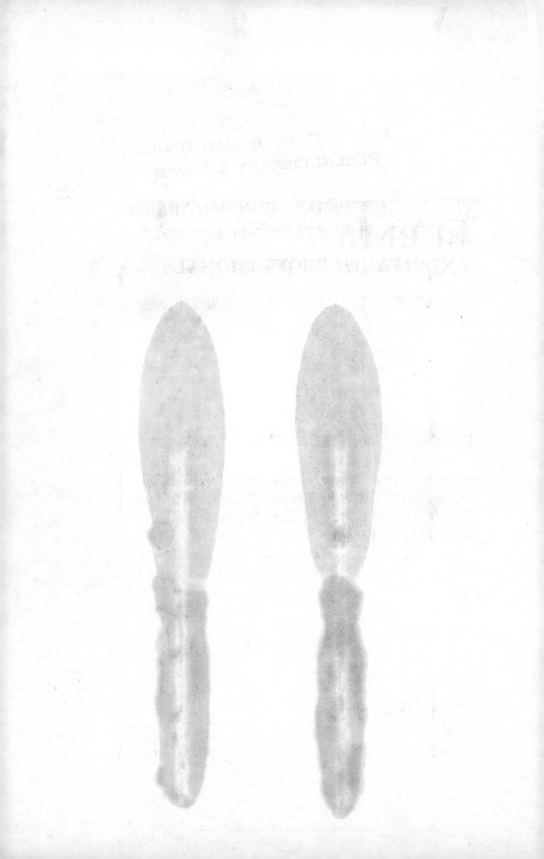

BURNOUT
AND HEALTH PROFESSIONALS:
Manifestations and Management

by
Thomas W. Muldary, Ph.D.

Psychologist in Private Practice, Ann Arbor, Michigan;
Lecturer, Psychology, Eastern Michigan University,
Ypsilanti, Michigan; National University,
San Diego, California

A Capistrano Publication

APPLETON-CENTURY-CROFTS / Norwalk, Connecticut

0-8385-0892-8

Copyright ©1983 **by Capistrano Press, Ltd.**
All rights reserved. No part of this book may be reproduced in any manner without written permission from the publisher.

Capistrano Press, Ltd.
12882 Valley View, Suite 15, Garden Grove, California, 92645

83 84 85 86 / 10 9 8 7 6 5 4 3 2 1

Library of Congress Cataloging in Publication Data

Muldary, Thomas W.
    Burnout and health professionals.

    Bibliography: p.
    Includes index.
    1. Medical personnel–Job stress.   2. Burn out
(Psychology)   I. Title. [DNLM: 1. Health occupations.
2. Attitude of health personnel.   3. Stress, Psychologi-
cal.   4. Job satisfaction. WM 172 M954b]
R690.M78 1983   610.69′019   82-25295
ISBN 0-8385-0892-8

Publisher, B. Wallace Hood, Jr.
Editor, Carmen Germaine Warner
Production Editor, Barbara L. Halliburton
Cover Design, Carolyn Hesse
Internal Design, B. Wallace Hood, Jr. and Alice Harmon

Printed in the United States of America

CONTENTS

FOREWORD

As the author of this comprehensive work points out, the pervasive phenomenon of burnout among health professionals is easy to describe but hard to define. The subtle negative changes that steal into an individual's behavioral repertoire and culminate in burnout are often recognized last by the person experiencing them. One nurse reported that her colleagues had been telling her she was "burning out," but she dismissed their descriptions of her negative behavior as circumstantial. However, when one of her patients, with whom she had developed a close relationship, died and she stood at the bedside and laughed hysterically, she suddenly realized that her colleagues were correct. She was experiencing burnout and she needed help.

Every health professional who cares and cares deeply is at risk where burnout is concerned. And, every health professional should have available comprehensive and authoritative information on the subject. *Burnout and Health Professionals: Manifestations and Management* explores nearly every aspect of burnout, including the elusiveness of its definition, theoretical perspectives, a description of its manifestations in both individuals and organizational structures, and prescriptions for prevention and management. The author stresses the dialectical nature of burnout in that it does not reside solely either in the individual or in the environment but in the relationship between the two and in how the health professional perceives self and situation.

The management of burnout is not merely a personal "go-it-alone" affair. Therefore, the author treats, in a comprehensive fashion, not only individual strategies for managing the manifestations but managerial ones as well. Organizational strategies for the assessment and prevention of burnout are explored in great detail.

Reading *Burnout and Health Professionals: Manifestations and Management* is like conducting a comprehensive assessment of oneself and the work setting. Readers may reach some sobering conclusions about their own situation, but the book can serve as a valuable resource in choosing a course of action for management and prevention.

Gloria Ferraro Donnelly, R.N., M.S.N., F.A.A.N.

PREFACE

Day after day, health professionals are intensely involved with the suffering and distress of human beings under their care. And, day after day, they are faced with unprecedented demands for efficiency and accountability for the quality of care they provide. Until recently little attention has been given to the question of what happens to professionals who work so intimately with others, wavering the peaks and valleys of emotion, against the background of enormous social, professional, and institutional pressures. It seems to have been a foregone conclusion that health professionals naturally retain their objectivity and remain unaffected by such conditions. However, the question now begs for serious attention since it is currently accepted that many health professionals are overloaded with stress and unable to cope with the mental and emotional strain of unrelieved job pressures.

The effects of these kinds of pressures are quite varied, but the composite reaction has been named *burnout*. Most health professionals have experienced at least some of the prominent symptoms of this job-stress reaction. Most of those who have experienced the full force of burnout have felt a general exhaustion and a loss of energy, enthusiasm, and commitment to their work, their patients, and to their profession. Feeling alienated, hostile, resentful, frustrated, unable to give any more, and powerless to change things, many "burned-out" health professionals ultimately leave their profession forever. Those who remain cope with the stresses of their work by detaching themselves emotionally from the people they serve. For the health care professions, and for the human beings served, burnout has far-reaching implications. In light of the complexity of burnout and its debilitating effects on service providers, recipients, and society as a whole, it is imperative that we strive to understand this problem, its causes, its manifestations, its consequences, and its management. Nowhere is this task more important, and nowhere is our responsibility more apparent, than in the allied health professions.

The purpose of this text is to review the current state of knowledge and the most salient questions about burnout: What is it? How is it manifested? What are the most common causes? What are the effects of burnout on the physical, mental, and emotional functioning of professional helpers? How does it affect behavior and work performance? How can the problem be successfully managed?

The text is organized around three fundamental assumptions. First, health professionals can do little to manage stress and burnout unless they become *aware* that there is a problem. Second, awareness, or the recognition that a problem exists, must be followed by a *commitment* to doing something about it. Third, awareness is no more than static insight, and commitment is no more than a good idea, unless *action* is taken to bring about positive change.

To facilitate awareness, commitment, and action, the material in this text is ordered into ten chapters. Chapter 1 examines the nature of burnout, its general appearance, and its impact on health care delivery. Chapter 2 places burnout within the broader context of stress, and burnout is reviewed as one response to chronic stress. Chapter 3 points up the prominent features of the burnout syndrome in terms of its effects on mental and emotional functioning. The effects of burnout on behavior and work performance are outlined in Chapter 4. Primary causes of burnout are examined in Chapter 5, in relation to factors within health organizations, and in Chapter 6, in relation to the unique characteristics of people who help others for a living. Chapter 7 presents a range of strategies that "front-line" health professionals can use to manage stress and burnout, while Chapter 8 presents various approaches supervisors can follow to curb the problem of burnout among staff. Chapter 9 outlines strategies that can be pursued by health care administrators, and Chapter 10 offers some practical suggestions that health professionals at all levels can use to manage stress and burnout.

Although this text is written primarily for front-line health professionals, it is not assumed that they must bear sole responsibility for managing burnout. Very often, supervisors and administrators impose unnecessary stress on front-line people. As occasional sources of stress, supervisors and administrators must become aware of how they may affect staff and, more importantly, what they can do to reduce the level of stress experienced by personnel in their charge. Many authorities seem to believe that the responsibility for managing stress belongs to the individual worker since organizations are not subject to change. The implicit, and often explicit, assumption seems to be that because organizations will continue to be as rigid as they are, it is up to individuals to do what they can within the unchangeable "givens" of the system. Clearly, individual workers *do* have a large measure of responsibility. And, when it is not possible to change certain stressful features of health care organizations, the only recourse *is* to train individuals to cope more effectively. However, it is dysfunctional for any organization to train workers how to cope with organizational stressors that need not exist in the first place. It is time for the literature on stress and burnout to move beyond the individual worker and to stimulate a movement toward controlling stess at higher levels within organizations. This is not a novel idea, but the active involvement of health care administrators in creating more positive work environments—those wherein the potential for burnout is reduced—has been slow in developing.

For the front-line practitioner, the supervisor, and the health care administrator, perhaps the material in this text will facilitate a continuing search for understanding and managing the problem of burnout. Indeed, perhaps the most important benefit of this text is the extent to which it provokes new perspectives and new learning. For professionals in training, this text may orient them toward the job stresses that they might expect and suggest some ways of preparing for and coping with the realities of helping people in distress. As new professionals proceed through their training, their professional socialization will not be complete without some understanding of the problem—burnout—that is taking its toll on those before them.

BURNOUT
AND HEALTH PROFESSIONALS

CHAPTER 1

Nature of burnout

There once was an infamous conqueror who was known to ride upon a mighty elephant as he led his armies into attack against defenseless cities. One night the conqueror and his armies approached a city and camped in the nearby desert, awaiting the light of dawn to signal their attack.

It so happened that all inhabitants of the city were blind. They feared the great conqueror, yet they feared even more what legend had told them about the terrible beast that trampled everything in its path. Since they knew neither the form nor the shape of the elephant, the blind populace grew anxious to learn the truth about this dreaded creature. Some ran like fools into the darkness, groping sightlessly until they were sure they had found the elephant. Each gathered information by touching some part of it.

Upon returning to the city, groups gathered around their team of investigators, eager to learn the truths that might help to save their lives.

The one whose hand had reached an ear proclaimed, "It is a very large, rough thing, wide and broad like a rug!"

Another, whose hand had touched the trunk, countered, "No! It is actually long and fat like a python, but straight and hollow like a pipe!"

One whose hand had felt its feet and legs declared, "The truth is that it is mighty and firm, like a stone pillar!"

(Eastern Folklore)

Recently, few topics in the allied health field have been as popular and controversial as burnout. Burnout is a phenomenon thought to undermine the morale and well-being of health

1

professionals, reduce the quality of care given to patients, and, in general, trample the overall operation of human service programs in its path. It is a problem that has aroused the concern of practitioners, captured the attention of administrators, and inspired the imagination of many authors. And yet this phenomenon is somewhat like the proverbial elephant—firmly entrenched in the consciousness of health professionals, but neither wholly conceptualized nor fully understood.

For some the term *burnout* is little more than a popular buzzword in the professional vernacular; it is a trendy catchword that they often willingly and indiscriminately use as a "diagnosis" for almost any problem of living that they experience. This view is not without merit because *burnout* is a popular term and something of a fad these days. Those closest to the problem, however, are not willing to dismiss the concept of burnout simply because it has become popular. They recognize that legitimate definitional problems do not preclude the use of the term since *burnout* is a causal term rather than a technical one. As such, it does have considerable communicative value, and many people have little trouble recognizing burnout. As Bolles (1980) explained, "Burnout is kind of like pornography. I'm not sure I can define it, but I know what is is when I see it" (Forney, Wallace-Schutzman, and Wiggers, 1982, p. 436).

Like many psychological terms, *burnout* is one loaded with diverse meanings. Consequently, it is much easier to describe than to define. For most people, however, burnout suggests a general loss of energy. The phenomenon is often conceptualized in a metaphorical sense that equates it with a wearing out or exhaustion from constant drains on personal resources. It is common sense to conclude that someone who "burns out" must have been "on fire" at one time. In this connection the term was once used as a loose psychiatric label for psychopaths whose chronically antisocial behavior seemed to die out after the age of forty. It was also used, and still is in some contexts, as a street label for people who appear to be emotionally spent and mentally disorganized because of chronic drug use. Currently the term is applied most frequently in the world of work, where morale and problems of performance efficiency are attributed to burnout. As a work-related concept, burnout was formally introduced by Freudenberger (1974) in an article that addressed the problem of the "staff burnout syndrome" among front-line human service workers who were undertrained and overloaded with work. Subsequent research has demonstrated that the syndrome occurs among teachers (Hendrickson, 1979), police officers (Ellison and Genz, 1978), social workers (Pines and Kafry, 1978), mental health workers (Pines and

Maslach, 1978), lawyers (Maslach and Jackson, 1978), career counselors (Forney, Wallace-Schutzman, and Wiggers, 1982), agency administrators (Maslach and Jackson, 1978; Pines and Maslach, 1978), the clergy (Kammer, 1978), and health care professionals (Hall and others, 1978; Pines and Maslach, 1978). There is an abundance of anecdotal evidence in the allied health literature to suggest that burnout is a critical problem among health professionals.

In allied health, as in other fields, *burnout* appears to be a new label for a traditional problem that received little formal recognition until recently. Inspection of the *Cumulative Index to Nursing and Allied Health Literature* reveals that no articles with the term *burnout* in their titles were published prior to 1978. Between 1978 and 1980 only four articles on burnout were recorded. However, by 1980 the number of articles about burnout had increased dramatically in an explosion of awareness.

Unfortunately, this burgeoning literature has not yet provided a complete picture of the phenomenon. In fact, this literature consists of numerous perfunctory articles and a range of unsubstantiated opinions concerning the etiology, symptomatology, and control of burnout. This situation is understandable since burnout is a very young area of study. Yet it is also clear that burnout warrants more serious study than it has received so far. To date, our understanding of burnout in allied health is grounded mainly on impressions, anecdotal evidence, and comparisons with other helping professions. As compelling as some of this information is, findings from systematic research are necessary to unify our thinking about burnout in health care.

It would be naive to assume that the ambiguity surrounding the concept of burnout has gone unnoticed by health professionals who consult the literature for concise information. They have found that the literature on burnout in allied health is all-inclusive. When viewed as a whole, this literature offers a description of burnout that is so broad as to exclude almost nothing as a symptom of that condition. This description has developed through an accumulation, ad infinitum, of adjectives that enumerate the symptoms of burnout. In many ways this body of literature resembles a broad-brush classification system for an exclusive syndrome encompassing everything from depression and alcoholism to stooped shoulders and the common cold. This is an unfortunate situation for many practitioners because the grouping of several distinct phenomena under the heading of burnout has left them confused about the definitional boundaries of the concept. Many of these practitioners have learned to pay little attention to theory and the efforts of research to delineate the parameters of burnout because so far the payoff for them has been minimal.

The broad range of the concept of burnout clearly causes difficulty from a heuristic standpoint. This range incorporates those on the left, who consider burnout a popular fiction; those on the right, who consider it a concrete reality; and those in the middle, who consider it a syndrome of varied etiology, symptomatology, management, and outcome. Underlying the positions of the latter two groups is the assumption that there is such an entity as burnout and that all we need to do is to agree on the fundamental signs and symptoms that define it. Then we can move from trial-and-error approaches to treatment to systematic strategies. Yet even if we come to agree on the defining characteristics of burnout, this consistency would be of little value if the concept itself is not valid. However, if we can establish conceptual criteria that implicate the possible etiology of burnout and suggest viable approaches to managing those causes, then we may be addressing more clearly the problem of validating the concept of burnout. If diagnoses of burnout are reliable and valid, their usefulness will be reflected in their ability to generate predictions in the form of prognoses.

Although burnout is a multidimensional phenomenon that defies simplistic analysis, the validity of the concept is compromised when it is viewed so comprehensively that virtually nothing is excluded as a cause, symptom, or effect. Aside from the pressing need for published research, several conditions in the literature on burnout in allied health must be remedied. For one thing, the literature must do more than record impassioned tales of demoralization and refrain from equating burnout with the whole of human dysfunction. The parameters of burnout need to be clarified and its symptoms viewed in terms of extremes. Etiological explanations must take into account the fact that some people "burn out" and others do not, even though they are exposed to the same conditions. It must be recognized that several concurrent factors may interact in various ways and thereby lead to different effects for different individuals. Explanations that identify universal causes of burnout are overgeneralizations. Any discussion of the problem that offers formula approaches for managing burnout is also suspect. The individualistic nature of burnout must be recognized as a function of the individual's relationship with the environment—with each individual relating to the environment in unique and qualitatively different ways.

The remainder of this chapter suggests parameters for the phenomenon of burnout. From the tremendous range of signs, symptoms, and manifestations found in the literature, the most salient features of its appearance are identified. Definitions of burnout, from the general to the particular, are discussed and synthesized into a working definition for this text. Finally, the significance of burnout in health care is briefly discussed in terms of its impact on service providers and service delivery.

CHARACTERISTICS

The burnout syndrome appears as a highly variable combination of symptoms, behaviors, and attitudes (Lavandero, 1981). Table 1-1 lists a range of manifestations cited throughout the literature. Although this is an exhaustive list, certain features of burnout are manifested more frequently than others, with the presenting pattern made unique by each person. Some signs of burnout are readily apparent to others, while some are covert and part of the individual's private, subjective experience. For example, certain kinds of thoughts and feelings tend to occur with some regularity in the burnout syndrome, yet they are not observable by others until the individual expresses them through words and actions. Physical symptoms may or may not be noticeable to others.

Among this vast range of symptoms, which ones tend to appear most frequently? To answer this question, let us begin with some examples. Pines and Aronson (1981) noted that the most striking examples of burnout encountered in their research involved nurses working with terminal cancer patients. Nurses working in this setting were initially very idealistic and deeply committed to caring for their patients. After a short period of time, however, the stress of helplessly watching person after person die seemed to cause a shift of attitude. The nurses began insulating themselves emotionally. In order to avoid being overwhelmed by their feelings of powerlessness and grief, they detached themselves emotionally from their patients. With less attachment to the dying patients, the nurses came to develop a resentment toward them and viewed them as overly demanding. The growing resentment toward the very people the nurses were initially committed to helping led to feelings of guilt and shame. As hard work and feelings of powerlessness, hopelessness, resentment, guilt, and shame continually recycled, feelings of exhaustion and malaise set in and, in turn, led to more resentment toward

Table 1-1 Signs and Symptoms of Burnout Identified in the Literature

PHYSICAL	PSYCHOLOGICAL	BEHAVIORAL
Fatigue	Feelings:	Dehumanization of patients
Sleep disturbances:	Anger	Victimization of patients
Difficulty sleeping	Boredom	Fault finding
Difficulty getting	Frustration	Blaming others
up	Depression	Defensiveness
Stomach ailments	Discouragement	Impersonal, stereotyped communica-
Tension headaches	Disillusionment	tion with patients
Migraine headaches	Despair	Applying derogatory labels to
Gastrointestinal	Apathy	patients
problems	Guilt	Physical distancing from patients
Frequent colds	Anxiety	and others
Lingering colds	Suspicion/Paranoia	Withdrawal
Frequent bouts of flu	Helplessness	Isolation
Backaches	Pessimism	Stereotyping patients
Nausea	Irritability	Postponing patient contacts
Muscle tension	Resentment	Going increasingly by the book
Shortness of breath	Hopelessness	Clock watching
Malaise	Attitudes:	Living for breaks
Frequent injuries	Cynicism	Absenteeism
Weight loss	Indifference	Making little mistakes
Weight gain	Resignation	Unnecessary risk taking
Stooped shoulders	Self-doubt	Use of drugs and alcohol
Weakness	Other:	Marital and family conflict
Change of eating	Loss of empathy	Conflict with co-workers
habits	Difficulty	Workoholism and obsessiveness
	concentrating	Use of humor as a buffer from
	Difficulty attending	emotions
	Low morale	Decreased job efficiency
	Moodiness	Suicide
	Decreased sense of	Overcommitment or
	self-worth	undercommitment

the patients, who were perceived as causing the nurses' exhaustion. As the vicious cycle intensified, guilt and shame increased.

The burnout problem for these nurses was complex. According to Pines and Aronson (1981), because of the nurses' initial idealism, they came to believe that their current feelings and attitudes toward patients were unacceptable, inappropriate, and especially shameful. They convinced themselves that of all people *they* should not be feeling the way they did. The nurses' guilt and shame became tremendous burdens that they carried hidden within themselves. They tried to mask their inner turmoil by appearing undaunted and efficient on the outside. Pines and Aronson noted a supreme irony in this: The nurses felt miserable but looked cool and efficient, and as they looked around at other nurses (who were also hurting on the inside) they saw no evidence that anyone else was experiencing similar feelings. Consequently, they came to envy others who, like themselves, *appeared* untroubled. The next step in the nurses' logic was to conclude that, because no one else appeared troubled, there must be something inherently wrong with them. At this point feelings of inadequacy and failure emerged. Not surprisingly, with increasingly frequent doubts about their own professional competency, some nurses concluded that they were not cut out for health care and opted to leave the profession.

This example points out several common components of the burnout syndrome. The nurses experienced a *loss of idealism*, a *decreased commitment* to helping those in need, an *emotional detachment* from patients, *negative attitudes* toward patients, feelings of *powerlessness* over the conditions of their work, and *mental and physical exhaustion*. With these nurses, as with many individuals who have experienced burnout, there was an erosion of spirit and a general demoralization under conditions perceived as highly stressful. It is this aspect of the burnout phenomenon that has received the most attention to date—its direct connection to chronic *stress*. The burnout syndrome represents one response to unrelieved stress. In the example given here, the stressful conditions of the nurses' work are easily appreciated. Yet it is clear that one does not have to work with dying patients to appreciate stress or to experience burnout. Consider the following cases.

Steven H. has been a high school teacher for four years. He recently decided to make a major career change because he felt that his work had no real impact on his students. He saw his students as uninterested, unmotivated, and resistant to learning. Given those conditions, Steven became convinced that it was futile to continue teaching. He reported that each year he experienced the same problems with a new class of students and that he felt much like Sisyphus of Greek mythology, rolling a huge stone up a hill, only to have it roll down again each time. In his frustration Steven referred to his students as "animals" and shifted his approach to dealing with them by becoming a rigid disciplinarian, going strictly by school policy, and treating students inflexibly. Like the nurses, Steven experienced a loss of enthusiasm for his work. His attitude toward his students became progressively negative. He even managed to *dehumanize* them in his own mind, as a means of facilitating and justifying his detachment from them. Steven grew more easily angered and irritated with his students, and he adopted a *rigidly technical* approach to teaching and interacting with them.

Mary T. is a physician specializing in internal medicine. During her first few years of practice she enjoyed conversing with her patients as she made her hospital rounds. Now she no longer enjoys chatting with her patients and, in fact, sees it as a waste of time. Paradoxically, Mary's time seems to her to be spent mainly in mundane, routine work that is rarely challenging or interesting. So she puts less time and effort into her work than she once did.

Grace A. is an ICU nurse at a large metropolitan hospital. She has used up almost all of her sick leave this year because of various phychosomatic ailments and frequent feelings of being "run down." She was recently reprimanded by her supervisor for frequently being late for work. Grace explained that she often slept right through the morning alarm on weekdays, but that for some strange reason she awakened at 6:00 A.M. each morning of her days off. When Grace goes home after work, she cannot seem to unwind and relax without having several drinks. Some nights Grace continues thinking about her job to the point of being obsessed with reviewing her performance that day.

John R. is a clinical social worker whose caseload in a protective services department involves child abuse. He stated:

I've been here for five years, so I had enough seniority to survive the recent layoffs in our department. But I kind of wish I hadn't. I suppose I should be thankful that I have a job, but I'm really not. I've had it. You wouldn't believe how draining it is to work with these cases. I get so emotionally involved and so uptight when I see what's happening to some of these kids. Lately, I've been having headaches that I know are caused by this job. And, it's crazy, but even though I really get into these cases, a lot of times I'm just going on "automatic," and it's like nothing bothers me because I'm going through the motions and I'm really numb to all of it.

Tracy R. is an alcoholism counselor who gradually developed a contemptuous attitude toward her clients. She confided to a friend, "I get sick and tired of these drunks coming in here and playing games with me. They just spew out whatever they think you want to hear, and then they go right out and drink again. You can't believe anything they say." Tracy's co-workers do not share her views, and, because she has been complaining to them about clients more and more, they have been avoiding her. They have noted a change in Tracy over the last six months: She appears to be much less sensitive to the needs of her clients. She has been cutting her counseling sessions shorter and shorter, spending about half the time on them that she formerly did. Her approach to treatment has become noticeably "standard" in that she writes treatment plans that reflect the same activities for each client.

Mary, Grace, John, and Tracy are experiencing burnout in some ways that are similar to how Steven is experiencing it. Their initial enthusiasm and commitment have decreased, they have become less efficient in their jobs, and they are all responding to the pressures of their jobs. Also, their symptoms are manifested in extremes. John is overly involved in his work, while the rest are detached from it. John seems to care too much, while the others seem to care too little. John is trying very hard at his job, while the others have stopped trying. The symptoms of burnout in each case encompass a range of human functions, and—at least in John's case—physical, emotional, cognitive, and behavioral areas are clearly affected.

There is a common thread running through each of these cases: Each person works in a human service occupation. Their jobs require frequent emotional contact with other human beings—unlike various technical occupations where individuals interface with machines or objects of some kind. Although burnout can occur in any occupational group, it is especially prevalent among persons working in human service occupations. People whose jobs are to help other people seem to be the most vulnerable to burnout, for reasons that are discussed later in the text. This being the case, we would expect some very critical implications for the delivery of human services. Before examining some of those implications, let us narrow our discussion and move toward a formal definition of burnout.

A DEFINITION

The examples cited in the preceding section provide broad descriptions of burnout. Describing the problem is much easier than defining it, even though burnout is a multidimensional problem that can present itself in a variety of ways.

In the allied health literature burnout is sometimes equated with job stress (Bailey, 1980). Job stress is generally viewed in relation to factors in the work environment that interact with a worker's personality in such a way as to disrupt the worker's psychological or physical functioning (Margolis and Kroes, 1974). Although intrinsically related, burnout and job stress are *not* synonymous. Burnout is typically considered as one consequence of job stress. Job stress appears to be a necessary condition for burnout to occur. Many workers experience job stress and do not burn out, but none burn out without experiencing job stress.

Among the formal definitions of burnout there are direct or implied links to the stress experienced in one's work. For example, Veninga and Spradley (1981) made an explicit connection with job stress in their definition of burnout as "a debilitating psychological condition brought about by unrelieved work stress." They maintained that this work-related condition results in "(1) depleted energy reserves, (2) lowered resistance to illness, (3) increased dissatisfaction and pessimism, (4) increased absenteeism and inefficiency at work" (pp. 6-7). Edelwich and Brodsky (1980) emphasized the stressful aspects of one's job in defining burnout as "a progressive loss of idealism, energy, and purpose experienced by people in the helping professions as a result of the conditions of their work" (p. 14).

Edelwich and Brodsky restricted their use of the term *burnout* to the helping professions. Although they did acknowledge that burnout can occur in virtually any profession, they maintained that it tends to occur with more regularity, carry higher social costs, and assume special intensity and character in the human service professions. These authors argued that human services have several built-in sources of stress that are unique to helping and that these stress factors tend to increase the vulnerability of health professionals in comparison with those in other professions. What are these factors, these conditions of work in the helping professions that may predispose professionals to burnout? Many of them are discussed in detail in Chapter 5. Here the discussion focuses on what Pines and Aronson consider the most important general factor.

Pines and Aronson (1981) highlighted the applicability of the burnout concept to the helping professions. They defined burnout as "the result of constant or repeated emotional pressure associated with intense involvement with people over long periods of time" (p. 15). The authors further viewed burnout as a "state of mind that frequently afflicts individuals who work with other people . . . and who pour in much more than they get back from their clients, supervisors, and colleagues" (p. 3). These investigators suggested that burnout is a syndrome that includes physical, emotional, and mental fatigue; feelings of helplessness and hopelessness; and a lack of interest and enthusiasm for work and life in general. As an erosion of spirit, burnout affects precisely those professionals who had once been the most idealistic and enthusiastic. According to Pines and Aronson, these are the professionals who had at one time been "on fire."

Cherniss (1980) implied this erosion of spirit in his definition of burnout as a "process in which a previously committed professional disengages from his or her work in response to stress and strain experienced on the job" (p. 18). It appears that a prerequisite condition for burnout among health professionals is an initially strong humanitarian commitment to helping the less fortunate. This commitment is grounded in altruistic values and entails an investment of one's whole self in the purpose of one's work. Burnout robs health professionals of that investment and leaves them bankrupt of enthusiasm and purpose. Helping becomes either just another job or more of a problem than it is worth. The fire and sense of mission in one's calling fades and dies.

Perhaps the most widely cited definition of burnout is that proposed by Maslach. She defined burnout as

The loss of concern for the people with whom one is working [including] physical exhaustion [and] characterized by an emotional exhaustion in which the professional no longer has any positive feelings, sympathy, or respect for clients or patients. (Maslach and Jackson, 1977, p. 3)

Maslach's definition characterizes burnout as a phenomenon common to personnel in human services. Subsumed under this definition is an attitude of detachment resulting from continual demands on emotional resources and a tendency to become rigidly technical in the performance of job duties. Thus, a salient feature of burnout appears to be a disruption of previously satisfactory relationships between professionals and their work environments.

These definitions reflect certain generally accepted dimensions of burnout. First, burnout is one response to a stressful work environment. It is not synonymous with stress. Rather, it is a consequence of unrelieved work stress. Second, although burnout may occur in any occupation, it is especially prominent among health professionals who come into repeated emotional contact with people in need of services. The type of work-related interactions that take place between providers and recipients is distinct from the kind of interactions between persons in business and industry. Providers of human services are typically inspired by altruistic values, with helping being a value in itself. Third, burnout typically manifests itself as a combination of physical, mental, and emotional exhaustion; loss of commitment; disengagement from one's work; and a general inefficiency in adapting to the unique demands of one's relationship with the environment that surrounds the delivery of human services.

Similarities among these definitions of burnout suggest that common elements can be synthesized to form a working definition for the purposes of this text. Burnout is defined here as the *process by which a once-committed health professional becomes ineffective in managing the stress of frequent emotional contact with others in the helping context, experiences exhaustion, and, as a result, disengages from patients, colleagues, and the organization.*

In emphasizing the connection between burnout and stress in the workplace, it becomes necessary to examine the nature of stress in general, for burnout cannot be understood apart from this phenomenon. Stress is the background against which burnout is understood. Therefore, Chapter 2 briefly examines the nature of stress. Because the conceptualization of burnout advanced here also points out the importance of the individual's relationship and interactions with the work environment, Chapter 2 outlines a theoretical framework for viewing those interactions. Before considering these topics, however, it is important to highlight the significance of burnout in health care.

IMPACT ON HEALTH CARE

Contemporary health care practices are more technically efficient, sophisticated, and complex than ever before. As a result, the chances of producing positive changes in the health and well-being of patients are much more favorable than they were in the past. However, the stress and strain associated with delivering health care services can have various adverse effects on providers and ultimately on the overall quality of medical and nursing practice. It is certainly possible that iatrogenic effects of treatment may occur.

For one thing, chronic stress can gradually produce a state of tension and irritability that is incompatible with performance efficiency. A chronically aroused, tense, and irritable health professional is a person with an impaired ability to respond to continually changing conditions and demands. Such a professional may not adequately meet the treatment needs of patients, and, therefore, patient neglect becomes an increasingly probable outcome.

Second, as enthusiasm and commitment wane, there is a decline in overall motivation to provide quality health care. Health care becomes just a job—one that is performed grudgingly by a demoralized health professional and only well enough to get by without any seriously adverse consequences.

Third, under prolonged stress the burnout syndrome may come to include an impairment of the ability to attend, concentrate, and engage in complex thinking and problem solving. Because medical and nursing practices are so complex, they require critical thinking, problem solving, and decision making on a regular basis. When these functions are impaired in the provider, the outcome of work performance can be disastrous for patients.

Fourth, with a decline in enthusiasm and liking for one's work, there may also develop a loss of empathy, caring, and respect for patients. It is much easier to neglect—and in some cases even consciously harm—people whom we do not understand, care about, or respect. They become medical or surgical entities, stripped of humanity and deserving of no more concern than one would show for the cleanliness of one's uniform.

Fifth, as health professionals burn out, they tend to become more concerned with their own well-being and less about the welfare of others. "I've got to take care of myself before I can be effective in taking care of others" becomes more than a sensible piece of advice. Burned-out health professionals may protect and defend against any perceived imposition on their time and energy. They may become unwilling to help a colleague ("It's not my job," "I don't ask for help, so don't ask me," or "If you can't do your own job, then maybe you shouldn't be here"). If several members of the same staff are experiencing burnout, frequent conflicts over duties may occur. Staff members may withdraw from interactions with one another, breaking the cohesiveness of the staff, closing off channels of communication, and disrupting team functioning.

Sixth, burned-out health professionals who cope with the stress of their jobs by heavy drinking or drug use or both are more than a liability—they are dangerous. They represent accidents waiting to happen. They are the most serious threat to the well-being of patients.

Finally, every year health care organizations lose hundreds of their most competent and committed practitioners to burnout. The effects of this turnover ripple through all levels of these organizations. High turnover is associated with increased expenditures for training new personnel to replace those who have left. It is also associated with lowered morale and the disruption of patient services (Edelwich and Brodsky, 1980). As morale falls and staff-patient relations are disrupted, other staff members become disposed toward burnout, and the cycle repeats itself.

These are just some of the ways in which burnout can impact the delivery of health care. As the subsequent chapters will show, the implications for allied health are even more extensive.

SUMMARY

The popularity of the concept of burnout is readily apparent in a burgeoning literature that decries the ravages of a recently labeled but traditional problem among health professionals. Although there has been a significant increase in awareness of this problem, the current data base on burnout in allied health is limited. Numerous accounts of the burnout phenomenon have blurred the definitional boundaries of the problem, while emphasizing its multidimensional nature. As a complex problem with no single set of antecedents or consequences, burnout represents a significant challenge to those concerned with managing it. Its symptoms are highly variable and typically appear in a syndrome with manifestations in physical, emotional, cognitive, and behavioral areas of functioning. Among the most frequently noted symptoms are the following:

- Loss of idealism

- Decreased commitment to helping

- Emotional detachment from patients

- Negative attitudes toward patients and one's work

- Feelings of powerlessness over the conditions of one's work

- Mental and physical exhaustion

- Adoption of a rigidly technical approach to one's work

- Increased escape and avoidance

- Appearance of various psychosomatic ailments

For the purposes of this text, burnout is defined as the process by which a once-committed health professional becomes ineffective in managing the stress of frequent emotional contact with others in the helping context, experiences exhaustion, and, as a result, disengages from patients, colleagues, and the organization. This definition emphasizes burnout as a response to stress experienced in the context of human services. The impact of burnout on the delivery of human services is highlighted in terms of increasing the potential for patient neglect, reduced performance efficiency, impaired mental functioning of providers, staff conflict, substance abuse, and turnover.

REFERENCES

Bailey, J.T. Job stress and other stress-related problems. In K.E. Claus & J.T. Bailey (Eds.), *Living with stress and promoting well-being: A handbook for nurses.* St. Louis: C.V. Mosby, 1980.

Bolles, R. Personal communication, March 20, 1980. In D.S. Forney, F. Wallace-Schutzman & T. Wiggers. Burnout among career development professionals: Preliminary findings and implications. *Personnel and Guidance Journal*, 1982, *60*(7), 435–439.

Cherniss, C. *Staff burnout: Job stress in the human services.* Beverly Hills, Calif.: Sage Publications, 1980.

Edelwich, J., & Brodsky, A. *Burnout: Stages of disillusionment in the helping professions.* New York: Human Sciences Press, 1980.

Ellison, K.W., & Genz, J.L. The police officer as burned-out samaritan. *FBI Law Enforcement Bulletin*, March 1978, pp. 1–7.

Forney, D.S., Wallace-Schutzman, F., & Wiggers, T. Burnout among career development professionals: Preliminary findings and implications. *Personnel and Guidance Journal*, 1982, *60*(7), 435–439.

Freudenberger, H.J. Staff burnout. *Journal of Social Issues*, 1974, *30*, 159–165.

Hall, R.C.W., Gardner, E.R., Perl, M., Stickney, S.K., & Pfefferbaum, B. The professional burnout syndrome. *Psychiatric Opinion*, 1979, *16*(4), 12–13; 16–17.

Hendrickson, B. Teacher burnout: How to recognize it; what to do about it. *Learning*, 1979, *7*(5), 36–39.

Kammer, A.C. Burnout: Contemporary dilemma for the Jesuit social activist. *Study of the Spirituality of Jesuits*, 1978, *10*(1), 1–42.

Lavandero, R. Nurse burnout: What can we learn? *Journal of Nursing Administration*, 1981, *12*(11), 17–23.

Margolis, B., & Kroes, W. Occupational stress and strain. In A. McLean (Ed.), *Occupational stress.* Springfield, Ill.: Charles C Thomas, 1974.

Maslach, C. Burnout: A social psychological analysis. San Francisco: American Psychological Association Convention, August 1977, p. 3.

Maslach, C., & Jackson, S.E. Lawyer burnout. *Barrister*, 1977, *5*(2), 52–54.

Pines, A., & Aronson, E. *Burnout: From tedium to personal growth.* New York: Free Press, 1981.

Pines, A., & Kafry, D. Occupational tedium in the social services. *Social Work*, 1978, *23*, 499-507.

Pines, A., & Maslach, C. Characteristics of staff burnout in mental health settings. *Hospital and Community Psychiatry*, 1978, *29*, 233-237.

Veninga, R.L., & Spradley, J.P. *The work stress connection: How to cope with job burnout.* Boston: Little, Brown, 1981.

CHAPTER 2

Stress and burnout

Everyone experiences occasional stress on the job, but when occasional stress turns into prolonged and sustained tension, frustration, and anxiety, then job dissatisfaction increases and stress becomes more than a transient problem. Various physical, psychological, and behavioral changes gradually tilt the balance of well-being in an insidious process that may lead to burnout.

The term *stress* is actually an engineering concept used to refer to an external force applied to a physical object that produces strain on the object. From an engineering perspective, the resultant strain is a function of the magnitude of the stress and the properties of the object. This usage, however, does not bear a perfect correspondence to the meaning of stress as a physiological or psychological phenomenon.

In both lay and professional terminology there has been a tendency to use the word *stress* in two different ways. As a *stimulus*, stress is seen as something to which people are exposed from outside of their bodies. Stress is considered to be external to the individual. When conceptualized in this way, stress is viewed as a problematic environmental condition or force that demands adaptation from the individual. When stress is viewed as a *response*, it is inferred to be within the individual. Therefore, as a response, stress refers to an internal reaction to demanding environmental conditions. When conceptualized as such, another concept is often applied to those environmental conditions presumed to elicit the internal reaction: pressure. For example, a person may say, "I'm feeling a lot of stress [internal] because I've been under a lot of pressure [external] lately." This usage of the term *stress* is closest to the general psychological meaning of the concept. However, the psychological meaning of the term refers to a condition of the individual and, therefore, parallels the engineering concept of strain. Further, in psychological terms, the concept of pressure is replaced by that of *stressors*, which denote forces impinging on the individual. The concept of stressors parallels the engineering concept of stress.

Theorists and researchers are not in complete agreement about how to define stress. In some respects they are divided, like the lay public, on the issue of whether stress is a stimulus or a response. The literature on stress reflects the same basic confusion about whether stress is internal or external to the individual. As Monat and Lazarus (1977) suggested, response-based definitions that place stress within individuals cannot account for the fact that the same physiological or psychological responses may be elicited by quite different stimulus conditions. Stimulus-based definitions, on the other hand, suffer from an inability to recognize that any situation may or may not be stressful, depending on the nature of the situation and the meaning it has for the individual.

Not only is there disagreement over the issue of stress as stimulus or response, there are different levels of analysis from which the concept has been approached. For instance, at the psychological level stress is seen in terms of disruptions of thinking, emotions, and behavior. At the physiological level, stress is viewed in terms of disruptions of bodily functions. At the social level, stress is hypothesized in terms of disturbances in a larger system. Because of the numerous ways in which the concept of stress is approached, some critics have suggested abandoning the notion of stress altogether and replacing it with concepts that are more restricted in scope.

Several years ago Lazarus (1966) proposed that the term *stress* be used as a generic term for a whole area of problems that includes the stimuli that produce stress reactions, the reactions themselves, and various intervening processes. This approach would create a broad field of stress, including physiological, psychological, and sociological phenomena as a collective area of study. Lazarus further suggested that this broad area of stress should be defined in terms of *"any event in which environmental demands, internal demands, (or both) tax or exceed the adaptive resources of an individual, social system, or tissue system"* (Monat and Lazarus, 1977, p. 3).

The study of stress is concerned with how individuals adapt to various conditions that tax or surpass their resources for coping. It is also concerned with the antecedents and consequences of success and failure at adaptation. The following section examines the ways in which the body responds under demands for adaptation. Stress is explored at the physiological level. Lazarus's *transactional model* of stress is then outlined to emphasize the role of perception in influencing adaptational outcomes. That is, in the transaction between the individual and the environment, it is the individual's perceptions and cognitive appraisals of demand that are hypothesized to determine whether or not the so-called physiological stress response has been activated at all. Such an analysis places stress neither within the individual nor in the environment, but in the person-environment transaction. As one response to chronic, prolonged stress, burnout is ultimately influenced by one's perceptions and appraisals of the circumstances one finds oneself in at work. Stress may be bad for you, it may affect your health, and it may lead to burnout *if you perceive your work as stressful and beyond your ability to cope.* Many people work extremely hard and "burn the candle at both ends," yet they may not burn out. In themselves, hard work and insufficient rest seldom lead to burnout (Veninga and Spradley, 1981). Many individuals simply do not define hard work and long hours as stressful; some people even seem to thrive on such conditions.

PHYSIOLOGY OF STRESS

The interdependence of bodily functions and electrochemical response patterns under conditions of stress have been of special interest to scientists since the early part of the twentieth century. The pioneering work of Walter Cannon, an American physiologist, was a major impetus to the study of stress during the 1920s and 1930s. Cannon (1932) theorized that demanding conditions—such as extremes of heat or cold, noise, pain, or emotional arousal—cause the body to rapidly mobilize its electrochemical systems in preparation for action. Cannon suggested that this reaction, called the *fight-or-flight* response, is fueled by an "emergency adrenalin secretion" that prepares the body quickly and efficiently for either meeting the challenge or escaping it. He further hypothesized that the fight-or-flight response has an adaptive function in assuring safety or promoting relief from danger and that it evolved in all higher organisms because of its intrinsic survival value.

According to Cannon, the body is mobilizing its resources for a physical fight or a swift escape. When faced with a threat to one's life, survival would depend on making the most appropriate and quickest response. Were threat to lead to paralysis, as sometimes happens when an animal or human "freezes" in the face of extreme fear, then serious harm or even destruction would result. The fight-or-flight response was seen by Cannon as a built-in mechanism for preventing harm by taking one of two other more adaptive courses of action. For example, perhaps you have had the experience of having to quickly run out of the way of a speeding automobile, slam on your brakes to avoid hitting a child darting onto the street, or rush to a patient's room when a "code blue" is signaled. In each case the value of the fight-or-flight response is clearly evident: All bodily systems are activated for emergency action. As Cannon would suggest, this rapid activation of the fight-or-flight response is necessary to protect your survival or someone else's.

The biochemical processes that comprise the fight-or-flight response are hidden from view. Yet hundreds of studies conducted since Cannon introduced the concept have demonstrated that a highly complex interplay between the functions of the endocrine and autonomic nervous systems underlies the general fight-or-flight reaction. It is now known that the "emergency adrenalin secretion" is only one aspect of a diffuse response to stressful, dangerous, or otherwise demanding conditions. A model that implicates the endocrine and autonomic nervous systems to explain the body's response to stress has been advanced by Selye (1936, 1956, 1976).

Stress Response

The first systematic attempt to identify the principal bodily systems involved in the fight-or-flight response was undertaken by Hans Selye in 1936. Now considered one of the foremost authorities on stress, Selye (1956, 1976) elaborated on the fight-or-flight concept, thereby developing a comprehensive theory of physiological response.

In this theory Selye outlined the *general adaptation syndrome*, or *stress response*, which is consistent with Cannon's fundamental premise that the body possesses a built-in reaction to a wide variety of demanding situations. The general adaptation syndrome (GAS) is a three-phase model of the temporal sequence of adaptation to stressful conditions, which are called *stressors*. Stressors refer to factors that produce a characteristic response in the body (i.e., the stress response). In other words, any internal or external stimulus condition that elicits the stress response is considered to be a stressor. Listing the characteristics of these stressors would be virtually impossible since any stimulus may have that potential.

The general adaptation syndrome is based on Selye's hypothesis that the body's response to stressors typically occurs in three major phases. The first phase, *alarm*, represents an emergency reaction involving the activation of the body's defensive forces. During this reaction a perceived stressor elicits an immediate "call to arms" within the body. The second phase is *resistance*, in which physiological adaptation is at a maximum level of operation in terms of the bodily resources used. The body uses its physical resources to resist the demands imposed upon it. The third and final phase is *exhaustion*, in which bodily resources are depleted and the individual loses the ability to resist continued exposure to the stressors. It is hypothesized that this is the stage at which coping patterns fail. The latter two phases correspond most closely to the syndrome of burnout. In all three stages the autonomic nervous system and the endocrine system are intricately involved. An understanding of the stress response requires that the biochemical functions of these systems be outlined, for the characteristic reactions of these systems are assumed to be at the very heart of one's subjective experience of both stress and burnout.

Endocrine System

The endocrine system consists of a series of glands that manufacture chemical products called *hormones*. Glands that produce hormones include the pituitary gland, thyroid and parathyroid glands, adrenal cortex, adrenal medulla, ovary, and testis. These glands release hormones as a result of direct nervous stimulation and/or as a result of hormonal secretions from another endocrine gland. Even small amounts of a hormone or combination of hormones may have dramatic effects on the body.

The pituitary gland performs a particularly important function. The *anterior* component of this gland secretes various hormones known as *trophic hormones*, which seek out other glands and stimulate them to secrete their own respective hormones. Because of this function, the pituitary gland has often been referred to as the *master gland*. The master gland (in particular, the anterior portion) secretes a hormone that directly stimulates the activity of the *adrenal cortex*. The specific hormone is called *adrenocorticotrophic hormone* (ACTH). This hormone is especially critical in the stress response. ACTH activates the adrenal cortex to secrete substances known as *corticoids*. The corticoids are of two general types. Members of one group, the *glucocorticoids* (including cortisone, hydrocortisone, and corticosterone), are involved in the metabolism of sugar. They promote an increase in blood sugar available for energy as well as a redistribution of blood in the body. They also have a paradoxical function: They inhibit the processes by which the body controls tissue damage, and they lower resistance to infection. During the alarm phase of the GAS, a high production of corticoids is generated. If the stressors persist, the body continues to produce glucocorticoids, which continue to hamper the ability of the body to control tissue damage and form immunological defenses against infection and disease. Yet the body strives to fight off tissue damage during the resistance phase. If, however, the stressors are excessive, unrelieved, and deplete the body's resources to resist, exhaustion occurs and the result is tissue damage or infection or both.

The second type of corticoids, the *adrenal corticoids*, produced during the stress response are metabolized in the body and create various metabolites. *Corticosteroids* are among the metabolites most often used in measuring physiological stress. There are two major kinds of corticosteroids: *17-ketosteroids* and *17-hydroxycorticosteroids* (17-OH-CS). Because the levels of these two steroid products are quite sensitive to stress effects, changes in their levels are often used to identify the presence of a stress response. The stress response effects an increase in the levels of both.

So far it would appear that the stress response is primarily a function of an orchestrated secretion of a family of hormones from the pituitary-adrenal axis. But this is only part of the overall picture. The rest of the picture includes the autonomic nervous system.

Autonomic Nervous System

The autonomic nervous system (ANS) is comprised of a collection of nerves that activate vascular and glandular structures. The particular nerves of the ANS are called *motor nerves* or *efferent nerves*. A typical nerve extends from the spinal cord and contacts a group of nerve cells whose cell bodies are located outside the spinal cord. At this junction point another nerve receives an impulse and carries it to a specific organ and stimulates the organ.

The ANS is divided into two main branches: the *sympathetic* division and the *parasympathetic* division. These divisions usually have opposite effects on the body. The sympathetic branch is associated with arousal, whereas the parasympathetic branch is related to relaxation. Thus, during the stress response motor nerves carry impulses from the sympathetic branch to the heart, organs, and muscles, and all bodily systems are aroused for fight-or-flight. When stressors are reduced or eliminated, messages are sent by the parasympathetic nervous system to those structures and a decrease in arousal is effected.

One gland that is stimulated primarily by the sympathetic nervous system is the *adrenal medulla*. Although the adrenal cortex is activated by ACTH from the pituitary gland, the adrenal medulla (center core) is activated by nerve impulses. When activation occurs, the adrenal medulla secretes its hormonal substances: *adrenalin, noradrenalin,* and *dopamine*. The three are collectively known as the *catecholamines*, and they have various effects on the stress response. For example, the relationships between adrenalin and anxiety or anger have been discussed for years. However, adrenalin and noradrenalin have been correlated with qualitatively different kinds of emotions. This fact suggests that there may be important hormonal differences in the various emotional states accompanying the stress response. As we shall see later, such findings pose some special problems for the theory of stress response.

The question still remains as to where this general bodily response begins. Through processes that are not fully understood, the stress response begins the instant a stressor is perceived by an individual. Selye (1976) suggested that when stressors are perceived, somehow the *hypothalamus* functions much like a central arousal mechanism and triggers the pituitary gland to secrete ACTH. When ACTH reaches the adrenal cortex, a characteristic reaction is set off whereby a host of corticoid hormones are released into the bloodstream. At the same time the sympathetic nervous system instantly activates the adrenal medulla to release catecholamines. All these substances reach organs and muscles and bring the body to a highly aroused state.

This state of arousal—coordinated by an electrochemical mobilization of glands, organs, and muscles—can be appreciated by taking a moment to imagine that your professor has suddenly asked you to come to the front of the classroom and give an oral report to the entire class. Or, if you are currently a practitioner, you might think of a time when you had to respond to a patient who had gone into cardiac arrest. In either case your stress response would be essentially the same (at least that is what the theory maintains). How might you experience this arousal?

Immediately your attention narrows to the task at hand. Your heart rate increases, your muscles become more richly supplied with blood. As tiny blood vessels constrict and divert blood away from your extremities, your hands may begin to feel colder. Your brain is supplied with more needed glucose, which has been converted from glycogen stored in the liver. As your breathing becomes more rapid, the amount of oxygen in the blood is increased, thus enabling your brain and your muscles to burn glucose efficiently. As blood rushes to your brain, electrical activity in the brain is intensified and you assume even greater control over your bodily movements. Your hearing becomes more acute, your pupils dilate, and your vision becomes more acute. As bodily systems are gearing up for fight-or-flight, it may be more difficult to think clearly because the brain is focused more on the motor aspects of your response. It should not be difficult to appreciate the survival value of this kind of bodily reaction to perceived stressors. Yet contemporary living does not usually place us in situations where the fight-or-flight response is activated in the face of repeated threats of serious bodily harm. Nor do we typically deal with threats by outward aggression or by running away, even if we would like to. Giving an oral report to your class is not a life-threatening event, and running wildly from the classroom is not the appropriate response to the threat you may perceive. Nor is it acceptable to approach and hit your professor with a textbook simply because you were asked to give an oral report. The primitive tendency to fight or flee must be overcome, and you must deal with the threat in more controlled ways. However, *the stress response still prepares you for fight-or-flight*. One of the demands of contemporary life is to find more effective avenues for managing the stress response. The demand is to do so in socially acceptable ways. Such responses are influenced by others' expectations, and these expectations themselves can intensify the experience of stress.

Thus, there is irony associated with the stress response. We often "stew in our own juices" because the stress response is activated for fight-or-flight, but we do not respond with physical fighting or physical flight. Some of the "juices" we stew in are the corticoids, steroids, and catecholamines. Fortunately, however, the complementary action of the parasympathetic nervous system helps to reduce the levels of various substances in the body. Whereas the sympathetic nervous system acts to trigger all systems at once, the parasympathetic nervous system acts in a slower, more specific manner on targeted organs to bring the body back to a state of relative balance or *homeostasis*. What these facts suggest is that it takes longer to relax than it does to become aroused. Today the lives of many people consist of repeated demands that stimulate arousal throughout the day, with only infrequent periods of relaxation. Because this type of low-grade arousal persists on a chronic basis, it becomes more and more difficult for the body to repair the effects of the stress response.

Everyone has an occasional bad day at work, and everyone experiences occasional crises and emotional upsets. Usually we have little trouble adapting to these stressors because they are short-lived. The stress response operates to deal with such situations in the short run, within minutes or a few hours at most. But when hours turn into days, and when days turn into weeks, and weeks into months, a prolonged state of arousal exists from which the individual cannot escape. This prolonged arousal is what is meant by *chronic stress*.

Chronic stress is qualitatively different from *episodic stress*, in which the body's stress response is distinct and of short duration. Episodic stress allows the body to eventually return to a balanced state, a low level of activation. It occurs infrequently enough to allow the individual to recover and re-energize when the stressors have been removed or avoided. The person experiencing chronic stress, however, is an individual who is at a relatively continuous level of arousal, without sufficient recovery time. Health professionals typically work under conditions of chronic stress, functioning at above-normal levels of arousal for long periods of time without sufficient time for rest and recovery. Their work is not a low-stimulus variety with only occasional demands for fight-or-flight. It characteristically involves high levels of arousal that continue on a daily basis, without substantial relief from fight-or-flight mobilization. It is not episodic stress that leads to burnout among health professionals; it is chronic stress that gradually drains them of their resources for continued adaptation and coping.

Selye (1974) hypothesized that individuals use up a special energy source during the stress response. He posited that *adaptation energy* provides the power to mobilize the body and give it strength for fight-or-flight. According to Seyle, constant drains on this energy supply eventually deplete it. Selye maintained that each person has a finite supply of energy for adaptation at the time stressors are encountered. After using all that is available during a stressful experience, the individual is thought to need a period of rest so that this energy supply can be replenished. Because the parasympathetic nervous system is not engaged long enough to counter the effects of arousal, the stress response continues and the energy available for adaptation is expended. This is the point at which exhaustion, one aspect of burnout, sets in.

Physical Illness and Nonspecificity of Stress

Selye (1974) regarded the stress response as a stereotypical reaction of the body: *"the nonspecific response of the body to any demand made upon it"* (p. 14). Within this definition is a very important notion: the nonspecificity of the body's response to stressors. According to Selye, although every demand made on the body is specific and unique (e.g., cold temperatures, which elicit shivering to generate more heat; warm temperatures, which stimulate perspiration as a cooling effect; or exercise, which calls for increased demands from the muscles and cardiovascular system), *the body's overall response to those stressors is not specific*. Even though each demand may have some specific effects, each one produces general effects as well. According to Selye, it is immaterial whether the demand is pleasant or unpleasant because each stressor provokes the same biochemical stress response in the body. Stressors may vary, but the stress response does not. Each stressor makes a nonspecific demand that the body adapt itself. This stereotyped, nonspecific, and orchestrated gross bodily reaction called the stress response, or general adaptation syndrome, is, therefore, assumed to be the same, regardless of the particular stressors. Whether a person is surprised with a promotion or stunned by a layoff, the bodily response to those conditions is viewed as essentially the same.

Selye (1974) offered an analogy for the notion of nonspecificity of the stress response. Home appliances such as refrigerators, heaters, bells, radios, and light bulbs produce—respectively—cold, heat, sound, and light. But to function they depend on one common factor: electricity. A person unfamiliar with electricity would probably find it hard to believe that all these phenomena depend on one common source. Selye assumed that different outcomes emerged from the same prerequisite generalized response. Electricity is likened to the stressor effect: The specific results may be different, but the underlying process is the same.

The nonspecificity of stress, posited by Selye, has further implications. He argued that it is not only immaterial whether a stressor is pleasant or unpleasant but also equally *irrelevant if the stress response is somatically induced or psychologically induced.* For example, physical trauma elicits the stress response, but the same response can also be produced by the *thought* of being physically harmed. Somatically induced stress and psychologically induced stress are seen by Selye (1974) as biologically identical: "It is difficult to see how such essentially different things as cold, heat, drugs, hormones, sorrow, and joy could provoke an identical biochemical reaction in the body. Nevertheless, this is the case" (p. 16).

As suggested earlier, the stress response may be implicated in various physical illnesses. In fact, professionals and lay persons alike now seem to be making increasingly frequent attributions to stress as one of the most significant hazards to health. Chronic stress—the continuous, unrelieved level of low-grade arousal—is assumed to play a determinant role in serious health breakdowns (Pelletier, 1977). Chronic stress is also assumed to play a direct causal role in the development of the burnout syndrome (Veninga and Spradley, 1981). The process of physical deterioration believed by many to occur within the body under prolonged stress is not completely understood. Yet many medical experts consider the notion of a stress response to be one of the most valuable organizing concepts in science (Albrecht, 1979). It is a concept that suggests that the human body is capable of literally destroying itself under prolonged conditions of arousal without relief. Although stress is an organizing rubric for innumerable physical illnesses, from hypertension and heart attack to a host of gastrointestinal and even nutritional disturbances, it is still not clear which mechanisms are involved in the etiology of stress-related somatic illness.

What does the research suggest about physical deterioration under prolonged stress? There are at least three main ways in which stress may lead to physical illness (Monat and Lazarus, 1977). First, as powerful hormones are released into the bloodstream, significant alterations in bodily processes occur. When these changes are produced repeatedly by neurohumoral influences, permanent disruptions of tissue functions can result. As the fight-or-flight arousal response is activated in a chronically recurrent pattern, bodily tissues may simply wear out. Theoretically the weakest somatic link in the chain of bodily reactions would wear out first. Symptoms of disease or illness then would appear as signs of tissue damage in particular organs, glands, or muscles. A second possibility is that individuals may resort to self-defeating or self-destructive coping efforts in the face of stressful conditions. Maladaptive coping behaviors could include excessive smoking and drinking or spending more hours at work and fewer at leisure as part of an achievement-oriented life-style. Such patterns of day-to-day living are inherently noxious to bodily systems and may lead to somatic illness as tissues become damaged by the strain. Third, individuals may persist in judging physical symptoms as benign or meaningless when the symptoms are not. Consequently, they may habitually minimize signs of true illness and thereby avoid medical intervention and exacerbate the symptoms. On the other hand, they may attribute the symptoms to actual disease processes that are not amenable to medical treatment.

Of these three sets of possible cause-effect sequences, the first has received the most attention. Researchers have been especially interested in how stress produces bodily illness through hormonal secretions that alter tissue functions (Monat and Lazarus, 1977). Selye's collective work has generated this interest. The nonspecificity of the stress response hypothesized by Selye has been accepted for years as the characteristic physiological reaction that ultimately increases susceptibility to disease when stressors go unrelieved. There is an abundance of scientific evidence favoring the notion of a causative nonspecific stress response. Some recent findings, however, have suggested that adrenal cortical hormone secretions may *not* occur as part of a stereotypical stress response (Lazarus, 1974; Mason, 1971, 1975; Melton, McKenzie, and Saldivar, 1974). Instead, they suggest there may be some *specific* reactions that mediate between specific stressors and specific somatic illnesses.

Although the notion of a general adaptation syndrome may have considerable utility in helping us to understand stress, it now appears that there may be specific as well as general causes of stress-related disorders.

Psychological Factors and Stress Response

In a study of stress among air traffic controllers (ATCs), Smith, Melton, and McKenzie (1971) found no evidence that ATCs at air-ports with high-density traffic experienced more anxiety (which was used as a measure of stress) than ATCs at a medium-density airport. In another study, Melton, Smith, and McKenzie (1975) found that physiological stress among ATCs at a high-density airport was greater than the physiological stress of ATCs at a low-density air-port, but that there was no significant difference between the two groups on measures of psychological stress. Air traffic control may have no significant effect on the psychological state of ATCs

(Melton, Smith, and McKenzie, 1978), even where there are dramatic effects on their physiological states.

It appears that a critical variable in the psychological experience of stress is *perception* of stressors. As we shall see shortly, perception can be a critical factor in determining physiological stress as well. For example, it is assumed that the job of the air traffic controller is a particularly stressful one. Most people also assume that the job of a nurse is a stressful one. Although both occupations may correlate with significant physiological stress responses, they do not necessarily correlate with psychological stress. In the case of ATCs, Smith (1973) found that low-density shifts were rated less favorably because they provided less challenge. The same factors that effected increases in measures of physiological stress (i.e., the pressure of traffic density, the fast and changing pace of the jobs) were also those that provided the most satisfaction and facilitated the best performance. The unique pressures of air traffic control were identified as one of the most attractive aspects of the job. Although similar studies in the nursing field have yet to be undertaken, it would seem logical to assume that the same holds true. In fact, there is some evidence that indicates that ICU nurses perceive interpersonal relationships as a major source of stress on their jobs and, at the same time, one of their greatest sources of job satisfaction (Bailey, Steffen, and Grout, 1980).

As Grout (1980) suggested, although situational demands may indeed have the potential to elicit a stress response, *they should not be considered stressors unless they do*. Different individuals may appraise situations as stressful or nonstressful, and the perceptual and cognitive processes involved—psychological processes—may be the most crucial aspects of the experience of stress. Indeed, there may be no stress response at all unless environmental demands are perceived and judged to tax or exceed the individual's resources for adapting. Psychological factors must play a pivotal role in the stress response. For the hypothalamus to trigger the stress response, it is necessary for perceptual and cognitive processes to intervene.

Mason (1971, 1975) and Lazarus (1978; Lazarus, Cohen, and Folkman, 1980; Coyne and Lazarus, 1980; Lazarus, Averill, and Opton, 1970) maintained that the response of the body to stressors is mediated by *emotional arousal* and *cognitive appraisal*. In addition, they argued that this response may be stimulus-specific. During the 1960s, for example, Lazarus and associates conducted several studies that repeatedly showed that normally stressful events can be rendered less threatening through cognitive efforts to achieve control over emotions. In those studies where situations were manipulated to encourage subjects to use denial and intellectualization as defenses against anxiety, those subjects showed lower levels of the stress response. It was also found that lower levels of autonomic arousal among subjects were related to their "defensive dispositions" (Lazarus, Averill, and Opton, 1970). As a whole, the extensive research conducted by the Lazarus group accumulated substantive evidence in support of the hypothesis that how a person appraises and copes with a stressor has a significant effect on the emotional and adaptational outcome (Coyne and Lazarus, 1980).

Such findings suggest that the body's response to stress may not be absolutely nonspecific. They also suggest that if different response patterns are associated with different stressors, and if those different reactions are associated with various emotional states, then stress reactions may be mediated by the individual's perceptions and may even be specific to particular kinds of personal appraisals about the nature of different situations. Therefore, a model of stress response needs to account equally for the ways in which individuals cognitively appraise situations and for the kinds of stressors that are hypothesized to cause a physiological stress response. To account for stress without including psychosocial factors slants perspectives on etiology and treatment. If nothing else, excluding these factors precludes meaningful hypotheses concerning individual differences in stress response and coping. In understanding burnout as a consequence of prolonged stress, what is needed is a practical framework for conceptualizing the variable effects of stress among health professionals.

LAZARUS'S TRANSACTIONAL MODEL

The most extensively developed and influential approach to psychological stress is that described by Lazarus (1966, 1967; Coyne and Lazarus, 1980). It is a model of stress that exemplifies the current attention being given to interactions between individuals and their environments. The central focus is on the nature of interchanges, or *transactions*, between person and environment and the cognitive processes that intervene in the person-environment relationship.

Within the transactional model, psychological stress is seen as a product of the way an individual appraises and constructs a relationship with the environment. In this relationship environmental demands, cognitive appraisals, coping efforts, and emotional responses are interrelated in reciprocal ways so that each affects the others. Stress is not conceptualized as a linear phenomenon resulting solely from impinging environmental forces; nor is it hypothesized as arising solely from within the individual. Rather, stress results from the interaction of factors assumed to play causal roles. The model represents a departure from traditional stimulus-response approaches that emphasize a single order of events (i.e., where environmental conditions are identified as specific antecedents that exert a one-way influence on how an individual responds). The transactional model recognizes that different people experience stress in different ways because the seemingly identical conditions to which they are exposed are *not* really the same for each person. To account for these differences the model incorporates the pivotal concepts of *cognitive appraisal, threat,* and *coping.* These concepts include various important processes described by Coyne and Lazarus (1980).

Cognitive Appraisal

The notion of appraisal has assumed a prominent place in the literature on psychological stress (Arnold, 1967; Averill, 1973; Lazarus, 1966). In general, *appraisal* refers to evaluations and judgments of events and of one's reactions to those events. It is assumed that individuals tend to appraise the events to which they are exposed and that they appraise their own behavior in response to those events. It follows, then, that an individual's assessments of events and actions play a determinant part in the experience of psychological stress. Lazarus and Coyne outlined this process within the context of a cognitive appraisal mechanism. They defined *cognitive appraisal* as "the person's continually re-evaluated judgments about demands and constraints in ongoing transactions with the environment and his or her own resources and options for managing them" (Coyne and Lazarus, 1980, p. 150). These appraisals or judgments determine the person's stress reactions, the kind of emotions experienced, and the outcomes of attempts to adapt to perceived stressors.

Primary appraisal

A person's judgment about the significance of a stressor is called *primary appraisal.* It is the evaluation of the direct implications that a particular encounter has for one's well-being. According to Lazarus (1974), individuals formulate an answer to the question of whether or not a transaction is threatening: "Am I safe or in some kind of danger?" (p. 261). Primary appraisals come in three forms: *irrelevant* appraisals, positive appraisals, and stressful appraisals. *Irrelevant appraisals* are those judgments that an event is innocuous and non-threatening. For instance, irrelevant appraisals occur when we ignore events that we judge to have no bearing on our own health and well-being. A nurse may hear about a major staff change at a different hospital and pass it off as irrelevant to the immediate circumstances. A primary appraisal may lead to the judgment that an event is beneficial or *positive*. A CCU nurse, for example, may judge a patient's heart-monitoring data as indicating stability or improvement and, therefore, posing no cause for concern or action. Finally, a primary appraisal may involve judgments of harm, loss, threat, or challenge. These are called *stressful appraisals*, and they include negative evaluations of one's present or future well-being. One judges an event or transaction as having some immediate or probable adverse effect on one's welfare.

Stressful appraisals that involve judgments of harm, loss, threat, or challenge are dependent on the person's time perspective (as are all other appraisals). According to Lazarus (1978), harm and loss refer to damage already sustained, such as illness, injury, demotion, or loss of a friend. Threat, on the other hand, may relate to similar damages, but the temporal orientation is toward the future. It pertains to the anticipation of something that has not yet happened. Stressful appraisals involving judgments of harm, loss, or threat can occur simultaneously or alternately. For example, nurses transferred to a new department might focus on the loss of status, familiarity, enjoyment, and confidence associated with their former jobs. Or they might dwell on the threat of increased pressure, interpersonal conflicts, or restricted privilege and authority. They might even be preoccupied with both their losses and new possibilities as they try to come to terms with the circumstances. When a stressful appraisal concerns harm or loss, the person's attention is focused on how to deal with the harm or loss in terms of tolerating or overcoming either. When the appraisal focuses on threat, the individual's concerns tend to center on how to ward off or prevent expected harm, since it has yet to occur. Therefore, in the previous example nurses transferred to a different department may experience stress as they strive to deal with their perceived losses and prevent anticipated problems.

Stressful appraisals may also involve judgments of challenge. Situations evaluated as challenging are those that offer the potential for mastery or gain as well as the potential for harm or loss. Lazarus, Cohen, and Folkman (1980) suggested that judgments under these circumstances include beliefs that the demands of a transaction can be met and overcome. However, the perception of challenge versus threat (both of which relate to potential future transactions with the environment) is a complex phenomenon in its own right. In some instances this appraisal could depend on what the person selects for attention; that is, what aspects of the transaction are emphasized in the appraisal process and what aspects are de-emphasized. Depending on what a person perceives as significant in a transaction, the outcome of the appraisal can be a judgment of challenge or a judgment of threat. Furthermore, the appraisal of challenge may represent a distortion of reality. So could the appraisal of threat. Thus, the individual may perceive challenge where there actually is threat or may perceive threat where realistically there is none.

It is apparent within the transactional model that the effectiveness of a person's cognitive appraisal can be assessed by the extent to which those appraisals lead to behavior that maintains or promotes the individual's well-being and adaptive functioning. It may be that burnout is one indication of faulty appraisals. However, the picture is not yet complete because other factors are also involved.

Secondary appraisal

The individual's judgments about the resources and options available for coping with stressful transactions, the constraints on using those resources, and the consequences of using them represent *secondary appraisals*. As Lazarus put it, primary appraisal deals with the question Am I okay or in trouble?, while secondary appraisal concerns the question What can I do about it? The basic difference between primary and secondary appraisal is in the *content* of what is being evaluated. Apart from this distinction, the two are highly interdependent processes. For example, individuals may believe that they can handle most stressful situations. This is a secondary appraisal, and it may lead them to judge transactions as nonstressful (primary appraisal) that would otherwise be threatening. Conversely, if they believe that they are without adequate coping resources, they may appraise an event as threatening although it otherwise would not be (Coyne and Lazarus, 1980).

The ways in which a person tries to cope with events appraised as stressful are determined partly by secondary appraisal, which is guided by factors such as prior experience in similar situations, beliefs about self and the environment, and the actual availability of resources for effective responding. Thus, when a person appraises a situation as stressful, the answer to the question "What do I do about it?" depends on such things as whether or not the person has had prior experience in similar situations, whether or not previous responses to those situations were effective, whether or not the same or similar coping resources can be used for the present situation, whether or not the person believes the demands of the situation can be met, and whether or not the person believes that the stress can be managed.

The relationship between individuals and their environment is an ever-changing, fluid, and dynamic one. Because this relationship is never precisely the same over time, changing conditions of the relationship require that the individuals change their cognitive appraisals as those conditions change. For example, self-appraisal of an individual's relationship to the work environment typically changes as either the individual or the work environment or both change. Such changes in cognitive appraisals would be assumed to occur over time, from the point of initial employment, as the individual becomes socialized into the work place. The process of changing judgments is called *reappraisal*. Lazarus (1974) described reappraisal as basically a feedback process that takes two forms. The first form of reappraisal involves processing new information about the ways in which the person-environment relationship is different and the significance of changes for one's well-being. Thus, a reappraisal could involve the judgment that one's job seems more demanding now than it was two months ago and that the increased demands are eventually going to wear one down. It could also involve an appraisal of harm if one judges that the increased work demands have caused one to lose sleep and develop an ulcer. A second form of reappraisal is defensive in nature. It involves an attempt to reduce personal distress by reevaluating and changing an originally stressful appraisal into an irrelevant or positive one. What was initially judged to be threatening is reappraised as nonthreatening or beneficial. The intent of this defensive reappraisal is to reduce emotional distress, not to look more critically at a stressful person-environment transaction with an eye toward changing it. Defensive reappraisal is an evaluative process that crosses over into the kinds of adaptation-related behaviors typically associated with coping.

Coping

Cognitive appraisals may be conscious and deliberate or automatic, impulsive, and even unconscious (Coyne and Lazarus, 1980). Whether conscious or unconscious, cognitive appraisal is an integral step in moving the individual toward adaptation to conditions perceived as stressful. Within the transactional framework, stressful transactions are those in which demands tax or exceed the individual's adaptive resources. Stressful appraisals, of course, occur when individuals judge that demanding transactions push them toward the limits of their adaptive capabilities. The actual processes of responding to such conditions are collectively referred to as *coping responses*. *Coping* is defined by Lazarus and Launier (1978) as "efforts, both action-oriented and intrapsychic, to manage (that is, to master, tolerate, reduce, minimize) environmental and internal demands and conflicts among them which tax or exceed a person's resources" (p. 311). When we speak of coping, we usually think of some kind of serious problem that causes an individual considerable emotional distress and requires response to the problematic situation in new and unfamiliar ways. If problems can be dealt with automatically by the effective use of habitual problem-solving behaviors, little actual coping occurs because the person's resources have not been sufficiently taxed. Coping is a concept reserved for adaptation under *difficult* conditions (White, 1974), conditions perceived as stressful.

Within the transactional framework, coping is seen as serving two functions: (1) to alter the ongoing person-environment relationship and (2) to control stressful emotions. The first function, alteration of the person-environment relationship, is attempted through *problem-focused* coping strategies that include *direct actions* such as fight-or-flight or approach-avoidance. The aim of direct-action coping is to manage the perceived sources of stress in some way, either by changing one's behavior or by changing the environment or both. Coping is problem focused in that it is oriented toward the problem generating the stress and toward the trouble in which one finds oneself. Imagine, for example, that after years of preparation you must soon take your licensing examination. The examination is extremely important to you and your career, and it is very challenging. At the same time it is threatening because there is always the chance of failure. Think of how you might approach this examination. Your preparation would probably include a survey of pertinent books and articles, a review of your class notes, perhaps rehearsals of answers to expected questions, and maybe even discussions with people who recently took the examination. As you do all of this preparation, you are attempting to manage the problem situation. You are focusing on the task at hand and thereby attempting to modify a demanding relationship with your current environment. You are trying to gain a sense of confidence, readiness, and control of that relationship. If your efforts lead you to reappraise the upcoming examination as less threatening than you originally thought, then your emotional response to the transaction is altered. Your anxiety is reduced. Regardless of how accurate your appraisals and reappraisals are, you have addressed the problem confronting you. You have changed the ongoing relationship with your environment, and one consequence has been a lessening of your fear and apprehension.

The second function of coping is *emotionally focused*. It is aimed at the direct reduction of emotional distress and the maintenance of an internal state that is conducive to unimpaired appraisal and effective action. Thoughts or actions whose goal is to reduce the emotional impact of stress are referred to as *palliative modes* of coping. They are called *palliative* because they make the person feel better without actually changing the stressful circumstances. These modes of coping focus primarily on the stressful emotions produced by demanding transactions with the environment. To clarify this function, let us return to the hypothetical licensing examination. In your mind recapture the significance of such an examination. In some ways it represents the most formidable challenge of your career to date; it is a challenge to your developing professional identity. Success means formal and legal affirmation of a minimally acceptable level of competence. Failure not only implies the opposite but also prevents your planned entry into practice, causes you great embarrassment and humiliation, and probably generates considerable self-doubt. Stretch your imagination a bit to envision the anxiety you would probably feel as the examination approaches. You could cope with this stressful relationship with your environment by employing problem-focused efforts, such as those described before. On the other hand, you could bypass the problem causing your anxiety and try to cope directly with the anxiety. If this is the course you pursue, then you might try to divert your thoughts from the examination, do relaxation exercises, go out and run or play tennis, medicate yourself with tranquilizers or alcohol, or simply try to convince yourself that the examination really does not mean anything and that passing or failing is no reflection on your skills anyway. Whatever you choose to do in this case is aimed at controlling the disturbing emotions rather than the relationship that is causing your anxiety. This is not to say that these coping efforts are necessarily maladaptive. Sometimes they may be all that are available as options. The point is that they are coping efforts that *do* serve a function: They help regulate emotions. And, as Lazarus (1977) noted in relation to the kind of test anxiety considered here, sometimes problem-focused direct actions are impaired by an emotion that interferes with clear thinking. Indeed, when you are experiencing extreme anxiety, it becomes very hard to concentrate. Under these kinds of circumstances, then, it is sometimes necessary to reduce the intensity of an emotion in any way possible in order to facilitate coping efforts aimed at changing the stressful person-environment relationship. Thus, it may be necessary to reduce your anxiety level *before* problem-focused coping is undertaken.

The examples used here to point up the two basic functions of coping may suggest to you that coping is something that *follows* stressful emotions. Yet the transactional model suggests that many of our coping efforts are oriented toward the anticipation of future threat. Consequently, if you anticipate failing a licensing examination, your anticipation may lead you to begin preparing for the worst —just as you would prepare for the possibility of harm when a tornado warning is announced over your radio. By preparing for the expected threat, you may be able to prevent actual harm from occurring. To the extent that you accomplish this, you have effectively altered the nature of the transaction. You have also changed the emotions that might have been experienced if you had not expected the harm. As Lazarus (1977) stated, "Overcoming the danger before it materializes can lead to exhilaration rather than fear, grief, depression, or whatever, depending on the nature of the harm or loss that might have been experienced and the appraisal of the reasons for success" (p. 153).

Coping, therefore, is seen as an adaptive response that can either precede or follow emotions. It also plays a role in determining which environmental influences are brought into a transaction and what form they will take (Coyne and Lazarus, 1980). This way of looking at coping behavior parallels the social learning view that individuals play active roles in influencing the environmental forces that subsequently impinge upon them. In a reciprocal fashion, person and environment influence each other. Individuals typically choose and help to create the environmental conditions to which they must respond. (In Chapter 6 this point is pursued in detail as various coping styles and strategies are examined.)

SUMMARY AND IMPLICATIONS

Although there are various ways in which stress is conceptualized within a linear stimulus-response framework, significant limitations are apparent whenever the phenomenon is defined as either an environmental stimulus or an internal response. A practical alternative is the view that stress represents an imbalance between demands and the resources to deal with them. Such a view focuses on the role of stimulus and response as variables in person-environment transactions. Using these concepts within a transactional framework may permit hypotheses about how individuals appraise what is being experienced at any given moment and how they use that information to cope and affect their ongoing relationships with the environment. Transactions are appraised, coping processes are employed, and the effects of these responses are appraised and reacted to in a continuous reciprocal flow of information between the individual and the environment.

An implication of adopting such a process-oriented perspective is that the etiology of stress and burnout need to be conceptualized in nonlinear terms. The causes of stress and burnout may not be found in a perspective where causes are balanced against effects in a one-way relationship. Although there do appear to be certain environmental conditions that often function as common stressors, they do not function as stressors *unless individuals perceive them as such.* Some health professionals burn out and others do not. Further, while certain individuals may have learned characteristic styles of coping and responding to perceived stressors and, therefore, may be more or less predisposed toward burnout, burnout as an effect of perceived stress is still a function of how the person-environment transaction is appraised. Ultimate attributions of cause, therefore, are made to the person-environment transaction and not to static environmental stressors or to personality characteristics, although the latter factors are not totally excluded from a transactional perspective.

For example, suppose two nurses are asked to add five more patients to their respective patient loads. Both nurses view five additional patients as creating a workload that is more than they can be expected to handle. Because of their past experiences and individual personalities, Nurse Jones feels that her inability to handle five more patients reflects on her inadequacy as a health professional, while Nurse Smith feels just as pressured but sees the situation as one in which the administration is constantly trying to squeeze as much work out of him as it can. Both nurses experience anticipatory stress and try to cope with the problem situation by confronting their supervisor. Both experience anxiety prior to the confrontation because they have appraised the situation as threatening. In Nurse Jones, anxiety is accompanied by self-derogation, while in Nurse

Smith anxiety is mixed with anger and blaming. After an unsuccessful confrontation with the supervisor, Nurse Jones experiences greater self-deprecation and disappointment, while Nurse Smith feels mainly anger and resentment. The same set of demands has been appraised differently by these two nurses, and the outcomes of the confrontation are different for each.

Suppose, however, that their confrontation is successful. The nurses may still react differently, depending on whether they attribute their success to their own efforts or to luck. Nurse Jones may attribute the success to her perseverance and skills at persuasion and thereby come to feel much better about herself than Nurse Smith does about himself. Nurse Smith may attribute success to pure chance, in which case he would probably maintain his resentment and anticipate new demands for increased workloads in the near future. In either case, differences in cognitive appraisals affect differences between the two nurses in terms of the intensity of their respective physiological reactions, the intensity of their respective feelings, and the kinds of solutions they choose to pursue. In essence, their respective relationships with their environment are qualitatively different.

REFERENCES

Albrecht, K. *Stress and the manager: Making it work for you.* Englewood Cliffs, N.J.: Prentice-Hall, 1979.

Arnold, M. Stress and emotion. In M.H. Appley & R. Trumbull (Eds.), *Psychological stress.* New York: Appleton-Century-Crofts, 1967.

Averill, J.R. Personal control over aversive stimuli and its relation to stress. *Psychological Bulletin,* 1973, *80,* 286–303.

Bailey, J.T., Steffen, S.M., & Grout, J.W. The stress audit: Identifying the stressors of ICU nursing. *Journal of Nursing Education,* 1980, *19*(6), 15–25.

Cannon, W.B. *The wisdom of the body.* New York: W.W. Norton, 1932.

Coyne, J.C., & Lazarus, R.S. Cognitive style, stress perception, and coping. In I.L. Kutash & L.B. Schlesinger (Eds.), *Handbook on stress and anxiety.* San Francisco: Jossey-Bass, 1980.

Grout, J.W. Occupational stress of intensive care nurses and air traffic controllers: Review of related studies. *Journal of Nursing Education,* 1980, *19*(6), 8–14.

Lazarus, R.S. *Psychological stress and the coping process.* New York: McGraw-Hill, 1966.

Lazarus, R.S. Cognitive and personality factors underlying threat and coping. In M.H. Appley & R. Trumbull (Eds.), *Psychology of stress.* New York: Appleton-Century-Crofts, 1967.

Lazarus, R.S. The psychology of coping: Issues of research and assessment. In G.V. Coelho, D.A. Hamburg, & J.E. Adams (Eds.), *Coping and adaptation.* New York: Basic Books, 1974.

Lazarus, R.S. Cognitive and coping processes in emotion. In A. Monat & R.S. Lazarus (Eds.), *Stress and coping: An anthology.* New York: Columbia University Press, 1977.

Lazarus, R.S. A strategy for research on psychological and social factors in hypertension. *Journal of Human Stress,* September 1978, pp. 35-40.

Lazarus, R.S., Averill, J.R., & Opton, E.M., Jr. Toward a cognitive theory of emotion. In M.B. Arnold (Ed.), *Feelings and emotions.* New York: Academic Press, 1970.

Lazarus, R.S., Cohen, J.B., & Folkman, S. Psychological stress and adaptation: Some unresolved issues. In H. Selye (Ed.), *Selye's guide to stress research* (Vol. 1). New York: Van Nostrand Reinhold, 1980.

Lazarus, R.S., & Launier, R. Stress-related transactions between person and environment. In L.A. Pervin & M. Lewis (Eds.), *Perspectives in interactional psychology.* New York: Plenum Press, 1978.

Mason, J.W. A re-evaluation of the concept of nonspecificity in stress theory. *Journal of Pyschiatric Research,* 1971, *8,* 323-333.

Mason, J.W. A historical view of the stress field (Part 1). *Journal of Human Stress,* March 1975, pp. 6-12.

Mason, J.W. A historical view of the stress field (Part 2). *Journal of Human Stress,* June 1975, pp. 22-36.

Melton, C.E., McKenzie, J.M., & Saldivar, J.T., Jr. *Comparison of Opa Locka Tower with other ATC facilities by means of a biochemical stress index.* (Report FAA-AM-74-11). Oklahoma City: Federal Aviation Administration, Office of Aviation Medicine, December 1974.

Melton, C.E., Smith, R.C., & McKenzie, J.M. *Stress in air traffic controllers: Comparison of two air traffic control centers on different shift rotation patterns.* (Report FAA-AM-75-7). Oklahoma City: Federal Aviation Administration, Office of Aviation Medicine, September 1975.

Melton, C.E., Smith, R.C., & McKenzie, J.M. Stress in air traffic personnel: Low-density towers and flight service stations. *Aviation Space and Environmental Medicine,* 1978, *49,* 724-728.

Monat, A., & Lazarus, R.S. Stress and coping: Some current issues and controversies. In A. Monat & R.S. Lazarus (Eds.), *Stress and coping: An anthology.* New York: Columbia University Press, 1977.

Pelletier, K. *Mind as healer, mind as slayer: A holistic approach to preventing stress disorders.* New York: Dell Publishing, 1977.

Selye, H. A syndrome produced by diverse nocuous agents. *Nature.* July 4, 1936.

Selye, H. *The stress of life.* New York: McGraw-Hill, 1956.

Selye, H. *Stress without distress.* Philadelphia: J.B. Lippincott, 1974.

Selye, H. *Stress in health and disease.* Boston: Butterworth Publishing, 1976.

Smith, R.C. Comparison of the job attitudes of personnel in three air traffic control specialties. *Aerospace Medicine,* 1973, *44*, 918-927.

Smith, R.C., Melton, C.E., & McKenzie, J.M. Affect adjective check list assessment of mood variations in air traffic controllers. *Aerospace Medicine,* 1971, *42*, 1060-1064.

Veninga, R.L., & Spradley, J.P. *The work stress connection: How to cope with job burnout.* Boston: Little, Brown, 1981.

White, R.W. Strategies of adaptation: An attempt at systematic description. In G.V. Coelho, D.A. Hamburg, & J.E. Adams (Eds.), *Coping and adaptation.* New York: Basic Books, 1974.

CHAPTER 3

Effects of burnout on mental and emotional functioning

Prolonged, intense involvement with people in distress and illness is a major stress condition that health professionals are exposed to on a daily basis. In gradual response to the stressful conditions of their work, many health professionals develop a range of physical, psychological, and behavioral symptoms that indicate that they may be burning out on the job. This chapter takes a closer look at the experience of burnout in terms of disruptive effects on emotions and thinking.

As indicated in Chapter 1, the burnout syndrome is a highly variable complex of signs, symptoms, and manifestations. Some individuals who are experiencing burnout may, therefore, have mainly somatic symptoms, others may experience primarily psychological effects, and still others may reveal the effects of burnout in their behavior and work performance. In most cases the burnout experience represents a crisis for these individuals, and all areas of their functioning are impacted in some way. The precise manner in which burnout is experienced and manifested, however, is clearly an individual matter and depends on each person's relationship with the environment. The progression of the syndrome is also variable in its timing and pathogenesis.

When Does Burnout Occur?

In certain professions burnout may occur shortly after the individual enters the job (Pines and Aronson, 1981). In nursing, for example, one study revealed that 70% of staff nurses in American hospitals resigned from their jobs during the year of the study (Lysaught, 1970). In child protection services some departments turn over 50% to 100% of their staff each year (Kempe, 1978). In many human service professions where turnover is extraordinarily high, burnout may be involved. When it is, burnout may claim human service professionals within less than two years after they begin their jobs. Within this short period of time these professionals apparently perceive and appraise their work as being more stressful than they either want or are able to handle. They determine that they have reached, or perhaps surpassed, the limits of their coping resources and that nothing else can be done to alter the situation. While change is the obvious recourse for burned-out workers, often the kind of change believed to be necessary is a total withdrawal from the workplace.

Burnout does not always lead to a terminal point such as turnover or job change. Some individuals do not leave the profession at all, even though they have burned out. They may seek a change of some kind, however. Such persons may make a lateral transfer to a different department, or they may make an upward move into a position of different yet greater responsibility. Still others may remain in the job, burned out and less efficient than they once were. In some respects they become like driftwood, just putting in their hours and going with the flow of events, without resistance and wherever the course of daily events may take them.

For some individuals burnout may occur in *episodes* that last a few days or a few weeks. They recover from the debilitating effects of stress either by finding a useful solution or by having time to recover. Freudenberger (1975) suggested that an individual may burn out in a short period of time, recover, and then burn out again later. According to Freudenberger, there are longer periods of time between each episode after the individual has experienced and recovered from the first one. It seems that those who manage to come through an episode of burnout learn from that experience to pace themselves, protect themselves, and be more cautious about dealing with the stressful aspects of their work. In short, they find alternative coping resources that enable them to function in their stressful jobs without suffering the effects of burnout.

The issue of *when* burnout occurs involves the related question of whether it occurs in stages. Some authors have suggested that burnout progresses through identifiable stages (Cherniss, 1980; Edelwich and Brodsky, 1980; Veninga and Spradley, 1981). Cherniss (1980), for example, hypothesized that burnout is a process that occurs in three general stages:

1. Impinging job stress
2. Emotional response
3. Psychological accommodation

More stringent theories about stages have been postulated by Edelwich and Brodsky (1980) and Veninga and Spradley (1981). Edelwich and Brodsky hypothesized that burnout occurs in four sequential stages:

1. Enthusiasm
2. Stagnation
3. Frustration
4. Apathy

Veninga and Spradley proposed five stages through which the burnout syndrome progresses. Using terms characteristic of the self-help genre, these authors identified the stages as

1. "Honeymoon"
2. "Fuel shortage"
3. Chronic symptoms
4. Crisis
5. "Hitting the wall"

Hypotheses suggesting that burnout occurs over time and in stages are based on the assumption that burnout proceeds through some orderly development. These theories assume that the conditions observed at one point in time are related in a determinant manner to those that occurred at an earlier point in time. They imply that individuals undergo basic transformations during the development of burnout and thus become somehow qualitatively different. The sequence of these changes is fixed, but the rate of change may be modified by experience. Within this fixed sequence there is an attempt to identify critical happenings at different points. However, it seems premature to conclude that burnout does, in fact, progress through an orderly sequence of events and stages. Instead, burnout appears to reflect a process that takes place in a variety of ways, proceeds at different rates, and depends on the nature of each person's relationship with his total experiential world. It seems both reasonable and necessary to assume that there will be considerable individual variability in response to job stress and in the appearance of the burnout syndrome.

GENERAL PSYCHOLOGICAL EFFECTS OF CHRONIC STRESS

It can be argued that a person experiencing burnout is going through a crisis. To appreciate the parallels between burnout and crisis, it is useful to outline a theory of crisis posited by Caplan (1964). This theory sheds additional light on the possible psychological dynamics of the burnout phenomenon.

Caplan's crisis theory is grounded in the concept of emotional balance or *homeostasis*. According to Caplan, individuals are continually exposed to situations that threaten to upset the relative balance of their emotional functioning. In most instances these threats are short-lived because the individual successfully manages the demands of the situations through learned problem-solving skills. There is minimum tension during these episodes because they are usually brief and the individual has learned from past experience that the problem can be resolved. Therefore, the individual successfully copes with the situation. Sometimes, however, the situation cannot be easily mastered by using habitual problem-solving strategies. Then there is a rise in tension and the individual begins to experience a crisis.

Whatever the situation, its potential to precipitate a crisis is largely dependent upon how it is perceived and appraised by the individual. That potential is also a function of the availability of coping resources. When there is an imbalance between the perceived difficulty of the situation and the resources available for coping with it, a crisis may ensue. When a crisis develops, it tends to follow a certain pattern, according to Caplan.

At first, the individual is confronted with a problem that represents a threat to him personally. He responds to feelings of increased tension and anxiety by trying to use problem-solving methods that have worked in the past. If this method is successful, the crisis can be terminated at this point. However, when habitual problem-solving measures fail to solve the problem and restore homeostasis, tension increases further. With the threat looming before him, unresponsive to his attempts at removal, the individual begins to feel as if he cannot handle the situation. This conclusion is followed by random trial-and-error attempts to resolve and master the problem situation. After continued failure to bring about desired results, a further rise in tension serves as a stimulus for mobilizing emergency and new problem-solving measures. Within Lazarus's transactional framework, this may involve cognitive reappraisal—an attempt to redefine the situation to make it fit with past experience or to reappraise certain aspects of the situation as being irrelevant or benign. As Caplan suggested, at this point the individual may resign himself to the problem and withdraw or give up some of his goals. There is also the possibility that these new measures of problem solving may work and, therefore, bring about a restoration of psychological balance. When these efforts are still not successful, the problem continues unresolved and tension mounts toward what Caplan called the "breaking point."

Going through a crisis in this way is not a pathological process. Rather, it represents a struggle for adjustment and adaptation to problems that seem to be unsolvable. A person who comes through the crisis successfully will have experienced psychological growth and will be better prepared to handle similar situations in the future. On the other hand, a person may emerge from a crisis less psychologically healthy than he was prior to its onset. It is interesting to note that the Chinese combine two characters to express the concept of crisis. One means "danger" and the other means "opportunity." Together they represent the idea of crisis. This seems to be a cogent way of thinking about crisis: An individual in crisis is faced with a situation that can result in harm or growth, depending on how the crisis is perceived and responded to. Whenever a condition of danger and opportunity confronts an individual, there is a pressing demand for *change.* The person can change for the better or for the worse, but will not come through the crisis unchanged. In a similar way burnout may signal the need for change. Although it is common to think of burnout in exclusively negative terms, as something bad and inherently destructive, the symptoms of burnout may be helpful to the individual by signaling that some kind of change is necessary. Granted, the burnout experience is not a pleasant one, but change and growth are usually not smooth transitions either. Burnout can lead the individual toward personal changes that are ultimately beneficial, changes that may not have occurred if conditions had not brought the individual to a point of choice between regression and progression.

The crisis theory proposed by Caplan cannot be integrated with the transactional model to provide an accurate account of burnout when both models are taken in their pure forms. That is, the applicability of Caplan's model is limited for several reasons. First, Caplan noted that crises are typically self-limiting and will be resolved for better or worse within one to five weeks. Such resolution does not occur where burnout is concerned. Second, during a crisis an individual experiences an increased desire for help from others and signals this desire to them. Persons who are experiencing burnout may not recognize that they are burning out and are, therefore, in need of help. Consequently, no messages are sent to others to evoke their helping response. Third, during a crisis an individual is typically open to outside intervention. Persons experiencing burnout are not necessarily open to outside intervention since they may not be aware that intervention is necessary.

It is interesting to note that Klein and Lindemann (1961) observed that crisis does not occur in a vacuum. They maintained that an individual's crisis is often an indication that a crisis is being experienced by one or more of that individual's reference groups. Consequently, for them the basic unit of analysis is not the individual, but one or more of the social groups to which that individual belongs. In relation to burnout, the problem of "contagion" has been identified by Edelwich and Brodsky (1980). It suggests that group burnout is something that needs to be considered because it may be rare that an individual health professional is a sole sufferer of the burnout problem. Furthermore, given findings that suggest that group burnout does occur (Freudenberger, 1974; Johnson, 1979, 1982), there are clear implications that an entire organizational structure can be in crisis. Just as crisis represents a turning point for individuals to regress or advance, an organizational crisis confronts a system with the same situation. When group burnout is recognized within an organization, it is a symptom of crisis; and such a large-scale crisis has far-reaching consequences for the total service delivery effort.

Whether burnout, like crisis, can be approached most productively from an individual or a group perspective remains to be demonstrated by research. However, the pattern of responses necessary to manage either experience seems to be similar, regardless of whether those adaptive measures are taken at an individual or a group level. For example, Rapoport (1962) suggested that adaptive resolution of crises requires (1) accurate cognitive appraisal of the situation, (2) appropriate management of emotions in ways that allow for tension reduction, and (3) willingness to accept the help of others in mastering the demands of the situation. The same general approach seems necessary for managing burnout as a form of life crisis.

Fig. 3-1 depicts psychological balance as a function of accurate perceptions and appraisals and adequate coping resources. As a crisis, burnout represents a form of psychological imbalance that results from inefficiency in the appraisal of one's circumstances or the unavailability of adequate coping resources or both. Included in the category of coping resources are adequate *support systems* for managing stress. Support systems consist of *people* who are available to the individual to help work through the demands of problem situations. Often this is a key factor in cases of burnout.

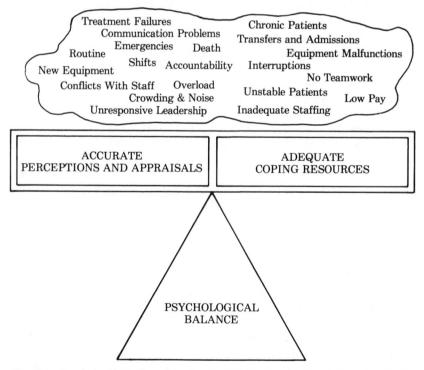

Fig. 3-1 Psychological balance is maintained in the face of stressful events at work when those events are accurately perceived and appraised and when the health professional has adequate resources for coping with perceived stressors.

That is, during times of stress and crisis, the individual does not tap into the resources available from other people as supports. In some cases those supports may simply not exist, even in health care settings. The importance of situational support will be discussed later (see Chapter 8). Here it is sufficient to emphasize that burnout may be prevented in some cases when support systems reinforce existing coping abilities of the individual.

As a way of thinking about the effects of burnout, the frameworks proposed by Lazarus and Caplan are helpful. Although these models have important differences, there are also basic parallels. Both emphasize the importance of cognitive appraisal and coping mechanisms, and both point out the adaptive functions that these processes serve. Caplan's theory offers a way of looking at the ultimate general psychological effects of chronic stress in terms of crises. It is important to note, however, that in most cases crises are precipitated by identifiable events that take place shortly before the onset of psychological disorganization. The events that contribute to burnout often are not clear-cut and do not occur in a close temporal contiguity with their ultimate effects. The essential point is that burnout is a phenomenon that can easily be conceptualized in terms that parallel the crisis experience.

MENTAL EXHAUSTION

There are various dimensions to the mental exhaustion associated with burnout. At one level mental exhaustion is evidenced by difficulty in paying attention and concentrating. At another level it involves an impaired ability to solve problems and make decisions. At still another level mental exhaustion is characterized by the development of negative attitudes toward health care recipients, colleagues, the work environment, and even toward oneself. This section will examine the dimensions of mental exhaustion.

Attention and Concentration

As noted in Chapter 2, our perceptions of the world are selective. This means that instead of responding equally to all the stimuli impinging upon us, we focus on only a few. This kind of perceptual focusing is called *attention* (Hilgard, Atkinson, and Atkinson, 1979). Through attention we manage to keep selected stimuli in focus, while either ignoring other stimuli or keeping them in the background of awareness. When we consciously focus our attention on something, we are said to be *concentrating*.

Attention is usually regarded as a passive and automatic reception of stimuli, without any effort to organize perceptual information into meaningful relationships. Concentration, on the other hand, depends in part on attention, but it is an active, effortful process of mentally manipulating and organizing complex information. Typically, a person who is having trouble paying attention to something attempts to compensate for the disruption by concentrating on processes that should have occurred automatically. The person who is experiencing burnout may have difficulty paying attention or concentrating or both. When burnout contributes to a disruption of these processes, the individual experiences some degree of difficulty in passively receiving information (attention) and in actively focusing on that information and organizing it (concentration).

We all experience problems in paying attention and concentrating from time to time. Individuals may be able to think briefly about something, but then their attention wanders to other things. The original focus is replaced by different material that environmental stimuli evoke or that emerge from within their minds. When individuals become intensely focused on thoughts or ideas stimulated by environmental events, their attention is distracted from thoughts arising from within. When they focus their attention on thoughts stimulated by internal events, on the other hand, they become less able to respond to external events. The latter experience is more common in the burnout syndrome than is the former condition. A person who is burning out may focus more on negative events of the past or negative prospects for the future, while giving less attention to immediate circumstances. Although appearing intently focused on current circumstances, the individual may, in fact, be attending primarily to thoughts arising from within. In effect, burnout may contribute to a *narrowing of attention to events outside oneself.* The individual becomes increasingly preoccupied with thoughts welling up from the inside.

Most people have little difficulty shifting attention from one direction to another as needed. This shifting is something the health professional must be able to do quickly, repeatedly, and without difficulty in order to respond to the ever-changing conditions of health care work. If a health professional is experiencing burnout, however, the ability to shift attention on demand may be impaired to some degree, depending on numerous factors—including the extent to which the professional has become absorbed with internal preoccupations. The ability to shift attention can be concentrated voluntarily, but individuals differ in this ability. In general, it depends on prior learning and on the absence of environmental stimuli or intruding thoughts that interfere with willful concentration.

There are various types and degrees of severity of disturbances of attention and concentration. Most pertinent to the overall experience of burnout is the narrowing of attention that frequently accompanies stress-related anxiety and other strong emotions. Under stress, individuals tend to narrow the focus of their attention in order to meet the demands before them. It seems reasonable to expect that under conditions of prolonged stress, attention remains relatively restricted in focus. Health professionals who are burning out may therefore run an increased risk of judgment errors and negligent practices because of a reduced ability to efficiently process information and solve problems as the problems arise. Naturally, when attention and concentration fade, accidents may happen.

Problem Solving

Problem solving requires that a logical pattern of reasoning be applied to a situation in which an answer is required for a question and there is no immediate source of reliable information (Black, 1946). In every instance where problem solving is required, the goal cannot be reached by resorting to learned habits only. Individuals must do something other than what they have done before. Before the individual *does* anything, however, the major means toward solution of the problem involves *thinking*. The individual must mentally manipulate perceptions, ideas, concepts, learned habits, and rules (McKeachie, Doyle, and Moffett, 1976). Although thinking may involve logical progressions from given information to conclusions, it may also involve a disconnected, illogical process in which one idea leads to another in a peculiar fashion. In problem solving, thinking usually follows a logical sequence of reasoning. The key is to generate thoughts and ideas that have a bearing on a possible solution and then to identify the appropriate solution from available alternatives. If alternatives cannot be generated, or if solving the problem requires more than the individual is able or willing to give, tension increases and psychological balance is upset.

In most instances health professionals routinely solve problems without much effort, sometimes even unconsciously. Practitioners who are burning out may experience increasing difficulty in finding proper solutions to problems. If these individuals place a high value on finding solutions to those problems, their levels of anxiety and arousal will increase proportionately. Increases in anxiety and general arousal tend to facilitate effective problem solving when they are kept within a moderate range of intensity. It is as if the anxiety fuels the mobilization of problem-solving resources. As anxiety, tension, and arousal increase, perceptual awareness and attention narrow and concentration is focused solely on the problem at hand. However, as one feels more and more pressure to identify the appropriate solution to the problem, concentration may become focused more on the *difficulty being experienced in problem solving itself.* Attention may be concentrated on the process rather than on the outcome. The ability to generate possible solutions then becomes impaired because the individual is distracted from the problem-solving task.

The health professional who is becoming mentally exhausted may recognize the importance of solving problems quickly and efficiently on the job yet find it increasingly difficult to expend the energy to do so. This situation may lead to more tension and anxiety which, in turn, impede the problem-solving process even further. One way to deal with this kind of dilemma is to resort to doing what was done in similar situations in the past—to fall back on former solutions to new and different problems. Such alternatives may not be real solutions at all, and the problem may continue in spite of the individual's satisfaction that it has been adequately resolved.

Problem solving is involved in the appraisal and coping processes discussed earlier. When the mechanisms of problem solving—thinking, in particular—are not functioning properly, appraisal and coping are impaired and stress continues on the road to burnout.

Attitudes

One of the most characteristic ways in which burnout is manifested is in the development of negative attitudes toward other people. An *attitude* is defined in terms of a predisposition to act in a particular way toward an identified object, event, concept, person, or group. An attitude is a state of mental readiness to respond in a particular manner. Thus, negative attitudes are associated with a predisposition to avoid the targets of those attitudes or to treat them negatively. When the negative attitude is directed toward the people with whom one works, the behavioral tendency is either to avoid them or to respond negatively when they are encountered. Actually, it is not so much the negative attitude per se that is problematic in the burnout syndrome; rather, it is the *behavior* that results from the influence of that attitude. Indeed, the only way to know about a person's attitude is to observe that person's behavior: what that person does and says. From a person's actions we infer the existence of a certain attitudinal predisposition. When making such an inference, we use the supposed attitude as a predictor of how that person is likely to behave in future situations. A negative attitude toward patients implies a general predisposition toward treating them in ways that are potentially incompatible with their well-being.

A "negative attitude" is an ambiguous notion. Yet it is assumed to include various specific predispositions. One such predisposition is especially prominent in the burnout syndrome. It is called *dehumanization.* When service providers develop a dehumanizing attitude toward service recipients, in effect the providers come to deny the human attributes of those they serve. They perceive patients as being devoid of humanity, as not having the same kinds of feelings, needs, aspirations, thoughts, and personal qualities that they have. This attitude precludes recognition of the personal identity—the uniqueness—of patients. As a result, it increases the likelihood that patients will be treated as if they were not human beings.

A dehumanizing attitude toward patients is often reflected in the language of health professionals—a language that makes patients seem more like numbers, objects, problems, or disease entities than individuals. It is also evidenced in language that is highly technical, scientific, objective, nonemotional, intellectual, or even cynical and demeaning. For example, a psychiatric patient may be seen as "the paranoid"; a medical patient may be identified as "the gall bladder in 238"; a surgeon may refer to a patient as "the bowel resection"; an emergency room nurse in the cafeteria may talk about "the CVA that came in this afternoon"; or a woman going through alcohol detoxification on a medical floor may be called "the drunk" or "the alchy." When labels are consistently used this way, human beings are being stripped of their individuality and thrown into stereotyped categories with millions of other faceless entities.

A developing attitude of dehumanization does enable the service provider to view patients in terms that reduce the intensity of emotional involvement with them. It is a distancing tactic. Lavandero (1981) noted that dehumanization is one of the extreme and most devastating features of burnout since it results in a decreased sensitivity to the humanness of others. Yet Lavandero also observed that dehumanization is *not always destructive.* Lief and Fox (1963), for example, found that medical students make extensive use of dehumanization to counter the distressing effects of witnessing and participating in autopsies in cadaver laboratories. The dehumanization apparently allows for a proper balance between feelings and objectivity. When carried to an extreme and applied indiscriminately in numerous situations, however, dehumanization becomes a maladaptive tactic used to maintain emotional control in the face of stressors that threaten to upset psychological balance.

An important implication for health care practice is that dehumanization encourages the justification of neglect. When patients are dehumanized by health professionals, the professionals absolve themselves from their responsibilities in an irrational manner and thereby attribute responsibility to the patients themselves for unfavorable treatment outcomes. As Maslach (1977) suggested, dehumanization may lead to *victimization*, wherein patients are seen as deserving their problems and their fates. In the cases of heart disease or renal failures, which inevitably deteriorate over time, health professionals may come to believe that patients are in some way personally responsible for their repeated admission to the hospital (Lavandero, 1981). In this connection Millman (1977) suggested that health professionals have developed techniques for justifying treatment errors and minimizing injuries caused to patients. According to Millman, one technique is apparent in mortality conferences where patient deaths are discussed in ways that support the decisions and actions of the physician. Patients may be blamed for their own deaths if they can be discredited as insane, alcoholic, uncooperative, or in some way undermining the treatment effort. Responsibility for treatment errors is shifted away from caregivers to patients in a strategy to rationalize deaths and defend against the severe guilt associated with making lethal mistakes.

Another change of attitude is evident in the health professional who becomes *rigidly technical* in the performance of job duties. This individual becomes increasingly steadfast in adherence to rules, policies, and procedures and begins treating everyone the same, allowing no room for individual differences in needs and circumstances. Special factors and considerations are not accounted for, unique requirements of patients are not acknowledged, and everyone gets treated the same, as the professional goes increasingly "by the book." Adopting such a rigid orientation to practice may be one way of coping with the difficulty experienced with problem solving: Since it takes too much out of the health professional to consider special circumstances and factors when moving toward solutions to problems, those factors are automatically exempt from consideration. Thus, the professional relies on pat solutions.

In addition to a change of attitude toward patients, health professionals who are experiencing burnout may come to feel negatively toward their colleagues. They may withdraw from group interactions and avoid others as much as possible. The health professional may feel as if colleagues discuss nothing but mundane topics, that they are all quite foolish and ignorant, and that the professional is tired of hearing the same things over and over again whenever they are around. The burned-out professional often develops a low tolerance for the peculiarities, sensitivities, and habits of co-workers.

Accompanying the change of attitude toward others is a change of attitude *toward oneself.* People who experience burnout often report a lowering of self-esteem. They feel inadequate, incompetent, powerless, helpless, ineffective, or inferior. They admit to feeling useless, impotent, and unimportant. They express feelings of being unable to make a real difference in the lives of those they serve. A nurse working in an alcoholism treatment unit might communicate this attitude through a cynical comment: "Why should I go out of my way for them? It makes no difference anyway. They're going to leave here and hit the first bar they come to. If not the first one, then eventually they drink; it's just a matter of time. Nothing I do changes that fact. And for this I got specialized training?" This communication is an expression of pessimism, futility, hopelessness, and powerlessness. Nurses in this state feel as if they can have no true impact on the drinking of their patients, so they simply put in their hours and take home their checks every two weeks. In the meantime they feel empty and useless. To them, nothing changes, nothing matters.

Detachment: Problem or Solution?

The most outstanding and frequently cited symptom of burnout is *detachment* from clients. It is characterized by the loss of concern and dehumanizing attitudes associated with mental exhaustion. Detachment manifests itself through actual avoidance of patients, physical distancing during interactions, absenteeism, tardiness, and the excessive use of humor similar to that portrayed in the television series "M*A*S*H." In an effort to maintain a delicate balance between concern and distance, the person experiencing burnout may seek refuge in distance from the distressing emotions felt in close relationships with patients. Such distancing is so much a part of burnout that sometimes it is considered the sole symptom.

Edelwich and Brodsky (1980) suggested that physical, emotional, and mental detachment is a symptom of burnout at one of its most critical points. They added, however, that caution must be exercised in interpreting the significance and meaning of detachment. A certain measure of "clinical distancing" seems to be necessary in order to be effective in helping others in the health care context. As Edelwich and Brodsky noted, detachment as a form of distancing is a part of overall professionalism that increases therapeutic effectiveness and minimizes the psychological consequences of failure. Therefore, care should be taken to avoid using the term *detachment* as being synonymous with burnout. A certain degree of detachment appears to be essential and sensible in actual practice.

Loss of Idealism and Enthusiasm

When people enter allied health professions, they start with a great deal of enthusiasm and idealism. They believe that they can somehow make an impact on the world, make some contribution that attests to their sense of personal competence, worth, or even power to make a difference. Somewhere in the process of exerting their influence on the world, the world pushes back and resists. The world does not always want to be changed in the direction intended by the health professional. Every time the world resists, every time a wound will not heal, every time a patient will not recover from an illness, every time a maladaptive behavior will not change, it becomes harder for the professional to push on and press forward with the same commitment and enthusiasm. As if to surrender to the law of physics, the health professional (as "irresistible force") cannot overcome the world of others (the "immovable objects"). The harsh realization that all their patients do *not* necessarily get better is an extremely difficult fact for health professionals to live with, especially when life and death are at stake.

Edelwich and Brodsky (1980), Kramer (1974), and Pines and Aronson (1981) stressed that a high level of idealism around the need to help may pave the way for eventual disillusionment. The professional idealism that new employees bring to the work setting often gives out under the continual stress of intense involvements with others who fail to change in the direction prescribed. The tragedy of burnout is that the highly motivated, idealistic, and enthusiastic health professionals who burn out are probably among the very best practitioners. Even more tragic is the fact that as the best professionals burn out the overall effectiveness of service delivery goes down.

With the loss of idealism comes a loss of enthusiasm for one's work. Enthusiasm is a motivational force that drives health professionals toward the ideal goals acquired prior to actual practice. When enthusiasm is lost, professionals limit their commitments, surrender to the realities of practice, set lower work-related priorities, and generally reduce their investment in their "calling." In a word, they lose their "drive." As a consequence of losing both idealism and enthusiasm, they become less able to cope with the disturbing realities and conditions of their work and more inclined toward complete resignation.

EMOTIONAL EXHAUSTION

Within the burnout syndrome, emotional exhaustion includes feelings of apathy, helplessness, hopelessness, dissatisfaction, and entrapment. A free-foating, generalized anxiety may also accompany these feelings. The burned-out individual feels emotionally depleted and, at the same time, often irritable and nervous (Pines and Aronson, 1981). A pervasive sense of discouragement and emptiness is also frequently reported by burned-out persons, who find that they need all of the little energy they have left to get through one more day. Some even feel that they have nothing left to give and that they cannot even go through the motions of their jobs.

According to Lief and Fox (1963), health professionals repeatedly encounter highly emotional situations in their daily work. These situations involve

Exploring, examining, and cutting into the human body; dealing with fears, anger, sense of helplessness, and despair of patients; meeting emergency situations; accepting the limitations of medical science in dealing with chronic or uncurable disease; being confronted with death itself. (p. 13)

Within the context of the provider-patient relationship, health professionals take access to the most intimate aspects of their patients' total beings. Exposure to the sights, sounds, smells, and touch of the human body in its most vulnerable or unpleasant conditions is an intensely emotional experience for caregivers. So is the ultimate realization that death cannot be conquered by medical science, that diseases may run their courses in spite of any intervention by providers, and that helping sometimes means failing. In response to these and other stressful conditions of their work, health professionals experience a range of disturbing emotions.

Apathy and Helplessness

There are obviously many responses to the stressful conditions of one's work. Many health professionals find it increasingly difficult to cope with the intense strain and chronic stress associated with the emotional demands of their work. They experience an emotional overload. Like a wire with too much electric current passing through it, the health professional short-circuits and shuts down emotionally. When this happens, *apathy* becomes the pervasive emotion.

Apathy is a common reaction against the frustration of being repeatedly unsuccessful in overcoming obstacles to one's goals. As health professionals find that they have no power to deal with stressful conditions by means of their own actions, they may resort to apathy and withdrawal when faced with subsequent frustrating situations.

Apathy may be a manifestation of *learned helplessness*. Findings from numerous investigations have demonstrated that individuals can learn to be helpless in the face of stressful situations. Animals also can learn helplessness in stressful situations. In a study by Seligman (1975), for example, a dog was placed in an apparatus with two compartments separated by a barrier. When an electric shock was delivered to the dog's feet through a steel grid on the floor, the animal quickly leaped across the barrier to escape the shock. The dog was trained to jump the barrier whenever a light came on because the light signaled impending shock. Thus, the dog learned to avoid the shock by escaping to a safe compartment. However, Seligman demonstrated that if the dog is placed in a situation where shocks are inescapable, it has significant difficulty in learning the avoidance response of jumping the barrier. In this case the animal does not respond but sits and takes the shock. As Seligman discovered, some animals never learn the appropriate response under these conditions, even if they are shown the correct response and carried over the barrier. In effect, the dogs *learned* that they could not avoid the shock (even though they could). They learned to be *helpless*.

Similarly, human beings placed in situations where they are unable to control aversive stimuli make few escape responses, even though escape is possible. The events that they are exposed to seem uncontrollable to them, and this appraisal seems to impair their ability to solve problems and cope with them. This learned helplessness is a behavior that is very difficult to change. Further, if one has learned to be helpless in one situation, this behavior tends to generalize or spread to other situations. Those other situations are perceived as similar, so it becomes extremely difficult for individuals to learn new responses that would enable them to avoid the unpleasantness of the situations.

What all of this material suggests in relation to burnout is that individuals may learn through repeated frustration that their actions make no difference in bringing about either pleasant or unpleasant outcomes. Therefore, they come to believe in their own helplessness. Even if they hit upon an effective way of handling a situation, they may still maintain a belief in helplessness if they attribute their success to luck or chance.

Health professionals who are frequently unable to find a way of dealing with the emotional demands of their work are likely to become apathetic because of the belief that they are helpless and ineffectual in coping. They appraise situations as stressful and conclude that they do not have the coping resources for managing their stress. Thus, psychological imbalance is created and emotional exhaustion goes unrelieved.

Empathy, apathy, and detachment

Apathy is intrinsically related to empathy and detachment. First, it is a mode of emotional detachment in response to repeated frustration. But the starting point is the empathy the health professionals feel for those they serve. Instead of reaching a midpoint where emotional detachment is counterbalanced by empathic concern, many health professionals progress toward an emotional numbness in which feelings are simply turned off. Once-empathic caregivers become indifferent and do their job because "it has to be done" or because "a job is a job." They put in "time" rather than themselves.

As Edelwich and Brodsky (1980) suggested, there is a downward cycle where apathy is concerned. First, the health professional is idealistic, enthusiastic, committed, and highly empathic. Then continual job frustrations cannot be managed successfully, and this state of affairs leads to anger and resentment and more attempts to remedy the situation. With continued failure, a sense of futility sets in and the health professional becomes indifferent. Helping becomes meaningless. One option is to follow the impulse to leave the profession. The professional who has reached the opposite extreme of empathy no longer feels for the patients. Seeing people suffer and die causes no strong emotions to well up from within. Feelings and concern have been blunted.

Anxiety and Defense

Any situation that threatens the well-being of the individual typically produces a stress condition. To understand the reactions of individuals to stress, psychologists often use the concept of *anxiety*. Anxiety is an unpleasant emotional state commonly known by terms such as *worry, apprehension,* and *nervousness.* Some forms of anxiety are realistic responses to perceived danger, and, as such, they are synonymous with *fear.* Other forms of anxiety, however, do not appear to be realistic emotional responses since they involve no realistic threat in the environment. In addition, there are various degrees of anxiety, from mild concern and apprehension to full-blown panic. And there are probably different degrees to which individuals are aware of the causes of their emotional discomfort (Hilgard, Atkinson, and Atkinson, 1979).

Because high levels of anxiety cannot be tolerated for very long, individuals develop their own unique ways of defending against it. As indicated in Chapter 2, one way of responding to the anxiety generated by a stressful situation is to take direct action. If direct action fails, however, the individual's level of anxiety may increase and different approaches may be pursued. One such approach is palliative by nature, in that stress is managed by trying to reduce the anxiety without taking direct action against the source of the stress. The individual focuses on defending against anxiety itself, while avoiding the anxiety-producing stressor. As discussed earlier, one mode of coping with the stress of health care is to detach oneself emotionally and mentally. What this detachment amounts to is *repression* and *denial,* two common defenses against anxiety.

As a defense against anxiety, denial involves a conscious or unconscious refusal to acknowledge the existence of external realities that are too unpleasant to face. Seeing people in distress and suffering on a continual basis is a stress condition that generates considerable anxiety for most health professionals. Over time, they often manage their anxiety by denying the severity of those conditions—by refusing to be overwhelmed by those situations. Repression, on the other hand, is a defense—not against external threats—against internal threats from one's own thoughts, feelings, impulses, or memories that are too disturbing to be permitted entry into conscious awareness. Although health professionals may feel extremely anxious during a response to a cardiac arrest, repression keeps that anxiety at bay so that they can respond to the situation effectively.

In such instances it is clear that repression serves an adaptive function. However, this response is not actually repression. It is called *suppression* since the health professional is deliberately controlling the anxiety and keeping it in check privately, while denying it publicly. The individual may be well aware of the suppressed anxiety. In contrast, repression is not a deliberate or calculated response. The individual is *not aware* of what is being kept from consciousness.

When anxiety or other feelings and thoughts are automatically kept below a level of awareness, they may persist in causing the individual considerable psychological distress, although the person may not be aware of the reasons for that distress. What usually happens is that repression is not completely successful. Therefore, repressed feelings find expression indirectly. Typically, the individual carries around a vague sense that something is wrong, but does not really know what it is. This vague sense may be part of the nagging thought that the burned-out health professional carries around with him: "Something is wrong, but I don't know what it is." At the core of this discomfort is anxiety.

In addition to repression and denial, anxiety associated with burnout is defended against by certain characteristic means. These defenses include the following:

- Intellectualization
- Reaction formation
- Rationalization
- Projection
- Displacement

Intellectualization is the attempt to gain emotional detachment by dealing with stressful events in abstract, intellectual terms (e.g., referring to patients in diagnostic terms). *Reaction formation* involves concealing an emotion from oneself and others by expressing the opposite emotion (e.g., the health professional who feels guilty about lack of concern for a patient may act as if that patient were the sole focus of attention; or the nurse who feels inadequate and ineffectual may try to appear crisp and efficient on the outside). *Rationalization* consists of attributing noble or socially acceptable motives to one's actions in order to create the appearance of acting responsibly and properly (e.g., the physician who explains that he did everything he could possibly do to save a patient but says the patient died because she would not follow his orders). *Projection* involves the attribution of undesirable feelings or motives to others when those feelings or motives actually belong to oneself. It may also involve the assigning of responsibility for failure to someone else when one should rightly claim that responsibility oneself (e.g., physicians who blame a patient for their own treatment mistakes). *Displacement* involves redirecting threatening feelings toward an object or person that is not the source of those feelings (e.g., health professionals whose anger toward a supervisor at work is taken out on their families at home. Although there are countless defenses against anxiety, these are the most common.

Defenses against anxiety serve a clear and useful purpose most of the time. When used to excess, or when relied upon when direct action against the source of stress and anxiety would be more appropriate, defense strategies are maladaptive for the individual. Although they are palliative and may provide temporary relief, they do not help solve the problem. In fact, they may enable the problem to continue and intensify.

SUMMARY

It is apparent from research that the highly variable and complex manifestations of burnout usually begin to appear within less than two years after human service professionals begin their jobs. Those who do experience burnout may reach a point of "no return"—where they perceive that terminating their employment is the only way to escape chronic job stress—or they may experience episodes of burnout from which they recover, and through which they learn more efficient ways of managing the stresses of their work. Whether burnout leads to job turnover or to more adaptive coping, the syndrome is hypothesized here as paralleling the *crisis* experience. In drawing this parallel the present chapter outlines the crisis experience as a function of the individual's appraisals of stressors and the ability to cope with those perceived stressors. The effects of burnout on *mental functioning* are discussed in relation to attention, concentration, problem solving, attitudes, detachment, and loss of idealism and enthusiasm. *Emotional exhaustion*, as a general effect of burnout, is examined in terms of feelings of apathy and helplessness, loss of empathy, increased anxiety and tension, and excessive reliance on ego defense mechanisms. Although the effects of burnout on mental and emotional functioning may be highly variable from person to person, the present chapter limits its focus to the most frequently reported psychological components of the syndrome.

REFERENCES

Black, M. *Critical thinking: An introduction to logic and scientific method.* Englewood Cliffs, N.J.: Prentice-Hall, 1946.

Caplan, G. *Principles of preventive psychiatry.* New York: Basic Books, 1964.

Cherniss, C. *Staff burnout: Job stress in the human services.* Beverly Hills, Calif.: Sage Publications, 1980.

Edelwich, J., & Brodsky, A. *Burnout: Stages of disillusionment in the helping professions.* New York: Human Sciences Press, 1980.

Freudenberger, H.J. Staff burnout. *Journal of Social Issues,* 1974, *30*(1), 159-165.

Freudenberger, H.J. The staff burnout syndrome in alternative institutions. *Psychotherapy: Theory, research, and practice,* 1975, *12*(1), 73-82.

Hilgard, E., Atkinson, R.L., & Atkinson, R.C. *Introduction to psychology* (7th ed.). New York: Harcourt, Brace, Jovanovich, 1979.

Johnson, S.H. *Preventing burnout,* Home Study Module, Health Update, 1979.

Johnson, S.H. Preventing group burnout. *Nursing Management,* 1982, *13*(2), 34-38.

Kempe, C.H. Child protective services: Where have we been? What are we now and where are we going? *Child abuse and neglect: Issues on implementation and innovation* (DHEW Publication No. 78-30147, vol. 5.) Washington, D.C.: U.S. Government Printing Office, 1978.

Klein, D.C., & Lindemann, E. Preventive intervention in individual and family crisis situations. In G. Caplan (Ed.), *The prevention of mental disorders in children.* New York: Basic Books, 1961.

Kramer, M. *Reality shock: Why nurses leave nursing.* St. Louis: C.V. Mosby, 1974.

Lavandero, R. Nurse burnout: What can we learn? *Journal of Nursing Administration,* November-December 1981, pp. 17-23.

Lief, H.I., & Fox, D.C. Training for "detached concern" in medical students. In H.I. Lief, V.F. Lief, & N.R. Lief (Eds.), *The psychological basis of medical practice.* New York: Harper & Row, 1963.

Lysaught, J.P. *An abstract for action. National commission for the study of nursing and nursing education.* New York: McGraw-Hill, 1970.

Maslach, C. *Burnout: A social psychological analysis.* American Psychological Association Convention, San Francisco, August 1977.

McKeachie, W.J., Doyle, C.L., & Moffett, M.M. *Psychology* (3rd ed.). Reading, Mass.: Addison-Wesley, 1976.

Millman, M. *The unkindest cut: Life in the backrooms of medicine.* New York: William Morrow, 1977.

Pines, A., & Aronson, E. *Burnout: From tedium to personal growth.* New York: Free Press, 1981.

Rapoport, L. The state of crisis: Some theoretical considerations. *Social Service Review,* 1962, *36*(2).

Seligman, M.E.P. *Helplessness: On depression, development, and death.* San Francisco: W.H. Freeman, 1975.

Veninga, R.L., & Spradley, J.P. *The work stress connection: How to cope with job burnout.* Boston: Little, Brown, 1981.

CHAPTER 4

Effects of burnout on behavior and work performance

U ltimately, the most reliable indicators of burnout are related to the individual's behavior. One aspect of the behavior of health professionals that is of greatest concern to administrators, patients, and the public in general is the way they perform their jobs.

There are various ways of approaching the problem of how burnout relates to human behavior and work performance. This chapter uses a descriptive approach. First, the focus is directed to outward behavioral signs that are frequently associated with burnout. The actual number of behaviors that may indicate that a person is experiencing burnout is virtually impossible to document. Therefore, the most outstanding behavioral symptoms are discussed here. The effects of stress and burnout on the work performance of health professionals are examined in the latter portion of this discussion. It is crucial that those closest to the problem of burnout turn their attention toward those aspects of the problem that can have the most serious consequences for practitioners and the most potentially devastating consequences for service recipients. Those aspects pertain to *what health professionals actually do on the job and how they do it.*

GENERAL BEHAVIORAL EFFECTS

Behavioral symptoms of burnout include observable *actions* of individuals: what they do and what they say. A multitude of behavioral manifestations have been described in the literature. In general, however, a behavioral sign may take the form of virtually any deviation from the individual's usual way of doing things. Yet deviations from a behavioral norm may be desirable because they often indicate positive change. Consequently, the kinds of behavioral changes that suggest a person is experiencing burnout must be relatively limited. Table 4-1 identifies some of the frequently cited behavioral effects.

Table 4-1   Common Behavioral Manifestations of Burnout

- Spending less time with patients
- Reducing physical contact with patients
- Taking excessive and unnecessary risks
- Excessive use of humor about work
- Expression of anger toward patients
- Avoiding other staff persons
- Excessive blaming of patients or staff
- Frequent complaining about the job
- Ignoring patient complaints
- Tardiness at work
- Absenteeism
- Increased alcohol consumption
- Increased smoking
- Increased use of patent or prescription drugs
- Medication errors
- Increased difficulty in following orders
- Poorly charted notes and observations
- Sudden changes of expression and mood
- Taking fewer breaks or more breaks from work
- Nonverbal anger (e.g., slamming, tossing, etc.)
- Clock watching
- Fault finding
- Describing patients in derogatory terms
- Impersonal, stereotyped communication with patients
- Performing duties strictly by the book
- Search for transfer or relocation
- Decreased cooperativeness
- Inefficient patient care
- Reduction in overall performance efficiency

Activity Level

Since burnout is a problem that results in general exhaustion, one would expect that a depletion of an individual's energy would manifest itself in that individual's behavior or level of activity. Normally exhaustion produces a reduction of energy that is evident, among other things, in hypoactivity. However, as a person is going through the burnout experience, there is sometimes an increase in overall activity level. The person seems *hyper*active. In such cases the person may be attempting to ward off the anxiety and increased tension through excessive activity since slowing down only serves to "back up" the tension and cause considerable discomfort.

Consider some of the ways that people may show increases in their level of activity. Ellen K. never seemed to be able to sit still for more than a few minutes while at work. During her breaks she would smoke several cigarettes and either tap her feet or her fingers all the while she was "relaxing." As soon as it was time to return to work, she quickly and abruptly terminated her conversations with colleagues, turned, and walked hurriedly out of the staff lounge. Others noticed that lately Ellen seemed to have a real sense of "urgency" about her, as if something were always waiting to be done right away. John R. was observed by his colleagues to have developed an extremely tense appearance and manner about one year after beginning his job as a nurse anesthetist. His verbal communications were punctuated with forceful emphasis even when discussing trivial matters, his fists were clenched when he talked about matters of personal significance, and the general flow of his speech seemed pressured and strained. Robert H. seemed to be "up" all the time. He was the first to tell a joke, the first to laugh at someone else's, and he was a "cheerleader" for the entire work group. Robert gradually seemed to be trying harder and harder to be popular among his peers. He was always talking, it seemed. He could be heard talking or laughing all the way down the hall. It got to the point where many of the staff began avoiding Robert because they could not get away from him once he got their attention. And no one could understand why Robert eventually had to take an emergency sick leave because of his "nerves."

Accelerated work activity and a preoccupation with working may be symptomatic of burnout, according to evidence that suggests that workoholism may be a part of that syndrome. The person called a *workoholic* has an apparent abundance of energy that is always being channeled into the job. What that person fails to acknowledge or accept is that there is a limit to one's energy supply. The rate at which the workoholic is going is a fast course to burnout, just as a speeding automobile is on a faster rate of energy depletion than an auto going at moderate speeds.

As Veninga and Spradley (1981) explained, "When the major source of stress comes from your job, working harder can become a blind alley that looks like a thoroughfare to recovery" (p. 136). Workoholism can also be a self-defeating strategy that develops after burnout has closed in on the individual, according to Veninga and Spradley.

The activity of workoholics is geared toward accomplishing as much as possible in a short period of time. When they fail to accomplish their goals within the time frame established for themselves, they double their efforts and try to make up for lost ground. As they become clenched in the grips of burnout, workoholics conclude that the only way out of its clutches is through more hard work. This is the "blind alley" referred to by Veninga and Spradley, for more hard work is just that—more hard work.

In contrast, burnout may lead to a decrease in general activity level. A person's movements may appear slow and sluggish, and it may seem as if it takes a great deal of effort to do anything that requires physical exertion. Some individuals may seem to have a slowed reaction time (e.g., some nurses may respond to call lights with considerable delay). Speech may be slow, monotonous, halting, and hesitant, punctuated with frequent sighs, and generally consistent with what is observed in people who are depressed. Although there may be strong similarities with depression (especially since both depression and burnout may involve a decreased level of energy), burned-out health professionals are usually not clinically depressed; they are burned out. Yet, this is not to say that the burned-out professional cannot *also* be depressed. Depression may accompany burnout, but it is not synonymous with it. Reduced activity levels may be more indicative of depression than of burnout per se.

Communication Problems

It was noted in Chapter 1 that burnout often involves a loss of empathy and respect for patients. Although both empathy and respect are attitudes or feelings, they are manifested in the actions of people. The only way to infer that someone is empathic or respectful is by observing how that person behaves toward others. When empathy and respect for others decrease, there are observable changes in the ways the individual communicates with them. Let us take a look at the behaviors that communicate empathy and respect and those that do not.

Muldary (in press) defined empathy in terms of the re-creation of the experience of another person within one's own frame of reference. As such, empathy involves seeing things as another person sees them, putting oneself "in the other person's shoes." It includes an ability to sense what another person is feeling and thinking. Empathy is true interpersonal understanding, and it is communicated in a variety of ways (e.g., by orienting one's body toward the other person and facing the other squarely, by maintaining eye contact, by leaning slightly forward, by maintaining an open posture, by verbally reflecting both the feelings and the facts contained in the other's communications). The type of caring that underlies effective health care services is necessarily rooted in empathy. When health professionals burn out, they seem to care less and feel less empathic, and their communications to patients indicate this attitude.

The absence of empathy, or a low level of empathy, is communicated both nonverbally and verbally. At the nonverbal level it is evident, first and foremost, in health professionals' *avoidance of patients*. They limit the amount of time they are in contact with patients. When they do come into contact with patients, they may avoid *eye contact*, keep their bodies *oriented away* from the patient (if possible), or communicate with patients at "consultative" distances (four or more feet away). Health professionals may *occupy their hands* with instruments of some kind, and they may respond only to the *content* of what patients communicate and not to the feelings that accompany the words. Detached professionals may try to fake empathy, but this attempt usually does not work. If they are faking empathy, they will miss important statements and simply rely on patent responses such as "ummm" or "um-hm," then perhaps change the subject. Their *tone* and *manner* may not be appropriately matched with those of the patient's communication. They do not need to sound as distraught as the patient, but neither should they seem gleeful or totally objective when the patient tries to relate distressing feelings to them. Their *language may not match* the language of the patient, in that it may be condescending or highly technical. Detached professionals may respond to the patient's communications in a *long-winded* fashion, as if giving a lecture or shifting the focus away from the patient and to themselves. Or they *may not respond at all* to the patient's communications. These are just some of the many ways in which health professionals may show a low level of empathy for those they serve. These examples are behavioral in that they suggest how the professionals may act when there is a reduction of empathy as a consequence of burnout.

Respect is such a fundamental notion that it almost eludes definition (Egan, 1975). Basically, however, it involves a prizing of another person simply because that person is human. It is difficult to imagine that persons committed to the allied health profession would not hold an attitude of respect for those they serve. Burnout often undermines the respect that professionals have for their patients. In extreme cases respect turns into revulsion.

Respect is communicated through the actions of the health professionals. When they orient themselves toward working with or for the patient, they demonstrate respect. They do not avoid the patient but seek to meet the patient's needs. They do not ignore the patient, but listen to what the patient needs to say. They pay attention to the patient rather than communicating indifference by not taking the time to listen. When health professionals avoid their patients, ignore their patients, and do not take the time to listen, they demonstrate not only a lack of empathy but also a lack of respect. They also show a lack of respect when they begin making increasingly negative judgments and expressing those judgments to the patient or others. Referring to patients in technical terms and applying derogatory labels to them communicate a clear lack of respect for them as human beings. But the burned-out professional cannot see patients as being truly human because they have become problems or annoyances. A lack of respect is also revealed through a lack of warmth toward patients. These are a few of the behavioral indications of lack of respect for service recipients. These kinds of actions can be manifested toward other staff as well. When such actions are displayed more and more frequently, they may be a good sign that the individual is burning out.

Some symptoms of burnout in the communication behavior of health professionals are more subtle. Communication is not simply a matter of sending messages. It involves an equal emphasis on receiving messages. As noted in Chapter 3, burnout may impair the individual's ability to pay attention and concentrate. Thus, persons experiencing burnout may have difficulty *listening* to others. They may not be able to fully process the verbal and nonverbal messages they receive. Often the ultimate measure of this condition is an inability to respond correctly to comments or questions stated by others. Health professionals who have not accurately perceived the messages sent to them will simply not make the appropriate verbal or nonverbal responses. Being preoccupied with something other than what is being discussed or presented suggests that attention is being directed inward and not outward toward the speaker. At a time when the demand is for an external focus, inner focus precludes efficient information processing. An immediate effect is the disruption of the smooth flow of back-and-forth communications.

Withdrawal from Professional and Social Contacts

Not only do many burned-out health professionals withdraw from contact with patients, they may also withdraw from other relationships. It is not uncommon for those professionals under chronic stress to become so preoccupied with themselves that they isolate themselves from others without even being aware of it. They spend more time alone and less time interacting with their colleagues at work. They may go on breaks by themselves, perhaps because they just want some private time. Others may dissociate themselves from the rest of the staff because their peers are no longer sources of satisfaction and enjoyment for them. Peers may be perceived negatively and, therefore, may be avoided.

It may become increasingly frustrating for the burned-out health professional to interact with a staff of people who frequently complain about how bad the work conditions are. Some tire of this situation very quickly and avoid the other staff because they want an escape from the pressures. Talking about the problems over and over again during breaks never provides the professional with the brief escape that is so desperately needed. For some, withdrawal (both on and off the job) is seen as the only means of getting away from the habit of talking about how frustrating it is to be in their job. For others, escape and withdrawal are not consciously planned. They seem to drift away from social contacts without being aware that they are doing so. Others can see it happening, however, because others are often the first ones to notice symptoms of burnout in the individual.

For example, nurses who burn out lose enthusiasm for their work and show little concern for and patience with other nurses. One way that they deal with their feelings is through a physical and emotional separation from the people they perceive so negatively. For some nurses, burnout affects nonprofessional relationships as well. Often frustrations that are encountered at home would not be bothersome at all if frustrations at work were adequately resolved. Nurses may become increasingly intolerant of family members and friends as burnout progresses without relief. Family and social conflicts then complicate the effects of job burnout and, in fact, aggravate the condition. Frequently the cycle of frustration, resentment, and intolerance of work recycles into the home life and then back to the workplace. Gradually the nurses' social relationships are jeopardized, and they begin withdrawing from them just as they withdrew from peer relationships at work. Everyone seems to be an annoyance for the person in the very depths of burnout.

Open Expression of Anger and Hostility

Health professionals who are experiencing burnout are more inclined to express anger toward patients than those who are not burning out. This inclination results from their reduced tolerance for people and from the sense of helplessness, hopelessness, futility, and anxiety that they feel. People burning out have emotions that are very close to the surface. Some even wear their emotions "on their sleeves." Consequently, it does not take too much additional stress to elicit strong emotional responses (e.g., anger and resentment) from them.

People under severe or chronic stress may not have the degree of control over their emotions that they formerly had. Nurses who have been targets of the angry outbursts of patients can appreciate this fact because they realize that patients who are under a great deal of stress may react with blatant hostility, although the patients would not ordinarily respond that way. Burnout often impairs the control mechanisms used to regulate emotional expression. Thus, when the mechanisms are malfunctioning, symptoms of burnout may appear in open expressions of anger.

Search for Transfer or Change of Job

Many individuals who are burning out believe that things would be better if they made a change to a different unit, department, or organization. In some cases this change may be just what they need; and when changes have been made, the symptoms of burnout may not appear again. For others, however, different avenues of escape are chosen.

Some individuals believe that their only escape is to leave the profession altogether. Convinced that they can no longer function as health professionals, these persons begin searching for other career alternatives. Some may take a series of night-study courses to explore other areas of interest and to see if other occupations they have considered are viable options for them. Some may take additional coursework as a means of enhancing their credentials and raising their prospects for promotion out of the circumstances that are presently so stressful—provided that promotion promises duties that are not comparable to the helping function. Still others do not wish to leave the profession forever. They want a change, but they want to change within the profession, not apart from it. Thus, they attempt to bolster their qualifications and take advantage of every opportunity for advancement up the organizational ladder. These people escape, not by going out, but by going up.

When individual health professionals begin looking around for other job opportunities, either within their employing organization or in a different context, they may be demonstrating a level of dissatisfaction brought about by unrelieved stress and burnout. Of course, one does not have to be under a great deal of stress to seek a job change. It is only when the search for alternatives combines with other behavioral, emotional, mental, and physical manifestations that burnout can be inferred as a causal influence.

Drug and Alcohol Use

People under chronic stress behave in ways that provide relief from their emotional discomfort. Drinking alcohol is one of the most popular means people use in attempting to modify their emotional and mental states. Using prescription medications is another means of altering one's mood and bringing about relief from debilitating anxiety. Both drugs and alcohol provide temporary relief because they medicate the effects of stress. The disturbing emotions that accompany stress are briefly anesthetized because pleasant feelings are substituted for unpleasant ones. However, these are a drastic and primitive means of stress management. They may also become maladaptive and detrimental to the user's health and well-being.

Excessive use of alcohol and drugs is often cited as a symptom of burnout. It would be a serious mistake, however, to conceive of alcoholism and drug dependency—the two extreme consequences of excessive use of mood-altering substances—as symptoms of an underlying pathology related to stress or burnout. Alcoholism and drug dependency are not symptoms, *they are the problems*. It is true that many individuals seek to reduce the effects of stress and burnout through chemical means. In some cases it may be that excessive drinking and a reliance on prescription medications are side effects of burnout. But we must never be fooled into accepting either as a symptom of another problem.

In certain cases stress and burnout may not be antecedents to drinking; *they may be consequences.* The problem drinker is someone who helps to create a stressful work environment. In cases where drinking is seen as part of the syndrome, *excessive drinking may be as much a problem contributing to burnout as it is a behavioral effect.* The heavy drinker and drug user has a greater likelihood of being overwhelmed by stress than does the moderate drinker or the nondrinker.

Performance Efficiency

A large body of research has consistently shown that moderate levels of stress and anxiety may facilitate performance on tasks. Too little stress may leave an individual unmotivated to perform well. Too much stress may interfere with smooth performance. The latter condition is problematic for health professionals going through burnout. Various aspects of impaired work performance related to chronic stress in allied health are examined in the following sections.

Bedside manner

As noted earlier, one response to chronic stress in the helping context is the rigidly technical performance of job functions. In the health care professions this response may involve what Reich (1948) originally termed putting on "character armor." Character armor is a defense used to protect oneself from anxiety and guilt. An example of character armor is the bedside manner assumed by many health professionals.

Bedside manner is acquired as a product of repeated encounters with people who are distressed and suffering. It enables nurses, for example, to go about their duties without being disturbed by the emotional threats of their work. They adopt a style of relating to patients that may involve patronization, being funny, acting as if one is always in a hurry, or being excessively cheerful. By acting according to a stereotyped bedside manner, nurses effectively reduce the probability that patients will display upsetting feelings or express disturbing thoughts. One unexpected effect of the bedside manner is that patients are prevented from revealing information that may relate directly to their medical condition and their treatment. A vital source of information comes from patients' self-disclosures, but the bedside manner neatly blocks it (Jourard, 1971).

Burned-out health professionals who become rigid in the way they interact with patients, by using techniques such as the bedside manner, can ultimately obstruct the delivery of effective patient care. This approach prevents patients from making important disclosures about their condition. In addition, it prevents the health professionals from being in touch with their own selves—after all, they are playing a professional role. With a reduction of insight into the self, there is a reduction in self-understanding and a reduction of the ability to recognize the experience of stress when it occurs. At the same time there is a restriction of the ability to be empathic toward patients. Because the professionals lack self-understanding, they cannot be expected to have a high degree of understanding for others. As Jourard (1971) noted, the bedside manner "desensitizes a nurse to her own experience and handicaps her attempts to know her patient" (p. 184).

In short, the bedside manner helps health professionals to keep their relations with patients impersonal and distant. Over time it may become as easy for nurses to slip into the bedside manner as it is for them to slip into their uniforms. The bedside manner is probably most evident among nurses and other health professionals who are experiencing burnout.

Increased tardiness and absenteeism

Tardiness and absenteeism are often indications of troubled employees. Whatever the causes, tardiness and absenteeism are bottom-line performance measures that say a good deal about the costs to the organization of having personnel problems. Virtually every publication on burnout identifies tardiness and absenteeism as symptoms of burnout. These two performance-related behaviors may result from other serious problems being experienced by workers. For example, they are both often cited as possible indications of alcoholism in employees. At the very least, it seems fair to say that tardiness and absenteeism are related to personal problems that employees are experiencing. *One* such problem may be burnout, although it would be premature to conclude that any employee who is frequently late or absent from work is experiencing burnout.

Inattention to details

Stress often has a facilitative effect on performance. However, in cases of chronic stress, stressors may impair the ability of individuals to pay attention to job-relevant information. The existence of of stressors in the work environment may attract a certain amount of their attention, so that some of their attention capacity is being used up as they unconsciously or consciously lock onto stressful stimuli. When their attentional capacity is reduced under stress, so is their capacity for efficient information processing, decision making, and problem solving. As an individual's attention is focused farther away from job-relevant information and tasks, the probability of missing vital bits of data is increased. Whether the person's attention turns inward or outward (toward a perceived stressor), the ability to differentiate essential from nonessential information decreases. What these facts suggest is that health professionals may pay less attention to details under stress. When they are observing patients for data relevant to the patients' medical conditions, it may become harder for these professionals to notice subtle changes or signs.

If one's attention is being distracted away from job tasks, then the likelihood of making mistakes or having accidents increases. Mistakes and accidents in health care carry potentially lethal consequences for patients. In recent years there has been a tremendous increase in malpractice litigation against health professionals. While inattention to one's job may be one contributing factor, the overall problem of burnout may be a more important consideration. Consider the fact that many physicians work more than 60 hours per week, with office hours on Saturdays as well. They may see anywhere from 20 to 40 patients per day. They are subject to interruptions through telephone calls not only at their offices but also at home. The constant physical and emotional strain under which they work is often dealt with through the increased consumption of drugs and alcohol. Obviously, not all physicians try to cope in this way. But even those who choose more adaptive means of managing stress find only temporary relief because the demands of their work supersede any time they may have for relaxation. Under such conditions it seems likely that physicians would become prone to errors in diagnosis and treatment as their attention becomes divided into countless areas.

Bottom-Line Considerations

Administrators and managers like to talk about the "bottom line" when discussing organizational issues. For them, the bottom line means costs and revenues. It is impossible to provide an accurate estimate of the bottom-line costs of burnout in health care. These costs encompass such factors as tardiness; absenteeism; accidents;

sick leave; turnover; training of new personnel to replace those who leave; overtime; increased overhead from inefficient use of materials and equipment; performance inefficiency and task repetition; advertising for new employees; administrative costs of recruiting, interviewing, and hiring new employees; processing; compensation benefits; and numerous other factors that serve to *raise the dollar cost of stress and burnout* among health professionals.

It would be helpful for administrators to make systematic estimates of the actual dollar cost of these factors in their health care organizations. Even if they do not understand the "human costs" of stress and burnout, they can appreciate the value of the numbers they derive. Administrators should calculate the average salary of employees and add to that the costs of overhead for those employees. Then they should compute the absenteeism rate and turnover rate for their organization. (The president of a small corporation once consulted me about a turnover problem in his organization. When I asked him what the turnover rate was, he stated that he did not know. Further, he did not even know how to compute it!) The cost of turnover should be computed in terms of factors such as expenses for advertising, recruiting, hiring, processing, and training. Conservative estimates should then be made of the percentage of these factors that are directly related to stress in the organization. For example, 10% of the 20% turnover rate may come from natural causes (e.g., retirement; job termination because of other opportunities, a spouse's transfer to a different part of the country, or serious illness; or dismissal of employees for specific reasons). What remains is an estimated 10% of the turnover attributed to stress. All the figures should then be added to show a total dollar amount that represents the bottom-line cost of stress for the organization. The total cost can then be divided by the number of employees in the organization to derive an estimate of the person-by-person cost of stress. It would then be an interesting mental challenge to multiply the person-by-person cost to the organization by the estimated number of health professionals in the national work force. That figure would be staggering.

SUMMARY

It takes time for symptoms of burnout to manifest themselves in behavior and work performance. People do not burn out on their first day on the job. The effects of stress show up gradually over a period of time. Stressors seem to have a cumulative effect that leads to burnout. It should be noted also that some effects of stress may be *delayed*, occurring after chronic stressors have been eliminated or reduced. Thus, a worker may appear to be adjusting rather well to the demands of the job, and then, for reasons not readily apparent, symptoms of burnout begin appearing. In most cases, however, people burn out in response to *chronic* stresses of their work. Although stressors may impinge on the individual on an intermittent, unpredictable basis over time, they *persist* in occurring.

It is important to emphasize that to talk about the effects of stress and burnout on behavior and work performance it is necessary to consider the conditions under which stress is experienced. Stress effects are dependent upon several factors:

- The amount of time a person works on a job task

- The level of experience an individual has on the job

- The level of familiarity a person has with the kind of stress associated with the work

- The kind of work the individual is required to do

- Aspects of the job that are most important to efficiency and effectiveness (e.g., precision, observation, manual dexterity, decision making)

- The ways in which different stressors interact (e.g., conflict with a supervisor, abusive language from a patient, malfunctioning equipment, and no opportunity to take a break are stressors that can combine in an additive fashion to exert a significant impact on the individual)

- Personal attributes and coping styles

In health care, the job itself, the physical factors of the environment, the interpersonal relationships, the time on the job, the job incentives and the reward structure within the organization (to name but a few) are factors that interact to determine the nature and magnitude of effects on the individual. Some health professionals will display in their actions more indications of stress and burnout than will others. But if they are, in fact, experiencing burnout, it will definitely appear in their behavior and work performance—what they say and what they do, what they fail to say and what they fail to do. Behavioral and work performance measures are the best indicators of burnout available. Why? Because they are readily observable, whereas thoughts and feelings are not.

REFERENCES

Egan, G. *The skilled helper: A model for systematic helping and interpersonal relating.* Monterey, Calif.: Brooks/Cole, 1975.

Jourard, S. The transparent self. New York: Van Nostrand, 1971.

Muldary, T.W. *Interpersonal relations for health professionals: A social skills approach.* New York: Macmillan, in press.

Reich, W. *Character analysis.* New York: Orgone Press, 1948.

Veninga, R.L., & Spradley, J.P. *The work stress connection: How to cope with job burnout.* Boston: Little, Brown, 1981.

CHAPTER 5

Structural causes of burnout within health care organizations

Structural causes of burnout are those found within the organizational environment in which the health professional practices (Lavandero, 1981). Numerous built-in causes of burnout have been postulated in the last few years. These causes include the qualities of the work setting that affect the health professional's interactions with clients and co-workers (Savicki and Cooley, 1982) as well as the general stresses of patient care, staff conflicts, professional relations, and the overall social climate of the helping context.

This chapter outlines factors that contribute to burnout potential in health care settings, focusing exclusively on structural antecedents that range from interpersonal relationships to policies, procedures, and noise. Chapter 6 follows with an examination of personal causes of burnout; those are considered apart from the present variables for purposes of organization only. It must be kept in mind that although structural and personal influences on burnout are discussed, they are not offered as static causes. The structural antecedents of burnout identified here may have especially strong influences on the appearance of burnout among staff, but ultimately the determinant influence stems from the individual's relationship or interaction with the environment.

PHYSICAL CONDITIONS OF HEALTH CARE ENVIRONMENT

Research in industrial and organizational psychology has demonstrated repeatedly that the physical quality of the work environment has both direct and indirect effects on worker performance. Recently it has been shown that the physical conditions of the helping context have a definite impact on the health professional's experience of stress (Claus and Bailey, 1980; Bailey, Steffen, and Grout, 1980; Baj and Walker, 1980; Kammer, 1978). Claus and Bailey, for example, found that overcrowded units, noise, poor lighting, poor ventilation, and malfunctioning equipment represented some of the physical stressors to which health care professionals are exposed.

Noise and Odors

Turner (1975) surveyed the ICUs of university teaching hospitals and found that the average minimum noise levels in those units were two times greater than the noise level required to disturb average sleep. In fact, in some cases these noise levels were two to three times greater than the level required to interfere with hearing normal conversational speech. In ICUs, as in other hospital departments, there are various mixtures of sounds, from the high-frequency beeps of monitors to the murmuring of respirators, the muffled cries of patients, and the crying of family members. When exposed to high levels of noise over a prolonged period, practitioners may begin developing signs of stress.

Noise in the health care environment is typically intermittent, unexpected, and reverberating; and that combination is irritating to most people. Not only is it psychologically irritating, but such noises arouse an autonomic response in the persons who must endure them. When this type of noise occurs over and over again, several times throughout the day, the fight-or-flight response is activated repeatedly—not to high levels of arousal, but to levels sufficient to have cumulative effects over time. One of the adverse effects of intermittent noise is that it generally interferes with performance more than continuous noise does (Landy and Trumbo, 1980). As performance of job tasks grows more frustrating for some health professionals, they experience more stress.

It is rare for the olfactory sense to be considered in discussions of stress in the workplace. However, in health care the olfactory sense is assaulted repeatedly by repugnant odors and punctuated by reeking or lingering medicinal odors. As Baj and Walker (1980) observed, the hospital environment emits repugnant odors such as fecal esters, acrid bile, and musty odors of superinfection. There are also the more subtle odors of cleaning solutions, food, flowers, and bodily odors of patients. These are generally negative stimuli that impose stress conditions on health professionals.

Facilities and Equipment

In a study of the stressors of ICU nursing, Bailey, Steffen, and Grout (1980) found that one of the stressors identified by staff nurses related to the quality of the physical work environment. The nurses perceived the workplace negatively in terms of its physical features. They also reported that it was stressful to be forced to rely on equipment that may malfunction or to be forced to do their jobs without proper equipment at all. These nurses perceived their respective work spaces as being insufficient and undesirable, and they complained that there were too many people in the units. Not all the nurses surveyed identified these as stressors; some kept their focus on factors that caused more significant problems (e.g., unit management, patient care, interpersonal relations and conflicts).

Many older hospitals do not provide adequate space for the number of patients and providers within them. There is often overcrowding, with two patients doubled up in a room that was formerly a private one. The nursing stations may not be adequate to accommodate new equipment and larger staffs. Storage rooms may be too small for the supplies that must be placed in them. Lighting and ventilation may be inadequate and, again, noise may be a problem in the older hospitals that do not have soundproofing. All these conditions may be stressful for the health professional.

Especially stressful is the lack of equipment within health care settings. One surgical nurse reported that a patient nearly died in surgery when a needed bronchoscope could not be found. That instrument was the only one of its kind in the hospital, and it had been sent out for repair the day of the surgery. This is not an isolated incident, for many similar ones reportedly occur day after day in hospitals where the equipment is either unavailable or malfunctioning. Given the seriousness of the consequences, it is easy to appreciate the stress these conditions impose on health professionals who need the equipment and need it to function properly.

Advances in health care technology have produced an ever-expanding range of complex and sophisticated equipment that health professionals must learn to operate. For example, as the nursing role proceeds through an unprecedented redefinition, nurses must adapt to the transfer of technology from medicine into standard nursing practice. This situation means that they must quickly and efficiently acquire the skills necessary to deal with not only people but also superintricate, highly sophisticated, and often mysterious machines. Thus, a source of stress that is often not recognized in the health care field—one that may become increasingly significant as technology continues to modify the health care function—is the so-called man-machine interface.

In health care, practitioners are interacting more and more with machines. The machines communicate with them through displays of information (e.g., dials, digits, gauges, printouts, and counters) that represent input for processing by human beings at the receiving end. That information may or may not be decoded properly by the individual, so the output of the machine actually constitutes potential sources of input for the human receiver. The output of the machine becomes real informational input for the receivers if their sensory apparatus is not limited or impaired and if they pay attention and concentrate on the machine's output. The output of the machine must be processed before appropriate responses can be made. It is the information-processing activities of the human being that represent both the strength and the weakness of the "man" part of the man-machine interface (Landy and Trumbo, 1980). In processing the machine's output, individuals have to classify and translate display signals to assure that the meaning of the output is understood. However, even if the meaning is precisely understood, there are no assurances that the individual will make the appropriate response to that information. As the complexity of machines increases, and as the stressors to which health professionals are exposed continue to permeate the work environment, the demands on individuals will probably intensify even further. In other words, holding all other stressors constant, it appears that technology will continue to produce ever-increasing numbers of complicated machines that must be mastered by health professionals in order to do their jobs. They will need to be more efficient than ever before in information processing because they must adapt to increases in both the *forms* and the *rates* of data provided by the machines. The machines may not "overload," but the persons in such a system may.

THE WORK ITSELF

In the face of stressors in the physical environment health professionals have a certain range of tolerance for functioning and for performing job tasks without activating emergency stress reactions. They can continually make minor adaptations to annoying stressors such as those discussed before and can do so without paying a serious psychological cost. But there are limits to the adaptations that a health professional can make on a continual basis. And when these limits are reached, symptoms of burnout may begin to appear. To appreciate the impact of structural antecedents of burnout, however, it is necessary to view factors of physical environment as a class of potential stressors that exert their stress effects within a broader set of factors related to conditions of the job itself—conditions that probe the limits of the professional's ability to perform efficiently.

Numerous aspects of the work itself can be stressful for health professionals. The *work schedule* required of nurses can contribute to burnout (Pines and Kafry, 1978). It is not uncommon for nurses to work many days without time off, and it is also not uncommon for them to work duty shifts that overlap into a different shift altogether. Two and three hours of overtime per day is a norm for some departments. In some settings health professionals can accumulate compensatory time for the overtime they put into their jobs. However, in those same settings there is often a limit to the amount of compensatory time they are permitted to use. Consequently, some health professionals accumulate more than the maximum allowable number of compensatory hours and are unable to use them. Another stressful aspect of the work schedule is that some individuals may be scheduled for time off and then be asked to work on those days off because of staff shortages or because someone is ill. For other professionals, days away from work are not really days off since they must be "on call" and available to the hospital as needed. The problem often is that these individuals are told by the administration that they should take time off from work, but when they attempt to do so they are asked to work instead. Repeated double-bind messages such as these can easily make a job frustrating and intolerable and facilitate the development of burnout.

Work overload is an important determinant of the extent to which health professionals burn out in response to structural factors. In fact, Maslach and Pines (1977) and Pines and Kafry (1978) reported that as the size or the acuity of the workload or both increased, burnout appeared to manifest itself more clearly among health professionals. Even if one's workload is not overwhelming, it may contribute to burnout if the health professional's job is sufficiently unpredictable in terms of how frequently routine tasks are interrupted by emergencies. Emergencies do not occur in a predictable fashion; they do not conform to time schedules; and they do not accommodate the normal flow of events. When emergencies do occur, they take health professionals to peak arousal. As the resulting fight-or-flight response is activated over and over again in a seemingly random sequence, an ultimate effect may be burnout.

French and Kaplan (1973) identified overload as a key variable in the stress experienced by workers in various organizations. They made a distinction between objective and subjective overload and between qualitative and quantitative overload. Objective overload is quantifiable in that it pertains to the volume of information individuals are expected to process within specified time periods. For example, objective overload may include the number of patient contacts expected of nurses each day, the number of telephone calls to make, progress notes to record, or medications to dispense. Subjective overload pertains to feelings that there is simply too much work to do or that the work is just too much to handle. Qualitative overload involves the discrepancy between the level of knowledge and skills required to do a job and the actual level of knowledge and skills possessed by the individual. Qualitative overload occurs when individuals do not have the prerequisite skills to complete tasks within required periods of time. Quantitative overload happens when individuals have more work than they can do in a given period of time. Both qualitative and quantitative overload are correlated with indexes of stress (Pines and Aronson, 1981).

These kinds of work overload are evident in many of the comments offered by health professionals: "There just aren't enough hours in the day to get all of these things done"; "We don't have enough staff to do what needs to be done"; or "I feel as if I never have a moment to myself, just a few minutes to relax." As Pines and Aronson (1981) suggested, the results of overload can be aggravated when tasks are imposed that have high priority for the organization but low priority for the service providers or service recipients. When the proper forms have to be filled out and document after document inserted into the recipients' files *before treatment is even provided,* both providers and recipients waiting for help are placed under a great deal of stress. *Paperwork and bureaucratic red tape often represent major work overload stressors.* And so do *meetings.* As one nurse commented:

It's comical, but sad. At our hospital we've got all chiefs and no Indians. Clinical specialists, supervisors, head nurses, nursing office staff—there are so many nurses who sit in meetings all day when they could be working on the units giving patient care. I wonder what they discuss at all those meetings. Probably, *the nursing shortage!* (Van Meter, 1982, p. 50; italics added)

Staffing problems represent another set of structural antecedents of burnout, and they can take various forms. According to recent estimates by the American Hospital Association, hospitals today cannot fill 100,000 budgeted, full-time nursing positions; consequently, there is an average of 72 openings at the typical hospital. Less than one-half of the 1.5 million registered nurses in the United States are working full time, and this statistic does not include those nurses who have let their licenses expire (Dolezal, 1982). The comments of one nurse reflect the tremendous psychological costs incurred by those who feel the direct effects of understaffing problems:

I remember one day we had 12 patients—five new surgeries, one girl who had just broken her neck in a car accident, and three patients who were having active seizures on and off. There were only two of us staffed for the floor. When patients wanted to talk, we had to say, "I'm sorry, honey, we're only doing what's absolutely necessary." On days like that, you do what you can and that's it. You work so hard, and then you go home feeling like you've done nothing.

The stress is so great in nursing, you can't understand it unless you're there. You come home not only physically exhausted from lifting patients and doing physical care, but emotionally drained from seeing patients die or dealing with families . . . Sometimes, my husband will say he's tired, too—he's in research—but his eight hours are equal to about three of mine as far as stress is concerned. (Dolezal, 1982, p. 8)

The most recognized staffing problem in health care, the *nursing shortage*, is documented and discussed in virtually every popular health care publication. As the exodus of health professionals continues, those who remain take on heavier workloads. The ratio of providers to patients sometimes increases to the point where caregivers must attend to an unmanageable number of patients. This increase in workload is one of the clearest effects of staff shortages, and it constitutes a significant stress condition for helpers who choose to stay on the job. The problem is that their jobs become more and more stressful as the workload peaks and levels off. As the workload peaks, there is often a need to put in more hours and take less time off from work. Under such conditions it would seem that burnout is inevitable.

Another staffing problem pertains to the decisions made by administrators about the placement of personnel. As Lavandero (1981) suggested, those who control the organizational structure may not understand the needs of their employees. Consequently, employees are often placed in departments where a "body" is needed —regardless of whether or not that "body" is either prepared to work in that department or appropriately matched with other staff in terms of professional and educational background, sex, age, or ethnic and racial characteristics. In such cases the result is a disproportion in the relative numbers of similar professionals (Kanter, 1977). For example, if two degree nurses are placed in a given department with several diploma nurses, the degree nurses may be perceived by their colleagues as "different" and, therefore, may not be afforded the same level of staff support as other "similarly situated" diploma nurses. By virtue of their training, then, health professionals perceived as being different may be isolated by the rest of the staff.

Another structural antecedent of burnout is the *lack of autonomy and power* of many health professionals. Health professionals may feel as if they really have no control over their work environment. And, as emphasized in Chapter 3, individuals who are repeatedly unable to gain a measure of control over their environments may acquire a "learned helplessness." Any successes they experience are attributed to factors external to themselves because they have learned that they are powerless to make a real difference in the way things are.

For some people the need for autonomy is so great that they will even blame themselves for accidents in order to maintain their sense of control (Pines and Aronson, 1981). Such compensatory beliefs may ultimately place more pressure on individuals as they assume responsibility for events that are, in fact, beyond their control.

In general, a lack of autonomy and power engenders feelings of frustration, victimization, and helplessness. Nurses are the most frequent sufferers of this experience because they are charged with tremendous responsibilities but are given no real power of authority. It is as if they are perceived as "second-class professionals" and "bed-pan carriers" who need no authority in their role of "carrying out doctors' orders." In the last few years nurses have emerged from this casted stereotype and revolted against conditions of deference to "higher authorities" who are frequently not in touch with the hard demands of professionals on the "front line." Nonetheless, such conditions generally prevail and, consequently, loom as structural causes of burnout.

The conflict for many health professionals (e.g., nurses) who attempt to solve the power and autonomy dilemma is that efforts to gain power are countered by what Kanter (1977) identified as the "lack of opportunity." As the powerless helpers strive to achieve a position of authority and autonomy within the health care organization, they find that the real opportunities for advancement are extremely remote.

Professionals are bound by law to conduct themselves with at least as much care as the "average, reasonable professional" in their profession (Cohen, 1979). For example, services rendered by a hospital ICU nurse must be at least as competently and skillfully performed as those of the *average* ICU nurse. If the professional rendering professional services acts in a manner that is in some way below the level of care that is expected from any reasonable person of the same profession under the same or similar circumstances, those acts are referred to in the legal context in terms of *negligence* (Cohen, 1979). If the professional in question is a health professional, the acts may be described more accurately in terms of *medical malpractice*. Since patients have a right to expect that the care they receive from health professionals is provided competently and skillfully, these professionals are *accountable* or *liable* for acts or failures to act in the course of rendering professional services. *Liability*, as a legal concept, and *accountability*, as a more general performance-related concept, represent additional stressors for health professionals. In health care there is such a high-risk element in the delivery of services, and often such a limited degree of control, that providers normally function in a condition of accountability overload. For most health professionals accountability is a threatening notion since the critical feedback typically concentrates on spelling out mistakes and incompetency. With the threat of such consequences hanging on their every action, health professionals are highly vulnerable to burnout. Further, the problem of accountability becomes all the more serious for these persons when it is viewed against the dilemma of being accountable and yet not having the requisite power and authority to balance the demand. This dilemma is especially problematic for nurses who have little power and authority relative to physicians and yet are highly accountable for their actions—sometimes more liable than the attending physicians.

One way of conceptualizing the structural antecedents of burnout is in terms of a generally *deficient reward system.* Health care organizations are so complex that they lose control of the efficient and equitable distribution of organizational rewards. Often such rewards take the form of *recognition, praise, encouragement, expressions of appreciation,* and clear *feedback* about job performance—regardless of whether it is for efficient or inefficient performance. The rewards people seek from the organizations employing them are not always money or promotions.

When health professionals do their jobs under the conditions already described here, and when they do their jobs without feedback, they tend to become discouraged. Even if all the other conditions identified remained totally unchanged, many health professionals could probably still cope with stress if they felt needed, appreciated, and acknowledged for their contributions. These are extremely powerful incentives—especially for people whose reasons for entering health care are directly related to these factors in the first place! Given their strong needs to make a difference, to be needed, and to be recognized for the help they give, health professionals may experience a particularly high level of discomfort about their work when these conditions are not satisfied. Thus, it is not only the negative features of the work environment that contribute to burnout; it is the absence of positive features as well.

When a health care organization fails to provide sufficient psychological rewards for its employees, the employees develop the sense that they are working hard—sometimes beyond the requirements of the job description—and that they still are not appreciated for what they do, either as expected or "above and beyond the call of duty." A popular cliche among people in virtually any organization is that "you never hear anything when you do a good job, but you always hear about it when you don't." What this cliche amounts to is the worker's perception that reprimand comes easily, but reward may not come at all. Again, "even when the quality and quantity of the workload is appropriate, the schedule is ideal, and the necessary power is available, an absence of feedback about job performance can lead to burnout" (Lavandero, 1981, p. 22).

Stressors of ICU Nursing

One factor that contributes greatly to the stress experienced by nurses is the performance-reward discrepancy relative to *salary.* The average nurse makes $14,000 a year, and salaries tend to stay low. On the average there is a mean difference of only $2,000 per year between the average salaries of recent graduates and staff nurses with 20 years of experience. As the nursing role has expanded and as new job responsibilities have increased, there has not been a commensurate increase in salaries. And even with these changes in roles and responsibilities, it seems that administrators have no incentive to raise nursing salaries because hospitals are closed labor markets: They do not need to pay anything beyond the going rate since they do not compete with other industries for nurses. The salaries of nurses today represent a travesty of social and professional justice, especially in view of the income gap between physicians and nurses. According to census data, in 1945 nurses made one-third of what physicians earned, and today they make *even less*—about one-fifth (Dolezal, 1982).

It is especially perplexing to health professionals that such low monetary value is associated with humanitarian functions. It is as if society believes that "helping the needy" is sufficient and just reward. Not uncommon is the health professional's experience of caring for someone whose job is perceived as less socially significant and yet worth much more in terms of wages. Many professionals can accept and live with such a disparity, but many cannot. Those who cannot accept the economic sacrifices of their work often become bitter and resentful when they begin to see others enjoying a higher standard of living, with all the trappings of a life-style they cannot afford. Indeed, for nurses who toil and struggle in the midst of death and suffering day in and day out, there is no rational explanation for why the salaries of professional athletes are *10 to 100 times higher* than the nurses', simply for entertaining people at leisure.

Bailey, Steffen, and Grout (1980) surveyed 1,800 ICU nurses in an attempt to elicit responses that would provide informative data on the stressors of ICU nursing. Several categories of stressors were identified by the subjects in this study. The three areas producing the greatest stress for these nurses were *management of the unit, interpersonal relationships,* and *patient care.*

Within the category of unit management several different stress factors were identified. Among them were inadequate staffing, apathetic staff, emergencies, transfers, admissions, unavailability of physicians, shifts, scheduling, paperwork, interruptions, charge position, and lack of continuity in patient assignments. Included under the heading of interpersonal relationships were personality conflicts with staff, physicians, administration, and residents; disagreement with physicians over patient treatment; unresponsive nursing leaders; lack of respect from physicians; lack of teamwork; and communication problems. Within the category of patient care were factors such as critical, unstable patients; death of "special" patients; inability to meet patient needs; chronic patients; emergencies; arrests; and decision-making.

Of these three major categories, interpersonal relations and patient care were seen as causing the most stress. Interestingly, they were also seen as contributing to the greatest satisfaction. That is, the most potent sources of stress for ICU nurses also had the greatest potential for providing a sense of satisfaction in their work. Thus, where patient care was concerned, patient deterioration was stressful for the nurses, but patient improvement was satisfying. With regard to interpersonal relations, interpersonal conflict was stressful, but cooperation and compatibility were satisfying. Another source of satisfaction for these nurses was the area of knowledge and skills, which included the opportunity for learning, intellectual challenge, pace, variety, and excitement.

The findings of Bailey, Steffen, and Grout are interesting for another reason. The data from their study suggest that those factors perceived as stressors by some nurses may be perceived as satisfiers by others. Perception and appraisal of one's circumstances are critical factors in determining one's experience of stress and burnout. It should be noted that these data further suggest that any attempt at helping nurses manage stress must focus on the processes of perception and appraisal.

It would be interesting to learn if the stressors identified by ICU nurses are consistent with the types of stressors identified by nurses working in different units. Logic suggests a close correspondence because health care in general is emotionally draining work that is not limited to areas where patients are seriously ill. Furthermore, one important category of stressors that is inescapable in health care, regardless of the department, is the area of interpersonal relationships. Health care is provided within the contexts of human relationships, and those social contexts can strongly influence the extent to which individuals experience stress and burnout. So important are interpersonal relations in health care that a separate section is devoted here to examining this critical group of stressors.

INTERPERSONAL RELATIONSHIPS

As indicated in Chapter 1, burnout is a response to the stress of repeated, intense emotional contact with people. It has been hypothesized that *people* are both the greatest source of stress and the greatest source of satisfaction in the practice of health care. There is a wide variation in the amount of contact built into the job tasks of health care. The laboratory technician, for example, has many fewer contacts with people than the floor nurse. And it could be argued that the nurse has more frequent and more intense contacts with patients than does the attending physician. Some functions may require few encounters at all with health care recipients (in some settings the pharmacist may be one example). For most health professionals, however, their jobs revolve around interactions with other people.

Just as health professionals can become overloaded with the technical requirements of their jobs, so also can they become over-loaded with interpersonal contact. One factor that contributes to this type of stress is the *state* of the individuals with whom one interacts. Most of the interactions of health professionals are with patients who are in varying states of suffering and distress and with colleagues who may be in different states of their own distress. Given such con-ditions, it sometimes happens that the mental and emotional states of patients and colleagues "rub off" onto an individual. When patients are interacting with a health professional, for instance, few of them are concerned about making the interaction a pleasant one for the professional. Instead they are focused primarily on their medical and emotional condition, and their own preoccupations often preclude consideration of the influence they may have on the health professional. When professionals go in and out of one room after another, encountering person after person in distress, it is not un-common for them to sometimes begin feeling a bit distraught, too. As discussed earlier, one way of responding to this situation is to detach and distance oneself emotionally, put on the professional armor, and press forward—unaffected and in total "control." Of course, this response is part of burnout.

To carry on one's duties in the face of forces that threaten to overwhelm emotionally is a monumental challenge. The implicit requirement seems to be that health professionals become super-human in controlling their emotions around other people. This necessity clearly produces an emotional overload that cannot be con-fined to the hospital environment or limited to an eight-hour shift. As Scully (1981) suggested, when a superhuman stance is carried over from job tasks to interpersonal relationships in general, tension escalates.

One of the common sources of stress from interpersonal rela-tionships is *conflict*. Some of the relationships among health professionals involve real or perceived differences in each other. Where the interests or values of one person are different from those of another person who is attempting to achieve the same goal as the first person, there is fertile ground for conflict. Not all conflicts are bad, nor are they all of the same kind. For example, *constructive conflicts* involve an open and honest dialogue between individuals in an attempt to reach a decision that produces results satisfying to both or all parties concerned. *Competitive conflicts* are win-lose situations in which each person follows set rules for relating to each other as each attempts to achieve mutually exclusive goals without becoming angry at another. *Disruptive conflicts* are not guided by rules, and the participants are not concerned with winning. These conflicts are typically associated with angry feelings, so the individuals in conflict are more intent upon harming each other in some way. Disruptive conflicts are thus the most stressful type of conflicts. They are the means used by individuals to defeat, harm, or strike a blow to another's person and are often used in an atmosphere of anger, tension, and stress. Obviously, these three kinds of conflicts are distributed along a continuum. Even in constructive conflicts, individuals may become angry for a time, but the anger dissipates and no harm is intended to anyone involved in the conflict.

Conflicts involve at least two persons (or groups) interacting with each other in an effort to reach mutually exclusive goals. The behavior of each person toward the other is designed to defeat or dominate the other or to gain a mutually designated outcome. These actions are opposing and generally incompatible. Let us now consider some relationships in which conflict between health professionals is often observed.

In spite of their complementary functions and roles, nurses and physicians are bred for interdisciplinary conflict. Their respective training programs socialize them differently. Physicians are predominantly male and have been socialized into positions of authority, status, power. Nurses, on the other hand, are socialized into a predominantly female profession that communicates that they should defer to physicians, even when the physician may be exercising poor judgment in patient care. Most of the time nurses and physicians avoid conflict and work cooperatively with the best interests of patients in mind. Sometimes, however, they come into intense conflict over matters pertaining to treatment. As Bailey, Steffen, and Grout (1980) reported, conflicts with physicians were significant stressors for many ICU nurses. Apparently such conflicts are often "set up" by nurses' perceptions that physicians show a lack of respect for them. If this is true, the physicians would tend to ignore the suggestions of nurses, defend their own opinions (sometimes in the face of clear evidence of error), and act in condescending ways toward nurses. When nurse-physician relationships are strained in these ways, the conflict is stressful for both parties.

Social Support Systems

Social support systems consist of other people. When they exist in the helping context, they can function as buffers that mediate the effects of stressful environmental conditions. Thus, social support systems consisting of one's colleagues can mediate the effects of burnout and help individuals to maintain psychological balance.

Effective, supportive relationships among members of any work group are important factors that contribute to the overall well-being of an organization. Organizational psychologists have frequently argued that the quality of interpersonal relationships and the communication within an organization are key determinants of the level of job satisfaction reported by workers. Good relationships are vital to the functioning of the organization as a whole and, at the same time, essential for curbing the effects of burnout on individuals. However, workers often get so caught up in their work and in habits and routine that they neglect each other (Pines and Aronson, 1981). They do not often provide the level of support that is necessary to provide optimum psychological benefits for one another.

Maslach and Pines (1979) reported that individuals who had effective social support systems at work tended to experience a reduction of burnout. Most likely this reduction occurred because the workers felt they were able to discuss their concerns with their colleagues. By sharing those concerns they could be helped to see the situation somewhat differently, distance themselves from the troubling situation, and obtain advice on how to handle it. Or perhaps it was simply consoling for them to have someone care enough to listen. It seems that in various human service settings burnout is less severe when providers have the opportunity to express their feelings and concerns and then receive constructive feedback and support. Stress is much greater for workers who feel that they are alone and that they must deal with their work-related troubles by themselves.

It is reasonable to expect that when health professionals are getting along with each other in their professional roles, they experience less stress on the job. In a study by Pines and Maslach (1978), for example, mental health workers expressed more positive attitudes about the institution, enjoyed their work, and felt more successful in it when work relationships were good. They also reported having many more "good days" than "bad days" at work when those relationships were satisfactory. During the good days they probably experienced their jobs as being much less stressful than the jobs seemed on bad days.

It is important to point out here that conflicts and "good" versus "bad" days at work are not direct linear functions of interpersonal relationships. That is, the immediate quality of those relationships, in terms of the level of satisfaction interacting persons derive from communicating with each other, must be viewed against the background of what has taken place in the recent and remote past of each person.

In every relationship, in every transaction with another person, there is for each individual a background of other concerns, moods, and feelings. When an individual goes to work and interacts with co-workers, the interaction occurs against a background of personal experience accumulated from other contexts. Thus, the individual may perceive work relationships against a background of countless other social relationships. If those social relationships are not satisfactory, or if they are causing the individual considerable stress, that dissatisfaction and stress may penetrate the work relationships. Conversely, if those relationships are satisfactory, the work relationships may be satisfactory also. An ongoing interaction with a colleague may suddenly make salient to the individual a broader problem faced outside of the work situation. The awareness may then elicit a change of mood and a change in the way the individual is perceiving the current interaction. As Lazarus (1977) suggested, "whatever the person is momentarily experiencing, be it emotional or not, happens against a background of other psychological conflicts and states, even if these are tentatively pushed into the background" (p. 149).

SUMMARY

Virtually any structural aspect of the health care environment can be stressful for health professionals, *provided it is perceived as such.* Despite the numerous antecedents of burnout that are identified in this chapter, the ultimate effects of environmental stressors depend on the individual's perceptions of them. It is the individual's interaction with the health care environment that is critical in the development of the burnout syndrome.

Structural antecedents of burnout include physical conditions of the health care environment (e.g., noise, odors, sights, facilities, equipment), the work itself, and interpersonal relations. Stressful aspects of helping are related to work schedules, work overload, mundane job requirements, staffing problems, shortages, placement of personnel, lack of autonomy and power, and deficient reward systems. Special categories of stressors include management of the unit, interpersonal relationships, and patient care. Interpersonal relationships constitute a prominent source of stress for health professionals, and emotional overloading through interpersonal contact is a common outcome. Conflict is a major source of stress generated by interpersonal relationships. Although the health professional may experience different kinds of conflicts, the nurse-physician relationship is a specific professional relationship that often creates stress for both parties. The effects of adequate and inadequate support systems are another important consideration in relation to burnout.

REFERENCES

Bailey, J.T., Steffen, S.M., & Grout, J.W. The stress audit: Identifying the stressors of ICU nursing. *Journal of Nursing Education,* 1980, *19*(6), 15–25.

Baj, P.A., & Walker, D. Management actions to humanize the health care environment. *Journal of Nursing Education,* 1980, *19*(6), 43–47.

Claus, K.E., & Bailey, J.T. (Eds.), *Living with stress and promoting well-being: A handbook for nurses.* St. Louis: C.V. Mosby, 1980.

Cohen, J.R. *Malpractice: A guide for mental health professionals.* New York: Free Press, 1979.

Dolezal, S. So tired of running, they're walking away. *Detroit,* February 7, 1982, pp. 7–13.

French, J.R., & Kaplan, R.D. Organizational stress and individual strain. In A.J. Marrow (Ed.), *The failure of success.* New York: AMACOM, 1973.

Kammer, A.C. Burnout: Contemporary dilemma for the Jesuit social activist. *Study of Spirituality of Jesuits,* 1978, *10*(1), 1–42.

Kanter, R.M. *Men and women of the corporation.* New York: Basic Books, 1977.

Landy, F.J., & Trumbo, D.A. *Psychology of work behavior.* Homewood, Ill.: Dorsey Press, 1980.

Lavandero, R. Nurse burnout: What can we learn? *Journal of Nursing Administration,* November-December, 1981, pp. 17–23.

Lazarus, R. Cognitive and coping processes in emotion. In A. Monat & R. Lazarus (Eds.), *Stress and coping: An anthology*. New York: Columbia University Press, 1977.

Maslach, C., & Pines, A. The burnout syndrome in the day-care setting. *Child Care Quarterly*, 1977, *6*(2), 100–113.

Maslach, C., & Pines, A. Burnout: The loss of human caring. In A. Pines & C. Maslach (Eds.), *Experiencing social psychology*. New York: Random House, 1979.

Pines, A., & Aronson, E. *Burnout: From tedium to personal growth*. New York: Free Press, 1981.

Pines, A., & Kafry, D. Occupational tedium in the social services. *Social Work*, 1978, *23*(6), 499–507.

Pines, A., & Maslach, C. Characteristics of staff burnout in mental health settings. *Hospital Community Psychiatry*, 1978, *29*(4), 233–237.

Savicki, V., & Cooley, E.J. Implications of burnout research and theory for counselor educators. *Personnel and Guidance Journal*, 1982, *60*(7), 415–419.

Scully, R. Staff support groups: Helping nurses to help themselves. *Journal of Nursing Administration*, March 1981, pp. 48–51.

Turner, A.G. Measuring and reducing noise. *Hospitals*, 1975, *49*(15), 85–86, 88–90.

Van Meter, M. A 'magic' solution for all our staffing ills. *R.N. Magazine*, January 1982, pp. 49–53.

CHAPTER 6

Coping styles and predispositions toward burnout

A reasonable question to ask when considering the phenomenon of burnout is Who are the people most vulnerable to it? At this point in the discussion only a partial answer can be offered. For example, we know that health professionals experience burnout with greater frequency than people in business or industry. However, we also know that burnout is a highly variable syndrome that is not peculiar to any single personality type, sex, age, race, or human service specialty. The syndrome appears to be individualized.

Are there certain people who have a greater risk for burnout than others? An answer to this question must be stated tentatively, for research must ultimately guide the response. Yet it seems from the available anecdotal evidence that some people in the human service professions are stronger candidates for burnout than others. This chapter will look at some of the behavioral characteristics of these persons in an attempt to clarify which persons carry significant risks for experiencing burnout while in their professional roles. First, the chapter offers a portrait of the health professional and suggests some predisposing factors that are common to people whose profession focuses on serving others. Then the discussion turns toward professionals who are especially high risks for burnout. The last portion of the chapter examines a range of assumptions that individuals may make about the nature of personal problems and their solutions. Recent findings from research in psychology suggest that the kinds of assumptions people make about who or what is to blame for their problems and who is responsible for resolving them may have a direct impact on their success in finding an adaptive solution.

PORTRAIT OF THE HEALTH PROFESSIONAL

Health professionals appear to be high risks for job burnout. If one assumes that it is not entirely because of environmental factors that they burn out, what is it about health professionals that predisposes them to burnout? To answer this question it is important to consider some special characteristics of people who choose to work in the allied health professions.

Most of the people who choose to work in these professions are individuals who are particularly sensitive toward others (Pines and Aronson, 1981). They have a high degree of empathy for others and, consequently, tend to experience more distress than do persons with less empathy when exposed to the suffering of those they serve. These individuals support humanitarian motives and values, and they are oriented more toward people than to things (Kadushin, 1974). They are dedicated to helping people in trouble because they are especially sensitive to the needs of others.

Pines and Aronson (1981) maintained that health professionals are predisposed to burnout because of their inherent *client-centered orientation*, which gives exclusive focus to the persons being served. The client's needs are paramount and define the professional's role. So long as the professionals continue to serve, suggested Pines and Aronson, their presence can be justified. The only noble motives are service motives. Therefore, individual needs and feelings are subordinated, and at times even denied, because the client-centered orientation suggests that it is inappropriate to satisfy one's own needs while in the professional role. Forced into using denial and repression as part of their job, health professionals block from awareness their feelings and needs that are being continually frustrated. Those repressed feelings find expression in other ways on the road to burnout.

Edelwich and Brodsky (1980) suggested that allied health professionals may have a particularly strong need to confirm their own sense of personal power to have an impact on the world. They want to make a difference to other people. They want to have positive effects on the lives of other people. Consequently, when this need is repeatedly thwarted by mundane bureaucratic obstacles, by people who do not get better in spite of the professionals' efforts, and by a society that appears to have withdrawn its full support of the helping motive, it becomes clear to many health professionals that their high aspirations must be changed. Burned-out professionals may simply resign themselves to the belief that nothing they can do will really make a difference.

It is generally assumed that health professionals are intellectually capable and interpersonally skilled and that they possess very good common sense. They respect other people and respond to others' needs as fully and as competently as they can. These professionals understand people, presumably because they understand themselves very well. They genuinely care for the individuals whom they serve, and they always look out for those individuals' best interests. Health professionals do not let themselves and their own problems get in the way of helping. They are psychologically healthy and the masters of their own fate. They do not submit to life but seize it and live it fully. These professionals are at home with others and not hesitant about entering the world of others, even though their own worlds may be disorganized and in turmoil, filled with suffering, and generally in crisis. Health professionals can readily mobilize their energies to handle any crisis, and they can act forcefully and decisively because they are "in control" all the time. They are more concerned with people than with money, for they have not become health professionals to get rich. They are willing to do whatever they can to actually live the values they hold, and they are willing to accept all the aforementioned expectations, even though many of these expectations may be unrealistic. In effect, health professionals often internalize the expectations associated with their role, and when those expectations are not lived up to, they experience guilt, tension, anxiety and then resentment, anger, and burnout.

Health professionals usually have certain expectations of their own. For one thing, they expect great things from themselves in their professional role. They believe that they will be able to function differently and perhaps more effectively than others who came before them. They may also expect that they should be able to serve virtually any kind of person and that there really is not a patient they could not reach if they just tried hard enough. They may expect that every patient they work with necessarily wants to get better. They may expect that the people they serve will appreciate what they do for these people. Health professionals may also expect that they will enjoy the environment in which they work; after all, everyone is there working for the same reasons. They may expect that working as a health professional will provide them with a greater sense of personal fulfillment than any other occupation could offer. They may expect that their efforts will be recognized by their peers and that their efforts will eventually pay off with various extrinsic rewards. They may expect that, although others may burn out on the job, they will not because they will see burnout coming and know what to do about it.

A humanitarian orientation, a high degree of empathy, a need to make a difference in the lives of others, expectations and stereotypes of health professionals, and personal expectations may collectively predispose the individual health professional toward burnout. These factors are certainly unique to allied health and human service professions.

HEALTH PROFESSIONALS AS HIGH RISKS FOR BURNOUT

Because of prior learning, family background, current life circumstances, job experiences, appraisal skills, coping resources, and various other factors, certain individuals in the allied health professions may be more predisposed to burnout than others. It is probably not possible to actually identify and distinguish separate personality "types" that are predisposed to burnout. Burnout is too highly individualized to accommodate static and rigid categorization of persons according to their degree of susceptibility. There is too much variability among individuals who experience burnout. However, it appears that there may be at least one style of interacting with the world that is connected with burnout. Various labels have been attached to this interactive style. For example, Friedman and Rosenman (1974) described it in terms of the "type A personality." However, what they described bears a conspicuous resemblance to what those in the mental health field call the "obsessive-compulsive personality." This collective pattern of ingrained responses to the world may constitute the single most significant predisposition to burnout.

The Compulsive Personality

Individuals described in clinical terms as "obsessive-compulsive" personalities have a certain rigidity about them that is related to an underlying need for order and organization in their worlds. A driving force behind much of their behavior is to ensure as much predictability and control in the world as they can. Things need to be orderly and to occur in a predictable manner. To the extent that events are in fact orderly and predictable, these individuals are able to exercise some degree of control over their occurrence. Because, for such persons, there is a place for everything and everything must be in its place, they are often seen as perfectionists, who cannot tolerate mistakes, flaws, or anything less than the ideal. A disturbing fact that these individuals never seem to be able to internalize is that nothing ever is perfect or ideal. Consequently, they repeatedly face the world as being imperfect, and this imperfection causes them considerable psychological discomfort.

To compensate for the lack of order, predictability, and perfection they seek in the world, compulsive individuals often strive hard to gain a measure of control over anything they can. Sometimes this need is manifested in their rigid adherence to policies and rules of conduct and their pattern of never deviating from the norm because of their inevitable guilt and anxiety over "going against the grain." These individuals seen preoccupied with matters of rules, order, and organization. They appear committed to an uncanny degree to efficiency and detail. Their compulsive attention to detail leads to a narrowing of their perceptual focus that precludes attention to matters at the periphery of their perceptual field and awareness. In other words, they give so much attention to specifics and particulars that they lose the ability to "get the big picture"—to see a total situation. Such narrowed perceptual focusing often causes them to miss some very important aspects of what is happening around them. They concentrate so intensely on specifics that other important information escapes their attention.

This narrowed attention is derived from a cognitive style—a general manner of thinking—that makes it difficult for them to think of several things together. Thoughts are compartmentalized and neatly organized so that the compulsive personalities may deal with one issue at a time. When satisfied that the issue has been thoroughly considered, then, and *only* then, are they able to make a transition to other thoughts. In short, they "obsess" over matters and cannot easily shift their attention to other things until they have organized their thoughts about the issues in an orderly, sequential process. When talking with compulsive persons, you often get the sense that, although they are looking at you, they are thinking about something else. This feeling may occur because they tend to lock onto a part of your message and then focus their attention solely on that particular aspect of the total communication. Or they may seize upon something you say and force an immediate focus on that issue, going over it and over it without being able to get on to other issues. They simply cannot shift their thoughts away from an issue until it is neatly tucked away in their unconscious.

An essential feature of the compulsive person is a restricted ability to express warm and tender emotions. The reason for this restriction is that emotional experience is something that few people have great control over. Emotions can be volatile and upset the order and neatness that is so greatly needed by compulsive persons. Consequently, these individuals strive to maintain control over their emotions. On the surface they often appear as formal and serious, clearly in control of themselves. They appear to lack the capacity for spontaneously expressing emotions to others. Therefore, when they do express emotions, the emotions sometimes have a forced and ungenuine quality. Given these factors, many of their everyday relationships have a formal and serious quality.

Work and productivity are of utmost importance to the compulsive individual. Often they are valued above interpersonal relationships and leisure. In fact, leisure does not come easily for the compulsive person because it must be worked for and planned. Leisure, and simply relaxing and doing nothing, are not orderly and organized events for most people. The compulsive person does not tolerate "doing nothing," so even during times away from work the person works. In many cases the individual will often postpone vacations and leisure activities.

An interesting thing happens to compulsive persons when the order and organization that they need cannot be controlled: They become depressed. When unable to control things, their mood changes. Because they frequently cannot control the events that they want to control, their mood may change often. Prolonged periods of depression may occur when these individuals continue to perceive a range of things they cannot control.

Compulsive persons are often oriented toward achievement in order to demonstrate their own worth as human beings. The job is a means for achieving and proving their worth. Therefore, they may take on an excessive number of jobs and projects as if they were counting their achievements by number. They get swallowed up in excessive devotion to work and productivity because this devotion is the means by which they can feel good about themselves. At the same time, however, they may resent that they need to work so hard while others approach work with less vigor. They become angry and hostile and carry these feelings around with them, suppressed and not permitted full ventilation. This anger and hostility are often expressed in indirect ways, for example, by being stubborn, argumentative, disagreeable, and insistent that everyone do things their way. Uncontrolled expression of feelings such as anger cannot be tolerated because it is so threatening to them. Also, expression of such feelings always brings with it the risk that others will disapprove, and acceptance and approval are extremely important to them because acceptance and approval by others are external measures of their worth as persons.

For many compulsive persons their most significant problem is an everlasting battle with time. These individuals are always conscious of time and always have a nagging sense of time urgency, similar to that described by Friedman and Rosenman (1974) in characterizing the type-A personality. They consistently feel the pressure of time. They want to get everything completed within a short period of time, so they always appear to be in a hurry. One consequence is that compulsive persons reduce the amount of time they invest in critical thinking and problem solving. Such matters simply take too much time. Consequently, these individuals respond to problem situations in noncreative, stereotyped ways because doing so saves time. They have the nagging sense that there is just no time to spare. They may eat in a hurry, talk in a hurry, and become generally impatient when forced to wait for anything. Even waiting for someone else to finish a sentence can be problematic for some compulsive persons. They may resort to repeated urgings that others finish speaking, or they may just complete sentences for the speaker. As one might expect, many compulsive persons are not good listeners. This situation occurs not only because of their impatience but also because they may get lost somewhere during the conversation as they lock their attention on to some detail in the communication.

Although there are various other secondary characteristics of the compulsive person, these primary ones serve to point out certain factors that make such individuals especially prone to burnout. Compulsive persons are high risks not only for burnout but also, as Friedman and Rosenman (1974) have argued, for coronary heart disease.

Other Predispositions

Obviously, the compulsive individual is not the only person who runs a risk of burnout in the role of a health professional. Some people, for example, may have a long-standing lack of self-confidence that carries over into their professional roles. Plagued by self-doubt for years, they may find this feeling intensified in the helping context whenever positive outcomes are not readily apparent. Because of their inherent lack of self-confidence, compulsive individuals may become especially anxious and fearful when left on their own to do a job as they see fit. Without continual direction and supervision, complemented by a concomitant steady assurance that they are, in fact, performing satisfactorily, *dependent* persons tend to experience considerable stress that may have a cumulative effect over time: It may lead to burnout. It is particularly hard for such persons to assume responsibility and initiate action because the fear of failure is so strong. Consequently, they often defer to others when important tasks must be undertaken or when important decisions must be made.

In their work relationships, as in their social and family relationships, dependent persons subordinate their own needs to those of others. They do so not because their role as a health professional requires such subordination, but because they have learned to assume submission toward other people in general. Other people are the supports on which they depend. Therefore, dependent persons avoid making demands of and displeasing others because of the fear that such actions will jeopardize those relationships to the point of forcing the dependent persons to rely on themselves for support. Since they believe that they are inherently unable to perform tasks with the same efficiency that others demonstrate, they may view even exceptional job performance on their part as a result of chance or luck. Their attitude is that they really do not have the ability to look as good as they did.

Given their long-standing dependency needs, dependent persons may receive considerable reward from their jobs as long as they feel needed and appreciated by those they serve. When this reward is not forthcoming as needed, the job may become more and more stressful for them. When they are asked to do certain job tasks, there is an implicit message that they are needed. Consequently, they may be prepared to accept as many tasks as they can. Whenever someone asks for something, such individuals may be unable to say no. The dependent individual lives by an unconscious dictum: Just tell me what you want me to do and I'll do it.

Some individuals interact with the world in a *passive-aggressive* manner. On the job this style is manifested in various ways, including a resistance to demands for adequate performance. The passive-aggressive individual resists in indirect ways. For example, when a nurse is told by her supervisor that she is scheduled to provide in-service training to staff nurses in three weeks, the nurse intentionally avoids reminding the supervisor that her vacation is to begin that week. When the vacation date arrives, the nurse goes on vacation without any word to her supervisor, thus leaving the supervisor to deal with what becomes an emergency situation—to salvage the in-service training. For the passive-aggressive person such actions do not come as isolated incidents. They occur frequently and sometimes predictably. As the supervisor in this example later commented, "I should have known she'd do something like this."

Passive-aggressive individuals habitually resent and oppose any demands made upon them by others to improve their performance or to maintain their current level of performance. Such demands are responded to with indirect resistance (e.g., procrastination, intentional inefficiency, or "forgetfulness"). Because of this passive-aggressive behavior, their relationships with both superiors and colleagues become strained. Promotions are not often given to such persons because of their work history. Consequently, their anger and general hostility increase, and their tendency to express these negative feelings in passive-aggressive ways increases further. The job becomes very stressful for such persons. However, they have helped to create the stressors they are reacting to.

In each of the styles described in this chapter, individuals *participate in shaping their own environments.* The environments they help to create may be stressful for them in that these environments demand certain adaptive responses that are difficult to make. The patterns described here represent characteristic coping responses that are engaged in by individuals in a range of situations, including the work environment. The consistency of behavior implied by the labels assigned to them may reflect their efforts to select and create environmental conditions that are typical for them and that they can respond to in characteristic ways, without having to change. Those stereotyped, long-standing patterns of interacting with the world may be the principal factors that set up the stress conditions these persons subsequently cannot adapt to. Burnout may become the most likely consequence of such patterns of behavior.

ASSUMPTIONS ABOUT PROBLEMS AND COPING

Whenever something happens to us, we automatically look for a reason to explain the event. When individuals are working under stressful conditions, they are likely to try to explain to themselves the reasons for what they are experiencing. The causes they come up with are explicit or implicit *attributions* to some set of factors since individuals are guided by various underlying assumptions about why things happen as they do. These assumptions have important implications for how individuals perceive problems and solutions. This section discusses four general sets of assumptions that people use when seeking to attribute responsibility for problems and for solutions. The implications of these assumptions for the management of stress and burnout are important since the logic that proceeds from the assumptions leads the person to determine who or what is to blame for those problems and who or what is responsible for a solution. These assumptions were originally presented by Brickman and associates (1982) as "models of helping and coping." The models, or assumptions, were identified as follows:

- The *moral model*—people are seen as responsible for problems and solutions

- The *compensatory model*—people are viewed as being not responsible for problems but responsible for solutions

- The *medical model*—people are considered responsible for neither problems nor solutions

- The *enlightenment model*—people are viewed as not responsible for solutions but responsible for problems.

Moral Model

As Brickman and his associates pointed out, the moral model holds that people are responsible for both creating and solving their problems. If, for example, health professionals perceive themselves as burning out, they may blame themselves for what is happening to them. For them, the solution lies in getting control of themselves or the conditions generating their negative experience. Brickman and associates suggested that the individuals who support these assumptions tend to see themselves as failing to make the critical efforts required to change things. Regardless of how hard these persons may be trying to manage burnout, for example, they consider the effort not strong enough, for the solution would be imminent (they believe) if only sufficient energy were expended. These persons believe that their fate is entirely in their own hands and that they must help themselves because that is the only road to solution.

According to Brickman and associates, the value of such an assumption about problems and solutions is that it encourages people to take control and start changing what they do not like about their lives, rather than sitting around complaining or waiting for someone else to change things. Also, if they choose not to take control of the situation, then they must accept things the way they are and quit complaining. On the other hand, a disadvantage of the moral model is that it may encourage the belief that victims of anything chose to be victims. Someone experiencing burnout would, therefore, be just as responsible for choosing to burn out as victims of violence would be for the harm they suffered. As Brickman and associates (1982) suggested, "The moral model is conducive to a pathology of loneliness" (p. 371).

When the assumptions inherent in the moral model are accepted by health professionals who are experiencing burnout, they are likely to see burnout as being their own fault entirely. Solutions to the problem are, therefore, seen as being totally dependent on what they do to undo the situation. Consequently, they may resist the efforts of others to help them manage the symptoms of burnout. And, if they are unsuccessful in reducing the severity of the problem for themselves, the problem intensifies and they reappraise the problem as one that continues only because they have not tried hard enough to correct it. Clearly, this may represent a critical error of judgment.

Compensatory Model

The basic assumption of the compensatory model is that persons are not responsible for their problems but they are responsible for solving those problems. Individuals who operate on the basis of this assumption see themselves as having to overcome obstacles thrown before them by their situation. Overcoming those obstacles is viewed as requiring special effort because the environment has dealt some unjust blows to these individuals. Health professionals who adopt the assumption of the compensatory model seek to find a solution by directing their energies at changing the situation in some way. After all, the situation is responsible for the problem. But, although the environment is viewed as responsible for the burnout, these individuals see that they must pull themselves up and fight back if anything is to be changed.

As Brickman and associates suggested, the advantage of this model is that it orients people toward solving the problem by changing the environment in some way without degrading themselves for creating the problems. The disadvantage is that persons who see themselves as always having to find solutions for problems they did not create may develop a very negative appraisal of the world around them. They may come to feel as if they must always "clean up the mess others have left." Such an assumption may increase the amount of stress these persons feel, particularly if they believe that such circumstances typify the work environment.

Medical Model

Brickman and associates (1982) used the term *medical model* to describe a set of assumptions in which people are not held responsible for either their problems or the solutions to those problems. This term is clearly the most appropriate label for these assumptions because current medical practice seems to be based on them: People are not responsible for their illnesses or their treatment.

Radical behavioral psychology represents a version of this medical model by viewing people as respondents to environmental stimuli beyond their control. When individuals who are experiencing burnout adopt such a view, they come to believe that they are incapacitated by forces outside their control. If a solution is to be found, it must come from someone else, someone who can properly diagnose the problem and prescribe treatment for the burnout symptoms. The advantage, according to Brickman and associates, is that the medical model enables people to accept help without feeling responsible for their personal weaknesses. However, they argue that this model may also influence individuals to become dependent on others for solutions.

Enlightenment Model

The enlightenment model is based on the belief that individuals are responsible for their problems but not for their solutions. In this model, individuals accept the idea that their problems stem from personal factors and faults that must be changed by submitting to some outside authority. They tend to see themselves as guilty and to blame for the problems they are faced with. In cases of burnout, health professionals may be convinced that their past actions have created the current problem or that some aspect of their behavior is out of control. The only way to resolve the problem, according to this model, is to turn oneself over to another person or an external force.

An advantage of this model is that it is highly appropriate for some kinds of problems, such as alcoholism. When alcoholics join AA, for example, they are encouraged to take responsibility for their drinking and, at the same time, admit that it is beyond their power to control. This model promotes a need for affiliation with others as a means of solving problems that are believed to be beyond one's ability to control. A disadvantage of this model is that it may encourage excessive focusing on certain problems and a reconstruction of a person's entire life around the relationships designed to help that person with the problems (Brickman and associates, 1982).

Consequences of the Assumptions

Brickman and his associates hypothesized that models in which individuals are held responsible for solutions are more likely to produce an increase in their competence than models in which they are not held responsible for solutions. From this perspective, the most beneficial models are the compensatory and moral models. Studies by Dweck (1975) and Seligman (1975), for example, revealed that individuals who believe they can control what happens to them are more likely to persist in their endeavors in the face of difficulty and that they are less likely to show the debilitating effects of stress. What these findings suggest in relation to burnout is that health professionals who believe they can manage or reverse the adverse effects of burnout—even though they did not create those conditions —are likely to maintain a sense of personal competence in the face of chronic stress. Therefore, they are apt to take responsibility for solving the problems associated with burnout and likely to assume an active role in working toward a meaningful solution.

One of the assumptions promoted in this text is that although health professionals may contribute to the stresses they experience, they are not solely responsible for the effects of those stresses. They are, however, obligated to recognize how those problems developed and to assume a measure of responsibility for managing or reversing the effects of burnout. This is the kind of assumption made by most approaches to stress management: Some stressors are unavoidable— and burnout may be largely an influence of threatening environmental factors—but the individual is ultimately responsible for coping with burnout. Individuals need to learn how to recognize and control the stresses of their work, monitor their responses to these stressors, and adapt their behavior accordingly.

LOCUS OF CONTROL

Another factor contributing to the development of burnout is the health professional's beliefs about the reasons for successes and failures on the job. When persons feel they have control over what happens to them in their jobs, they may respond to stress differently than if they believed otherwise. Rotter (1966) introduced the concept of *locus of control* to represent the degree to which individuals believe they have control over the outcomes of their actions. Persons who believe that they control the outcomes of their actions are said to have an *internal* locus of control, while individuals who believe that they have no control over the consequences of their actions are said to have an *external* locus of control. Thus, nurses who believe that the recognition they receive for their dedication to the job is because of the hard work they put in would see the outcome of their hard work (i.e., recognition) as resulting directly from their own efforts. In contrast, nurses who view their recognition as undeserved because their successes have resulted from luck, chance, or other factors beyond their control do not believe that their performance actually matters. The former nurses hold an internal locus of control, while the latter nurses hold an external one.

Every person in the allied health professions develops a set of beliefs about the extent to which an individual's performance produces various outcomes. As discussed earlier, one of the symptoms of burnout is a change of beliefs and expectancies to a point where health professionals lower their expectations about making an impact on the environment. Their initial idealism embraced an internal orientation that supported the professionals' belief in their own efficacy. However, as they repeatedly encounter obstacles that challenge those beliefs, a shift toward an external orientation may occur. No longer are they able to attribute the outcomes of their performance to the actions they take. They learn some painful realities, such as the fact that people will die regardless of what the health professionals do to prevent it. They learn that the system will not change, no matter how hard they try to force it. They learn that the collective world of others is more powerful than the health professionals are.

It seems reasonable to assume that individuals entering the allied health professions who are at either extreme of the locus-of-control continuum are at greater risk of burnout than those with moderate internal or external orientations. Persons with an extremely external orientation are fatalists to begin with, and events on the job may quickly reinforce and exaggerate their belief that they have no real power at all. Persons with an extremely internal orientation, on the other hand, are very idealistic and optimistic about the extent to which they can effect change in individuals and systems. The shock of reality may hit them like wind-shear forces that drive high-flying airplanes right into the ground. The difference between the two types is that the internally oriented one has farther to fall, and burnout may make that fall significantly harder and more painful for this type.

Health professionals whose expectations are relatively objective and realistic tend to find congruency between performance and outcomes within the helping context. In nursing, for example, the problem of "reality shock" (Kramer, 1974) can be tempered by socializing nurses to their profession in ways that promote the development of accurate perceptions of performance-reward linkages in nursing practice. Moderate or balanced locus-of-control beliefs can be promoted in relation to performance outcomes such as pay, autonomy, opportunity, mobility, job security, patient progress, and staff relations. Reinforcement of highly internal orientations encourages the development of unrealistically positive expectancies that may ultimately lead to burnout as health professionals gradually and painfully sense a lack of efficacy and fulfillment in the helping role. Reinforcement of highly external orientations is an opposite kind of setup for health professionals since they were predisposed to feel inadequate from the beginning.

In summary, when persons believe that they are in total control of whatever happens to them, they may repeatedly encounter stressors that they could have avoided if they had perceived that the stressors were beyond their control. They may fail to distinguish between stressors that are within their power to control and those that are not. Conversely, although externally oriented persons similarly fail to distinguish between forces within and forces beyond their control, they tend to see most stressors as inevitable and unchangeable. Like internally oriented persons, they may repeatedly encounter stressors that would be avoidable if they could only see that the stressors are *not* beyond their control. Both types could benefit by internalizing the "serenity prayer": God, grant me the serenity to accept the things I cannot change, to change the things I can, and the *wisdom to know the difference* (italics added).

RISK FACTORS

Women Professionals

Although there may be a current trend away from such occupations, Oakley (1975) reported that most women workers are found in human service occupations such as nursing and teaching. It is commonly assumed that women are more attracted to health care and human services than are men. It is also generally believed that caring for others is an extension of the nurturant female role. Whether women are, in fact, more nurturant than men and, therefore, more predisposed to channel their nurturance into professional helping roles is an issue perpetuated more by sex-role stereotyping than anything else. What does seem clear, however, is that those persons—male or female—who are sensitive and empathic enough to commit themselves to helping others are more inclined to experience distress upon witnessing the suffering of others. The characteristics that influence them to become human service professionals may be the same characteristics that render them vulnerable to burnout. *If* women have more of these characteristics than men do, then we would expect them to be more vulnerable to burnout than men are. Although some would argue that women do possess more nurturant, caring attitudes than men do, burnout among women professionals in the human services is probably caused less by the frustration of an innate nurturant need than by sex-role conflicts generated through psychosocial influences. The position taken here is that burnout among these women professionals is *not* a function of some frustrated female instinct but a consequence of the kinds of inter-actions women have with their work environments—environments in which major sources of stress come from expectations placed on them as women and in which the persons holding power positions are usually male.

When professional women are compared with professional men, women are often found to be at a disadvantage in relation to their work conditions (Pines and Aronson, 1981). In a study described by Pines and Aronson (1981), Pines and Kafry (in press) found that in comparison to professional men, professional women reported feeling that they had less freedom, autonomy, and influence in their work; less variety; less challenge; and less positive work environments. The women felt that they had fewer opportunities for self-expression and that they were less adequately compensated for their work. They were also exposed to more environmental pressures and were more inclined to overextend themselves in response to the demands of other people. Pines and Aronson (1981) commented that "these find-ings, plus research that showed women suffer from discrimination and harassment in male-dominated professions, support the findings of greater burnout and tedium among women" (p. 91).

Henning and Jardim (1976), in their book *The Managerial Woman*, contended that men and women differ in their overall orientation toward work. Women, they argued, see work as a means for self-fulfillment and personal autonomy. They consequently hold higher expectations for their careers. When these expectations are frustrated, they may burnout. It bears repeating that the persons with the highest expectations are often the ones most susceptible to burnout. In general, it may be that the expectations of women are somewhat higher than those held by most men. Of course, personal ideals and expectations are hardly the sole sources of burnout for either sex. But, in terms of gender differences, it appears that women experience more stress than men do when the quality of their interpersonal relationships are not satisfactory. Women may be more sensitive than men to the social aspects of their life and work (Pines and Aronson, 1981).

In relation to expectations held by others, men are typically seen as being less emotional, more detached, and less affected by the suffering they see around them. Consequently, it is considered more acceptable for men to be emotionally detached to begin with. Thus, when the woman professional begins to burn out and finds herself becoming more detached and calloused about her job, she may experience a sense of guilt because she is supposed to be more sensitive and nurturant than a man. A "hard shell" is somehow the designated property of males, and females are not expected to put one on and look like a male.

Women health professionals who manage a family in addition to their jobs have dual commitments that often cause special strains not experienced by men. Because these women are committed to their careers and, at the same time, committed to their families, they are often subjected to two sets of expectations. In one context they are expected to be professionals, and in the other context they are expected to function as wife or mother or both. Sometimes these expectations are incompatible, and women are thrown into a role conflict, which adds to the stresses they are already experiencing from both roles. In reality, women professionals have two full-time jobs, each with its own unique demands and requirements that they are forced to juggle and balance against each other. Under such circumstances these women have little time for themselves. If they are not responding to the needs of their families, they are meeting the needs of their patients. Therefore, the time available for meeting their own personal needs is limited. In addition, the pressures from each job often carry over into the other context: Home problems are carried into work, and work problems are brought home. Separating the two becomes very difficult as stress and tension increase.

Functioning in both areas may be adversely affected. Then women professionals may become confused about which area is causing the greatest stress and which area is in need of change. In most cases priority is given to the family, and job pressures are then perceived as something the women can do without. There are many complicating factors inherent in such role conflicts, and it is beyond the scope of this discussion to examine them completely. It is sufficient to note that women may be exposed to unique conflicts by virtue of the expectations associated with professional roles and feminine stereotypes. The resultant stress may predispose many dually committed women to burnout.

Another problem that women health professionals face is *sexism*. As Edelwich and Brodsky (1980) stated, "Sexism compounds the inequalities of position and power that exist throughout the helping professions" (p. 144). Nurses who must constantly defer to the authority of physicians cannot help seeing that most physicians are men. The nurses also realize that most hospital administrators are men. Indeed, many of the nurses I have talked with often refer to the administrators and physicians at their respective hospitals as "the boys' club." The sarcasm evident in this label reflects the underlying frustrations and resentments about the establishment of power bases along lines of authority that are reinforced by sexual polarization.

Whether or not conflicts with authorities in the health care setting are gender-free, the crucial variable is that such conflicts are often *perceived* and *felt* by women professionals as gender-based. When perceived in this way, women health professionals experience the added stress of anger, frustration, resentment, powerlessness, and restricted freedom.

Personal Factors

As individuals take on greater decision-making and leadership responsibilities, they are exposed to higher levels of stress. More of these kinds of responsibilities are assumed by persons with higher professional *credentials* than by those having few credentials. When a person is inadequately prepared—by virtue of training, experience, and general ability—to assume greater job responsibilities, that person may experience a very high level of stress as it becomes evident that the job is too much for the person to handle. Burnout may be right behind a promotion in such cases. On the other hand, even individuals who are adequately prepared for additional job responsibilities or new job functions may burn out just as easily. In fact, they may run an even greater risk than the less prepared individual. It is usually the norm for the most educated and most experienced persons in an organization to be the first considered for promotion. It is not only their current performance but also their professional *backgrounds* that make them likely candidates. Thus, if it is true that increased stress directly correlates with increased responsibility, then the level of one's training and experience may represent factors that increase the probability of being promoted into positions where increased responsibility is assumed. Once in such a position, a person encounters new and additional stresses that can contribute to burnout. In this connection, Patrick (1979) suggested that nurses with bachelor's degrees, associate degrees, or diplomas experience burnout more frequently than do licensed practical nurses, possibly because the former have greater decision-making and leadership responsibilities.

It might be expected that the more *experience* one has in a job, the less vulnerable one is to burnout. After all, with experience should come the ability to exercise greater control over one's feelings and behavior. However, a study by Pearlman, Stotsky, and Dominick (1969) suggested that experience may not provide such benefits for health professionals. In their study, nurses from a variety of institutions were investigated to determine if experience with dying patients was related to emotional discomfort and behavior toward those patients. The results indicated that nurses who had *more* experience with dying patients were more likely to avoid the dying and to avoid discussions about death. Thus, it may be that experience per se is not necessarily the "best teacher" of how to manage the stresses of one's work. It should also be noted that although burnout is especially likely to occur within two years of entering a human service profession, there is no guarantee that experience brings immunity. Indeed, many experienced health professionals are burned out.

One's *orientation* to the health profession may also be an important factor in the burnout syndrome. As indicated earlier in the text, for example, nurses are socialized into the profession differently than physicians are. Nurses are oriented toward the behavioral sciences, while physicians are oriented toward the biological sciences. Nurses generally rely on communication skills to develop relationships with patients, while physicians typically follow a clinical approach to patients. These respective orientations can create conflict because each group believes the other should handle patients as *it* does. Physicians may be angered by what they perceive as nurses giving too much attention to nonclinical matters, while nurses may view physicians as lacking genuine concern for patients as human beings. Neither group may understand the other's orientation to its work, and this lack of understanding may reinforce the felt conflict between them.

Finally, it is possible that *self-fulfilling prophecies* may contribute to stress and burnout. When individuals expect certain things to happen, they sometimes behave in ways that ensure that those events do indeed occur. For example, an individual may expect that another person will act in a certain way or manifest certain characteristics in a particular situation. Without being aware of it, the individual may then act toward the other person in ways that force that person to respond as predicted. In effect, the first person "sets up" the second person so that the prophecy can be fulfilled. Thus, the health professional who believes that members of a particular ethnic group are obnoxious and demanding may unknowingly treat members of that group in ways that "pull" obnoxious and demanding behavior from them. When those characteristics are manifested, the health professional has forced the fulfillment of the prophecy. Similarly, when health professionals are burning out, they may try to keep stress at a minimum by detaching themselves from patients. They may want to keep away from unappreciative, complaining patients, for example. When the professionals do avoid patients, however, they are behaving in a way that encourages patients to complain about their care. The complaints become more annoying, avoidance becomes a more frequent response, and more complaints result. The cycle generates more and more stress for the health professionals —but the stress may have been generated by the professionals themselves.

SUMMARY

This chapter examines the question of which individuals run the greatest risk of burnout in their role as health professionals. A general picture of the health professional has been outlined, including a group of characteristics common to members of the helping professions. In general, these individuals maintain a humanitarian orientation, a high degree of empathy, a need to make an impact on the world of others, and personal expectancies about their roles. Collectively these factors may increase the risk of burnout for health professionals. The professionals who may run the highest risk are compulsive personalities, individuals driven by their needs for control, perfection, and achievement. Others who carry high risk for burnout are individuals who are basically dependent and those who have a long-standing pattern of relating to the world in passive-aggressive ways.

Whatever one's style of coping and relating to the world, it is one's own participation in shaping the conditions one is exposed to that is the key variable in risk potential. Four sets of assumptions about the nature of problems and solutions are also examined. It is emphasized that the kind of assumptions an individual makes about the causes of problems and the sources of solutions has an effect on the individual's experience of stress and burnout. The concept of locus of control is described as a set of beliefs about the extent to which one has control over the outcomes of one's own actions. Special issues concerning women professionals are discussed in relation to the unique stressors that women are exposed to in the world of work. Finally, the chapter highlights some additional factors that may contribute to burnout: credentials and background, experience, orientation, and self-fulfilling prophecies.

REFERENCES

Brickman, P., Rabinowitz, V., Karuza, J., Coates, D., Cohn, E., & Kidder, L. Models of helping and coping. *American Psychologist,* 1982, *37*(4), 368–384.

Dweck, C.S. The role of expectations and attributions in the alleviation of learned helplessness. *Journal of Personality and Social Psychology,* 1975, *31*, 674–685.

Edelwich, A., & Brodsky, A. *Burnout: Stages of disillusionment in the helping professions.* New York: Human Sciences Press, 1980.

Friedman, M., & Rosenman, R. *Type A behavior and your heart.* Greenwich, Conn.: Fawcett Press, 1974.

Henning, M., & Jardim, A. *The managerial woman.* New York: Doubleday, 1976.

Kadushin, A. *Child welfare services.* New York: Macmillan, 1974.

Kramer, M. *Reality shock: Why nurses leave nursing.* St. Louis: C.V. Mosby, 1974.

Oakley, A. *The sociology of housework.* New York: Pantheon, 1975.

Patrick, P.K.S. Burnout: Job hazard for health workers. *Hospitals,* November 16, 1979, pp. 87–90.

Pearlman, J., Stotsky, B., & Dominick, J. Attitudes toward death among nursing home personnel. *Journal of Genetic Psychology,* 1969, *114*(1), 63–75.

Pines, A., & Aronson, E. *Burnout: From tedium to personal growth.* New York: Free Press, 1981.

Pines, A., & Kafry, D. Tedium in the life and work of professional women as compared with men. *Sex Roles* (in press).

Rotter, J.B. Generalized expectancies for internal versus external control of reinforcement. *Psychological Monographs,* 1966, *80*(1, Whole No. 609).

Seligman, M.E.P. *Helplessness.* San Francisco: W.H. Freeman, 1975.

CHAPTER 7

Individual strategies for managing burnout

In the clearing stands a boxer,
And a fighter by his trade
And he carries the reminders
Of every glove that laid him down
And cut him till he cried out
In his anger and his shame,
"I am leaving, I am leaving."
But the figher still remains.

—*The Boxer,* Paul Simon

Many administrators, supervisors, and other front-line people in the health care professions, those closest to the problem of burnout, suggest that the main focus of intervention must be on the individual worker since organizations are probably destined to continue functioning as they are. The assumption is that individuals must do what they can within the given parameters and constraints of their employing organizations.

Although it is true that the alternative is to train individuals to cope more effectively when it is not possible to change the conditions to which they are exposed, it is also true that many presumed "givens" of a system are changeable. Just as there are limits to what organizations can do to change, so too are there limits to what individuals can do to adapt. When individual workers reach the limits of their adaptive capabilities, one way they can deal with the givens of the system is to leave. This step is one of the ultimate effects of burnout. Unfortunately, many organizations perceive turnover as just another given in the system and make no effort to alter the conditions that are contributing to the problem. What individuals and organizations need to do is to determine what *can* and what *cannot* be changed within the system. At least then individuals can have a more accurate vision of reality and be in a better position to accept things as they are. Once the realities of the givens in the system are accepted, however, individuals need to determine what they can do to cope with them.

A central thesis of this chapter is that health professionals need to confront the different situations they find themselves in—with knowledge and courage. Because effective coping hinges on accurate perceptions and cognitive appraisals, these individuals must thoroughly and objectively assess their work environment in order to establish a reliable data base for engaging coping resources. A major part of this assessment must be directed at themselves. One of the most crucial steps in managing burnout is for the individual to recognize its signs and symptoms. Before any kind of intervention can be effectively implemented, one must become aware of the problem.

Unfortunately, many persons experiencing burnout are not aware that there is a problem; or at least they are not aware that their distress involves burnout. Once individuals become aware that a problem does exist, they must commit themselves to doing something about it. The focus of this chapter is that process. The discussion centers around a consideration of various modes of direct and indirect coping that individuals use with varying degrees of success. Acquiring or enhancing coping resources for managing chronic stress is a responsibility the individual must accept—whether or not the givens of the system can be changed or the changeable conditions can be altered. Indeed, taking an *active* role in coping with a stressful work situation may be the only way for individuals to manage the causes and consequences of burnout. If individuals do not take what is rightly their responsibility for managing their portion of the problem, they may not be able to count on the organization to meet its responsibility. The challenge is to learn to effectively manage those things that can be controlled, accept the things that cannot be controlled, and recognize the difference between them.

SELF-MONITORING

One way in which individuals can learn to recognize signs of burnout is by paying attention to signals of physiological arousal. *Self-monitoring* is a process of observing the signals one's body is sending about one's level of arousal. By monitoring arousal the individual can tune into sensations that might otherwise be ignored in stressful situations. Many individuals experience chronic arousal and fail to notice it because (1) it has become almost a norm for them and (2) it was never checked before it became a norm.

Despite the fact that health professionals usually appear cool and calm on the outside, even during emergencies, their composure masks an underlying physical arousal associated with the stress response. Some may not perceive these cues accurately, and, therefore, they become convinced that they are experiencing little stress. Others may perceive their bodily reactions accurately and conclude that they are not experiencing significant stress. As indicated in Chapter 2, it is one's appraisal of the situation that counts here.

With deliberate self-monitoring—not only of physical signals, but also of thoughts and emotions in different circumstances—individuals can develop an increased awareness of how they respond to a variety of stress-related situations. Self-monitoring is a concept that health professionals should understand easily because it requires observation of what might be called "vital signs" of stress. The only difference between monitoring patients and monitoring oneself is that one's observational skills are applied inward and not outward. By consciously monitoring themselves from time to time, individuals can develop an increased awareness of how they tend to respond to stress. This awareness provides them with a data base for change and growth.

CHARACTERISTICS OF EFFECTIVE COPING

As a form of life crisis, burnout is an experience that presents the individual with two possibilities: an opportunity for personal growth and the risk of further disorganization and distress. In responding to present demands, individuals may attempt to resolve the burnout crisis by resorting to habitual problem-solving actions, which involve minimum delay. If these measures do not work, they experience an increase in tension, anxiety, feelings of helplessness and strive to work out the problem in new and different ways. During this period of disorganization—a period in which usual modes of coping do not work—individuals have unique opportunities to draw from sources of strength that they never knew they had in themselves or their environment. It is during such periods that these reservoirs of strength can be discovered and new coping measures employed.

The usefulness of old or new coping responses is typically influenced by such factors as the individual's past experience and abilities; the form, intensity, and duration of stressors; social norms regarding the acceptability of behavior; and the availability of social support. Caplan (1964) suggested that coping strategies are effective to the extent that they meet certain criteria. He identified seven characteristics of effective coping behavior that apply to different kinds of life crises:

1. *There is an active exploration of reality issues and a search for information.* Effective coping involves a focus on the realities of the individual's current situation, without repressing, denying, or avoiding the issue or projecting blame outward. The individual examines any role that he may have played in creating the stressful circumstances to which he is now reacting. A search for factual information is undertaken as a means for ensuring accurate appraisal and cognitive representation of the situation. Through this process misconceptions and misperceptions are replaced with realistic assessments of the circumstances that are creating the distress.

2. *There is a free expression of positive and negative feelings and a tolerance of frustration.* With a reality focus the individual is able to express highly charged emotions safely, since they are kept at a conscious level where they are not denied, but managed appropriately. Frustration is tolerated as the individual begins to see the difference between factors under his control and factors beyond his control. In addition, the reality focus influences a recognition of unrealistic expectations or goals that are not attainable and are, therefore, destined to frustrate the individual and lead to further increases in tension.

3. *There is an active effort to engage the help of others.* The individual recognizes that he has not been successful in mastering the situation by himself and that others may be valuable sources of information or emotional support. This characteristic of effective coping should be emphasized for those persons who tend to avoid seeking others' help because they see it as a sign of personal failure or inadequacy. Attempting to "weather a storm" by oneself, when the storm is a hurricane, is a self-defeating path toward disaster.

4. *Problems are broken down into manageable bits and worked through one at a time.* There is an effort to articulate the problem in concrete terms. This means that the global sense that something is wrong is narrowed to a restricted set of specific conditions that make up the

overall problem. For example, the nurse who complains that "my job has got me so upset that I don't know what to do" copes with the problem most effectively when she is able to clarify the specific aspects of her job that are contributing to her distress. The underlying premise is that there is a limited range of job stressors that need to be managed. But first they must be specified, and then they must be approached in a systematic fashion.

5. *There is an awareness of fatigue and disorganization, a pacing of one-self, and the maintenance of control in as many areas of functioning as possible.* The individual recognizes that the psychological imbalance he is experiencing is a draining experience. Yet he avoids careless and desperate measures as he systematically endeavors to gain and maintain control over as many areas of his life as he can.

6. *Feelings are mastered where possible, and where mastery is not possible, the inevitable is accepted.* The individual recognizes those feelings that he has control over and those feelings that he cannot control. Those that he cannot control are accepted as such, and further stress is avoided as the individual ceases trying to gain control over situations that cannot, for the moment, be controlled.

7. *There is a fundamental trust in oneself and others and a sense of optimism that something can be done to bring about a positive outcome.* The individual's orientation to the life crisis is characterized by a belief in his own ability and the ability of significant others to work through the problem. There is a basic sense that there is an end to the stress, that it will not continue indefinitely, and that it will not lead to ultimately negative outcomes.

The characteristics of effective coping identified by Caplan can serve as useful criteria for assessing coping behavior. However, it should be noted that specific coping strategies vary in appropriateness, as a function of different person-environment relationships. The interaction of individuals with their unique situations is the ultimate measure of appropriate coping behavior because each one deals with stressful work situations in that individual's own unique way. Because burnout as a form of crisis is a very uncomfortable experience, it cannot be tolerated for long without the individual responding to the situation through active coping efforts—some of which may not be effective.

COPING STRATEGIES

There is considerable variability among individuals both in terms of preferred modes of coping and in terms of the relative effectiveness of their coping efforts. Whatever form coping takes, it involves overt or covert behavior aimed at managing conditions of stress and anxiety. Unfortunately, more is known about stress (the condition) than about coping (the behavior). To date, research has focused primarily on the conditions that lead to coping rather than addressing the issue of coping behavior itself. Consequently, much of the information available on coping is theoretical in nature.

As noted in Chapter 2, Lazarus (1966, 1974, 1977) and associates described two general modes of coping: direct action and palliation. Direct action is a mode of coping that involves efforts to master stressful transactions with the environment, while palliative modes involve attempts to make oneself feel better without changing the source of stress. Although palliative modes traditionally have been viewed as maladaptive (Monat and Lazarus, 1977), they can serve adaptive functions when they enable the person to maintain a reasonable level of psychological balance in the face of stressors that threaten with disintegration and total demoralization. The following sections discuss these two modes of coping in relation to strategies commonly used by individuals to deal with stress and burnout.

Palliative (Indirect) Coping Strategies

The palliative methods selected for discussion here are among the most frequently used modes of coping with stress indirectly. They include the following:

- Substance use
- Psychophysiological illness and collapse
- Defense mechanisms
- Escape and avoidance
- Relaxation techniques
- Exercise
- Diet

Drug and alcohol use

It is commonly assumed that some of the most popular forms of escape from stress and burnout are drinking alcohol and using other chemical substances to substitute pleasant feelings for unpleasant ones. So firm is this belief that many articles cite excessive drug and alcohol use as "symptoms" of burnout. It is often implied that these are palliative modes of coping and that they are, therefore, symptomatic of an underlying stress-related problem. Although many individuals use drugs and alcohol in an attempt to reduce the amount of stress they experience, the relationship between burnout and chemical excesses is more ambiguous than many authorities have apparently realized. For example, although numerous articles refer to alcoholism as a symptom of burnout, it is not at all clear that this is the case. In Chapter 4 it was argued that alcoholism and alcohol abuse are not necessarily symptomatic of anything. It is possible that excessive drinking and drug use may *predispose* individuals to burnout; or it is possible that these substance-use disorders are *concurrent with* burnout. The exact nature of the relationship remains to be clarified.

As palliative modes of coping, excessive drinking and drug use often serve to medicate individuals by reducing stress. But, at the same time, these methods may ultimately impair an individual's ability to function. They provide only temporary relief from stress and anxiety; as the effects of the substances wear off, the problems begin to resurface into awareness, in many cases with more severity. As a form of medicating against personal distress, drug and alcohol use may help to keep anxiety below the threshold of awareness. Therefore, one does not have to deal with the disturbing emotions or the source of the problem. The longer individuals keep anxiety and stress below a level of conscious awareness, the harder it becomes for them to understand the source of their problems. If they are blinded to the source of their difficulties, they are shielded from recognizing courses of direct action that can be taken.

If individuals see no escape from stressful work conditions, if the situation appears unchangeable and long term, and if the stress continues without letup, they may pursue any route of relief available. Frequently drinking and drug use are viewed as the only means of relief. It may not be a conscious and deliberate choice to seek relief through palliative modes such as drinking; many individuals seem to automatically turn to substances for such purposes. The problem is that they may feel a little better in the short run, but that period is extremely short and promises to bring them right back to the starting line.

Psychophysiological illness

Some people respond to chronic stress by developing clear-cut symptoms of physical illness. When such symptoms appear, the immediate concern becomes tending to the somatic symptoms, the systemic problem. In some cases this method diverts attention from the source of stress since the focus is now on the biological effects of stress. In other cases more stress is generated because individuals grow increasingly concerned about their physical health and well-being. In either case the bottom line is that physical illness makes the stress-related difficulties more serious. One might wonder, then, how physical illness can be considered a palliative mode of coping, one that makes the individual feel better in the face of unrelenting stress.

There are various ways in which physical illness can serve a relief function for individuals experiencing chronic stress. For some persons illness may represent an opportunity for temporary escape from the source of stress. It may provide a "time-out" period. After all, a "sick" person is absolved of most responsibilities during the period of illness. For some people physical illness may represent a form of surrender under unmanageable stress conditions. They give up resisting because that approach has not been successful. For others a total physical and emotional collapse may occur in response to the realization that nothing is working. When all resources have been tapped, there may be no alternative readily apparent to them.

It is important to emphasize that physical illness is not hypothesized as always representing a palliative response to stress. The connection between stress and psychophysiological illness is not fully understood, and theories abound to explain that relationship. The point here is that in some cases physical illness may constitute an individual's only perceived recourse for reducing the stress and anxiety.

Defense mechanisms

Defense mechanisms serve a purpose: They help individuals deal with anxiety without focusing directly on the problem. All human beings use defense mechanisms at times because these mechanisms are useful psychological devices. There is nothing wrong with using them for temporary relief. But when used excessively, defense mechanisms tend to distort reality and interfere with effective problem solving. An overreliance on psychological defenses may preclude the learning of adaptive direct-action coping strategies. For example, the staff supervisor who is failing at his job may be unable to admit that he does not have the requisite skills and ability to handle the demands of the position. He must therefore find a rationalization to account for his failure. Projecting blame onto staff members converts the supervisor's failures into their shortcomings. Stirring up interpersonal conflict disguises the problem and camouflages the supervisor's weaknesses; failures and liabilities can then be denied and kept from conscious awareness. A satisfactory solution to the problem is prevented because the realities of the situation are obscured. Stress continues and more relief is sought through palliation. In cases such as this one, it is often necessary to spend considerable time with the individual—within the context of a safe, supportive, and nonthreatening relationship—in order to provide feedback about the self-defeating effects of his behavior.

Escape and avoidance

As discussed earlier, one way in which health professionals attempt to cope with stress and burnout is through detachment. Detachment is a form of escape from situations that threaten the psychological balance of the individual. In the field of allied health, a measure of detachment is clearly beneficial. It becomes maladaptive when it is carried to an extreme. Detachment must represent a healthy balance between overidentification and underinvolvement. Lief and Fox (1963) referred to such a balance as "detached concern."

DETACHED CONCERN

Detached concern is a difficult ideal to attain because it lies midway between overidentification and depersonalization (Savicki and Cooley, 1982). The health professional must maintain empathy, concern, and caring while balancing them with professional objectivity. The role of humanist must balance the role of scientist. Numerous health professionals accomplish this balancing through intentional and regulated physical, emotional, or mental distancing from the health care environment. Many of these same persons cannot explain how they achieved an ideal balance between sensitivity and objectivity, claiming only that it "comes with experience." Unfortunately, detached concern, as a useful palliative mode of coping with job stress, is seldom a part of training programs. The importance of empathy is always stressed in the training of health professionals, but the importance of distancing is not given the same level of attention. Thus, to suggest that detached concern "comes with experience" is to imply that each practitioner must somehow independently find a way of achieving this balance.

A practical approach to training for detached concern is to provide opportunities for learning and practicing distancing in the same context as one learns and practices communicating empathy. For example, in role-playing exercises students could practice communicating *moderate* levels of empathy. Although high levels of empathy are associated with more satisfying and effective therapeutic relationships, high levels of empathy are also associated with high rates of burnout. Empathy training should include a recognition that there are clear and present dangers for the professional who is unable to moderate empathy with objectivity.

It is interesting to note that one way for practitioners to achieve detached concern is to use the defense mechanism of *intellectualization.* Intellectualization is an attempt to gain detachment from an emotionally stressful situation by dealing with it in abstract, technical terms (Hilgard, Atkinson, and Atkinson, 1979). This defense mechanism is a vital part of the repertoire of health professionals, who can ill afford to become overinvolved with patients. It is clear that a certain measure of this defense is essential for effective and competent health care delivery, for it can serve as a buffer against the threat of extreme anxiety caused by repeated contact with people who are suffering. It becomes a problem when used excessively, to the point of moving the provider to the opposite extreme: underinvolvement with health care recipients. Just as health professionals cannot afford to be swallowed up by their own emotions, neither can they afford to be cut off from their emotional experience.

Detached concern can also be facilitated cognitively through the kinds of statements one makes to oneself. Thus, it may be helpful to practice making self-statements that serve to mediate the arousal associated with stress. In the simplest terms this procedure may involve telling onself that the situation is not as threatening as it may appear or that in spite of the severity of the situation, one will not be overcome by it. (Other suggestions for intervening and mediating stress through *rational restructuring* are discussed in Chapter 10.)

PHYSICAL ESCAPE AND AVOIDANCE

Withdrawing from the health care environment represents one means of escape for individuals who are experiencing burnout. Frequent days off because of false illnesses are an obvious means of avoiding a stressful work environment. Other examples of palliative modes of coping that involve avoidance or escape include the following:

- Leaving early
- Avoiding peers

- Increased isolation
- Decreased patient contacts
- Increased distancing during conversations
- Long lunch breaks
- Spending more time on paper work

In these ways stress is dealt with indirectly since the source of the problem remains unchanged.

Relaxation techniques

One of the most promoted stress-management techniques is a palliative mode of coping: relaxation training. The premise underlying this training is that relaxation responses are incompatible with anxiety. A significant component of anxiety is muscle tension, and when muscle tension is reduced, individuals typically report a concomitant reduction in the level of anxiety they exeprience. With the aid of numerous relaxation-induction methods, individuals are able to achieve feelings of well-being through the anxiety-inhibiting effects of relaxing striated muscles. These methods include the following:

- Tension-relaxation
- "Letting go"
- Differential relaxation
- Hypnotic inductions
- Sensory awareness
- Meditation
- Yoga
- Autogenic training
- Biofeedback
- Sensitization

Any one of these approaches has the potential advantage of providing the individual with a learned skill for producing a state of relaxation that is incompatible with stress and anxiety. Each one requires training and practice since what is learned is a definite skill, and, like any skill, relaxation training is not effective until it has been mastered reasonably well.

Another advantage of relaxation methods is that they offer highly adaptive and efficient methods of reducing tension. In those situations where job stressors are perceived as unchallengeable and unchangeable, relaxation skills may be the principal means of coping. When used in combination with direct-action strategies, such palliative modes may help to reduce the anxieties associated with confronting or changing sources of stress. They certainly represent more constructive methods than resorting to chemical substances.

The mechanics of relaxation used in any of these procedures are so straightforward that they can be easily learned by anyone motivated to master the skills. Furthermore, in many cases self-instruction is the recommended mode of learning, either with the aid of books or with tapes designed for in-home practice. It is useful to think of relaxation training as a means for *re-learning* how to respond to stressful situations. Many approaches emphasize that people *learn* to be tense and nervous. In a similar way individuals can learn to relax—provided they practice the new response (relaxation) and provided they have the patience to deal with gradual change.

METHODS OF ACHIEVING DEEP RELAXATION

Benson (1975) described relaxation in terms of the demobilization of the sympathetic nervous system and the activation of the parasympathetic nervous system. When the parasympathetic nervous system is mobilized, the individual's level of general arousal is reduced. A state of deep relaxation is achieved through the mental activity associated with the various induction methods.

One of the simplest methods for inducing deep relaxation is called the *progressive relaxation* technique. The individual is instructed to assume a comfortable position and then systematically concentrate, with eyes closed, on various muscles, one at a time. Often the individual is instructed to begin with the toes and work up through the various muscle groups of the body, concentrating on the sensation of relaxation. The instructions may include using images of what the muscles would look like fully relaxed. After moving up the body, the individual may move back down, concentrating on each muscle in a progressive sequence aimed at producing complete muscle relaxation.

Another simple procedure involves a cycle of *tension followed by relaxation*. Each muscle group is tensed for 5 to 10 seconds followed by 20 seconds of releasing the tensed muscles. Two tension-relaxation cycles for each muscle group are usually used (Goldfried and Davison,

1976). Individuals are often told that the tension phase will enable them to become more attuned to sensations associated with stress and anxiety and that these sensations can serve as signals to induce relaxation. One of the major functions of this technique is to teach self-discrimination between states of tension and relaxation.

Relaxation may also be induced through *hypnotic induction.* There are numerous ways of inducing relaxation through hypnosis, and some approaches outline methods for self-hypnosis. Typically, self-hypnosis is learned by following instructions from a book, and this method presents one of the major difficulties with the procedure. It is easier for people to learn the technique through instruction by another person, preferably a reputable hypnotherapist.

Autogenic training is yet another method of achieving deep relaxation. It involves the use of mental imagery to effect changes in the body. Progressive exercises must be learned, preferably with the help of a teacher. The essence of the autogenic method is the ability to call forth images that are used as feedback messages to muscle groups. Sensations are vividly imagined and then transmitted to specific parts of the body in a procedure designed to cause a bodily response consistent with the image held in one's consciousness.

There are a number of techniques used in *meditation.* Each technique produces the same type of deep relaxation. Transcendental meditation, for example, involves the repetition of a mantra over and over as a person sits and allows the body to relax. The mantra, often a phoneme, is a pleasant sounding word with no real meaning. Meditation may also involve focusing on bodily sensations or abstract concepts (e.g., What is the sound of one hand clapping?).

Another effective mode of deep relaxation is *biofeedback.* In this method a technician connects various sensors to an individual's body. The sensors transmit data to a unit that displays visual or auditory information, and the individual is instructed to change the signal by intuitively altering various internal processes. Biofeedback is an effective means for learning relaxation, and many persons have found it a simple task to master, as it merely requires the individual to learn relaxation by learning how to change the display on the machine.

Exercise

For a long time exercise has been advocated as a means for coping with stress. Some exercise enthusiasts have managed to include in this category anything that makes one breathe heavily for more than five minutes. Thus, for some advocates any form of physical activity that is aerobic is also a valuable method of stress management. Notwithstanding the value of exercise (along with relaxation and diet), the danger may be that some individuals will see improved physical condition as the means to general wellness. And for some it may be. But the principal value of exercise is conditioning the body to withstand the harmful effects of stress—without changing the source of stress. Therefore, exercise must be placed in perspective. (Being an exercise enthusiast myself, I encourage rather than discourage it.) It is a palliative coping activity that may make it possible for the individual to continue working more comfortably in a stressful situation that has the potential for change. Exercise is *extremely* important to health and well-being, but it is hardly a panacea for managing stress as some writers suggest.

Diet

Reducing one's intake of alcohol, nicotine, and caffeine seems to make parasympathetic relaxation much easier. Furthermore, it contributes to healthy increases in one's energy level. There can be little question that proper nutrition and diet constitute vital means for maintaining physical health. Again, however, diet alone, or diet in combination with exercise and relaxation, will not *remove* the source of stress for an individual.

Direct-Action Coping Strategies

When individuals cope with stress by engaging direct-action strategies, they attempt to master stressful transactions with their environment. They may do so in various ways, including making personal changes, seeking the help of others, confronting the source of the stress, or actively trying to change the source of stress.

Confronting the source of stress

Direct action may require that the individual go directly to the source of stress and seek change at that point. In such instances the source of stress is often another person. Therefore, it is necessary that the individual confront the other person tactfully, sensitively, responsibly, and effectively. The process of confrontation is examined here because it may represent one of the most important interpersonal skills the health professional may have in managing stress.

Unfortunately, confrontation is often associated with attack, and therefore, for many people, it connotes an irresponsible, aggressive act. This view is inaccurate because confrontation is an interpersonal communication that can lead to more satisfying and less stressful relationships, when it is carried out in a positive and responsible way. Essentially, confrontation involves pointing out to another person one's perceptions of discrepancies, distortions, inappropriate behavior, and various other actions or facts that are causing one's interpersonal life to be stressful.

Berenson and Mitchell (1974) described five different kinds of confrontation. They are outlined here to suggest the kinds of things that others can be confronted with if these things are perceived as sources of stress. Because other people themselves are often sources of stress, these methods of confrontation can be used to facilitate a reduction of interpersonal stress.

INFORMATION CONFRONTATION

An information confrontation involves presenting another person with information that he does not have, but which is necessary for him to involve himself more effectively with others. For example, a supervisor may be generating considerable stress for her staff simply because she does not know what they think about a policy she has instituted. An information confrontation would present the supervisor with concrete information about other people's thoughts concerning the new policy. The staff's stress could be alleviated by simply letting the supervisor know about something she is currently unaware of.

EXPERIENTIAL CONFRONTATION

An experiential confrontation involves pointing out discrepancies between your experience of an individual and his apparent experience of himself. Stated differently, you may see a person one way, and he may see himself in a completely different light. There is some discrepancy between your respective experiences of that person. For example, a staff member may aggravate others with incessant complaining about the health care environment. Although this individual does not see the verbalizations as being negative or bothersome to others, this behavior is perceived quite differently by them. In another instance, a physician may not realize that his behavior toward a nurse is offensive to her. Therefore, the nurse may point out the discrepancy between his perceptions of his behavior and her experience on the receiving end. By confronting a staff member with the discrepancy between the way he and others perceive him and the way he perceives himself, a supervisor may help the staff member to examine his feelings about himself and how they affect the ways he interacts with others. What the supervisor asks is that the staff person consider a different point of view. It is important that the confrontation be stated as *tentatively* as possible because it may be highly threatening to an individual to be confronted with facts that are not open to any interpretation other than the one offered by the person doing the confronting.

Among the different discrepancies that may be pointed out in experiential confrontations are the following:

- How we see ourselves / how others see us
- What we communicate verbally / what we communicate nonverbally
- What we say we will do / what we actually do
- What we think we are / what we really are
- What we think / what we say
- How we feel / what we say

Confrontation may involve challenging the distorted views individuals seem to have of reality. By pointing out someone's distorted perceptions of reality, we may be able to help an individual escape from a pattern of behavior that creates stress for most people who interact with that person. For example, perhaps a supervisor is afraid of intimacy with her staff, so she avoids them during breaks and during lunch hours, keeping mainly to herself. She then claims that people on the staff are distant, cold, uncaring, aloof and that they are not interested in getting to know her. Responsible and gentle confrontation of these views may enable the supervisor to break out of this distortion and thereby increase intimacy and reduce the level of mistrust pervading the staff.

STRENGTH CONFRONTATION

Pointing out the strengths, assets, abilities, skills, resources, or knowledge that a person is failing to use is an instance of strength confrontation. Such a confrontation can be a highly rewarding experience for that individual since the focus is on the positive instead of the negative issues. Supervisors engage in this kind of confrontation when they point out to various staff persons that those persons do not seem to be performing at a level commensurate with their abilities. The prerequisite for strength confrontation is the ability to see strengths in other people. If you have this ability, this type of confrontation might be extremely helpful with a peer who is not currently doing a fair share of work on the unit. A positive approach, stressing that person's abilities, may be the impetus that induces him to "carry his load" and take some pressure off those who must cover for him.

WEAKNESS CONFRONTATION

Weakness confrontation is the opposite of strength confrontation. It requires that one point out to another person what that person is doing wrong, doing poorly, or failing at. This kind of confrontation requires a great deal of tact because an individual who is confronted with weaknesses often feels under attack. Consequently, that person may become defensive and fail to respond constructively to the confrontation. It is probably beneficial to balance weakness confrontations with strength confrontations. What someone perceives as criticism may be tempered by communications that point out that person's strengths as well. In this way it becomes an easier "pill to swallow."

ACTION ENCOURAGEMENTS

Action encouragements involve encouraging an individual to act in a particular way. The main focus is on the discrepancy between what a person says he is going to do and what he actually does. When such a discrepancy is pointed out, the individual may become motivated to act in accordance with his stated goals. This is the kind of confrontation that could be directed at the passive supervisor who states grand plans for the staff, yet fails to carry them out. It may also be highly appropriate for the supervisor who verbalizes support for the staff yet never takes a true advocacy role and represents their interests before the administration.

PROCESS OF CONFRONTING

Confrontation can be a positive experience for all parties involved when certain guidelines are followed. First, confrontation should take place in a context of empathic understanding. It is necessary to try to understand a person before confronting him, or else the confrontation may be totally ineffective. Second, confrontations should be stated assertively, but they should not take the form of accusations or condemnations. A certain amount of tentativeness is helpful. Third, do not confront someone simply because you are angry with that person. If you do, you will have nothing of substance to say since your statements will be guided almost exclusively by your emotions. Angry and wild accusations can do more damage and create more stress than currently exist. Fourth, do not present confrontations in the form of a "gangland massacre," with everyone voicing frustrations at once and effectively devastating the person confronted. Fifth, confront the person's *behavior*, not his personality. Focus on what the person said or did or failed to do or say. Sixth, do not accuse or label the person being confronted. Accusations immediately force individuals into defensive postures, and labels may be perceived as name calling. Seventh, avoid the "mum effect." In other words, resist the temptation to avoid calling unpleasant information to an individual's attention when it is important that the person have that information. It is not easy to be the bearer of bad tidings, but it may be more difficult in the long run to keep that information hidden from the person who may be generating a considerable amount of stress for everyone on the staff.

Changing oneself

Most assuredly there is some measure of personal change required in managing stress and burnout. One important change may involve a shift of perspective concerning the *attributions* one makes about the causes and solutions of problems. For example, health professionals often believe that successful patient care or successful psychotherapy is ensured if only they can make the appropriate interventions at the correct points. Such attributions of responsibility to oneself will lead to many experiences of failure and subsequent feelings of inadequacy. At the other extreme, some health professionals believe that what they do is only a "drop in the bucket" and that whatever they do really makes little difference. Such attributions of success and failure revolve around basic feelings of powerlessness and helplessness. The former orientation suggests an extreme *internal locus of control*, whereas the latter reflects an extreme *external locus of control*. Neither are conducive to successful coping, so a balance between the two is needed.

Because personal change is the topic of thousands of books and journal articles, it seems sufficient to note here that managing burnout usually does not require the individual to engage in a major project of reorganizing his personality. There are certain *behaviors* that may need to be altered in order to effect changes in the way one feels. But since the problem of burnout involves a restricted range of behaviors, only those behaviors should be the focus of efforts at change. Therefore, a primary step toward managing burnout is to determine *what actions need to be taken to produce desired outcomes*. Personal change then becomes something that is relevant, achievable, and verifiable.

It is argued here that the kinds of *immediate* changes necessary to manage stress and burnout involve the following:

- Self-monitoring of symptoms in order to become aware that a problem exists
- Identification of stressors that are causing or contributing to personal distress
- Accurate appraisals of transactions with the work environment
- Commitment to doing something about the problem once it is identified
- Acquiring or enhancing personal coping resources or both

The importance of major personality changes is de-emphasized in light of the pressing need for adaptation. Major personality changes are not necessary for most burned-out health professionals. *They simply need to learn how to do some things differently. It is not the individual that needs to be changed. It is the individual's transaction with the work environment.*

CLARIFYING EXPECTATIONS AND IDENTIFYING LIMITATIONS

As discussed earlier, many health professionals burn out because their professional expectations are too high and unrealistic and because they have not acknowledged their own limitations. Consequently, an important step toward managing burnout is a review of one's expectations of oneself and an inventory of one's professional strengths and limitations. I believe that the person who does not recognize his own limitations is a person sprinting down the road to burnout. The inevitable confrontation with his own liabilities and limits may rise in front of him like a concrete barrier that stops him dead in his tracks. When this person burns out, he will crash with a sense of failure that shakes the very foundation upon which he has constructed his personal identity.

Professional ethics mandate that practitioners recognize and practice within the limits of their training and experience. To do otherwise is not only unethical and potentially damaging to service recipients, it is a personal setup for unnecessary stress that can lead to burnout.

Changing the source of stress

Pines and Aronson (1981) proposed some concrete coping activities that individuals can use to manage stress and burnout. Those coping strategies include

- Reappraisal of goals
- Time management
- Acknowledging vulnerabilities
- Compartmentalizing life and work
- Self-reinforcement
- Change of attitude

REAPPRAISAL OF GOALS

Burnout involves a loss of idealism and enthusiasm, due, in part, to frustrated hopes and goals. Therefore, it is important for health professionals to continually reevaluate their immediate and long-term goals so that realistic goals and aspirations can be established. As a preliminary step, it is necessary to establish priorities in terms of what one wants from life and work. Doing so involves a values clarification exercise in which those things of greatest personal value are set as high priorities. These priorities then help the individual to set attainable goals. As Pines and Aronson (1981) emphasized, when setting goals it is important to distinguish between problems that can be changed and problems that cannot be changed:

The two most common mistakes are: giving up too early and hanging on too long. Individuals can both see how to solve a problem and distinguish the problems that can be solved from those that cannot. Some people have a dysfunctional tendency of focusing on fifty things that cannot be changed and thus either frustrating or depressing themselves. One can be most effective by focusing on the few things that can be changed. (p. 163)

TIME MANAGEMENT

Since the expectation of change usually produces some anxiety, individuals sometimes attempt to control the anxiety by postponing action. They intend to do something about a problem, but they keep putting it off because it just is not the right time. However, a good maxim to follow is that "there is no time like the present." If individuals who have made a decision about change consider that change to be an important one, the best time to implement the change is immediately. Time is a valuable resource that should be used constructively when making changes that promise to reduce stress and burnout.

ACKNOWLEDGING VULNERABILITIES

As Pines and Aronson noted, everyone must be willing to nurture themselves if they recognize signs of stress and burnout. If they are fatigued and tired, they should take time off and take care of themselves. During that time off they can evaluate what is happening to them and come up with some different strategies for coping. People must not ignore their own susceptibility to stress-related disturbances. If they recognize signs of burnout in themselves, they should take action to prevent the problem from becoming worse.

COMPARTMENTALIZING LIFE AND WORK

Pines and Aronson argued that it is important to keep a balance between the energy one puts into work and the energy available for outside interests. They suggest compartmentalizing life and leisure in a way that allows a person to leave work problems at work, instead of taking them home, where they will continue to cause distress. Reliving work stresses at home or with friends, Pines and Aronson contend, forces a re-experiencing of the stressful circumstances and does not enable the person to gain new insights into the problem, since he presents his perceptions only.

SELF-REINFORCEMENT

Health professionals cannot always count on supervisors and others to provide rewards at work. They need to be able to provide their own reinforcements, for they must first rely on themselves before relying on others. To the extent that health professionals are able to build their own self-esteem, they are able to respect and appreciate their own skills and their own selves, even when others do not communicate their appreciation.

CHANGE OF ATTITUDE

Health professionals should not take their job seriously at all times. There must be times when they can laugh at their own blunders (if they are not serious) and at some of the funny things that tend to happen on even the most solemn units. As Pines and Aronson suggested, people must be able to keep their sense of humor and not take themselves seriously all the time.

SUMMARY

This chapter provides an examination of various individual approaches to managing stress and burnout. The coping strategies described here are by no means exhaustive. (Chapter 10 provides a discussion of additional methods and approaches for managing burnout on the "front line" of health care.) Ultimately, managing stress and burnout is contingent upon the individual's belief that something can be done to effect positive change and a commitment to implementing the changes that are within the individual's power. Having confidence in one's own ability to get control of burnout may well be the most important factor in realizing that outcome. The belief that something *can* be done is the belief that pushes one forward toward *doing it.*

REFERENCES

Benson, H. *The relaxation response.* New York: William Morrow, 1975.

Berenson, B.G., & Mitchell, K.M. *Confrontation: For better or for worse.* Amherst, Mass.: Human Resources Development Press, 1974.

Caplan, G. *Principles of preventive psychiatry.* New York: Basic Books, 1964.

Goldfried, M.R., & Davison, G.C. *Clinical behavior therapy.* New York: Holt, Rinehart, and Winston, 1976.

Hilgard, E., Atkinson, R.L., & Atkinson, R.C. *Introduction to psychology* (7th ed.). New York: Harcourt, Brace, Jovanovich, 1979.

Lazarus, R.S. *Psychological stress and the coping process.* New York: McGraw-Hill, 1966.

Lazarus, R.S. The psychology of coping: Issues of research and assessment. In G.V. Collins, D.A. Hamburg, & J.E. Adams (Eds.), *Coping and adaptation.* New York: Basic Books, 1974.

Lazarus, R.S. Cognitive and coping processes in emotion. In A. Monat & R.S. Lazarus (Eds.), *Stress and coping: An anthology.* New York: Columbia University Press, 1977.

Lief, H.I., & Fox, D.C. Training for 'detached concern' in medical students. In H.I. Lief, V.I. Lief, & N.R. Lief (Eds.), *The psychological basis of medical practice.* New York: Harper & Row, 1963.

Monat, A., & Lazarus, R.S. Stress and coping: Some current issues and controversies. In A. Monat & R.S. Lazarus (Eds.), *Stress and coping: An anthology.* New York: Columbia University Press, 1977.

Pines, A., & Aronson, E. *Burnout: From tedium to personal growth.* New York: Free Press, 1981.

Savicki, V., & Cooley, E.J. Implications of burnout research and theory for counselor educators. *The Personnel and Guidance Journal,* 1982, *60*(7), 415–419.

CHAPTER 8

Managerial and supervisory approaches to burnout

You're either part of the solution or part of the problem.

—Eldridge Cleaver, 1968

In their research, Veninga and Spradley (1981) found that the behavior of charge persons is one of the most frequent sources of stress. Workers in any organization are often heard to complain about the pressures of dealing with their supervisors, managers, or bosses. In the health care field some charge persons are seen by staff persons as being autocratic, demanding, and generally "tough" as bosses. Others are perceived as silent and unpredictable, and they generate stress by creating a climate of uncertainty. No one knows what is on their minds, and no one is really confident about how to deal with them. Still others are passive, unresponsive, and seemingly willing to look more like figureheads than advocates of the staff. They generate stress by their inactivity, by their unwillingness to deal with controversy or conflict, and by a pacifist philosophy of appeasement, compromise, and capitulation. Of course there are many other styles and variations of leadership behavior that raise the stress level of subordinates. The critical issue for supervisors, however, is that they recognize their own influence as potential sources of stress for staff persons. If supervisors are part of the problem, they must become part of the solution. And, part of the solution involves making some changes in their own behavior to help reduce the stress of those persons they are supervising.

This is not an indictment against supervisors, for many of them are the primary agents of support for burned-out health professionals who are hanging on by a thread. But what is it about these supervisors who are able to influence a partial reduction of stress among their staffs? What do they do?

First, they recognize the stressors in the work environment, and they are aware of their own influence—for better or for worse. They also recognize signs and symptoms of stress and burnout among staff persons. They are *aware* of problems that exist. Furthermore, they are committed to doing something about those problems by capitalizing on their professional roles. Finally, they *act* on their commitment.

If supervisors are to increase their awareness of the problem of burnout, they need to develop a perspective from which potential solutions emerge. They can look at burnout from two such perspectives. From a *clinical perspective,* burnout can be viewed as a problem of *living*; from a *management perspective,* it can be seen as a problem of *working.* As a problem of living, burnout is manifested broadly—through physical, mental, and emotional distress and exhaustion that permeate an individual's interactions with the total environment. As a problem of working, burnout is manifested through job satisfaction and task performance indexes. Although supervisors should probably look at burnout from both perspectives, their immediate responsibility is to recognize performance-related problems. Generally speaking, if they suspect that burnout is a problem among their staff, they should proceed to collect and order their observations. Supervisors should gather baseline data through assessments of the mood, morale, behavior, and work performance of staff persons. They should use their observational skills as tools for identifying and specifying the problem as it is manifested in the health care setting. They should then avoid making the assumption that they know what the causes of the problem are, for it is vital that they involve their staff and get staff input about the conditions generating stress. Having identified the problem as objectively as possible, and having specified probable antecedent conditions, supervisors can then begin working toward solutions. This chapter will examine some general approaches that supervisors and managers can follow in combating burnout among their staff. These approaches are *not* solutions in themselves, but solutions may become apparent from them.

REACTIVE SUPPORT AND OPEN-DOOR POLICY

Supervisors and managers may be able to intervene in the stress experienced by staff by reacting to this distress in supportive, strategic ways. If they have an open-door policy that encourages staff members to approach them with some of their problems, strategic interventions can be quite helpful. But if supersivors do not have such a policy, or if they have one in name only, they will not have the opportunity to offer constructive interventions, since staff members will not approach them with their problems. Therefore, supervisors must be *available* and *accessible* to their staff. Both of these conditions must exist for an open-door policy to get off the ground.

To emphasize the importance of these two conditions, consider an analogy from models of information processing. When information is acquired by an individual through learning experiences, that information goes into storage and is available for retrieval when needed later. However, although the information may be available in storage, it may not be accessible when the individual needs to pull it out of storage. The individual may not know where to find the information in his memory. When he is repeatedly frustrated in his attempts to retrieve information that he knows is there, he will eventually give up his search. In an analogous way, supervisors may communicate to staff members that they are available whenever anyone wants to see them. Staff members may acknowledge that the supervisors are indeed available, but if all their attempts to get in and see the supervisors are unsuccessful, they will eventually stop trying. The staff will see that although the supervisors are available, they are not accessible; for whatever reasons, they cannot be approached. Thus, an open-door policy does not mean that it is sufficient to literally keep the door open and be visible in the office or on the floor. *It means that supervisors themselves are open*—open to paying attention and listening to what staff members need to say, open to working with staff members to find solutions to problems, open to giving information if necessary, open to providing crisis intervention where necessary, open to using reactive strategies for helping their staff manage the effects of stress and burnout.

Baldwin and Bailey (1980) argued that nursing managers and supervisors can use certain work site interventions to help mediate the stress experienced by staff personnel. For example, they recommended that reactive interventions such as "lending ego" during a stressful event, "debriefing" after a stressful event, and "consultation" can be highly appropriate schemes for dealing with work stress among staff. In lending ego, an approach analogous to active listening, supervisors attend fully to the feelings and facts being communicated by another person. They listen empathically and with genuine respect for the thoughts and feelings being expressed. They respond meaningfully and appropriately to those communications, demonstrate understanding, support, calmness, and add a measure of objectivity to the situation. In short, the supervisors enter into a mutual problem-solving alliance with the staff person because they truly care. Debriefing is similar to lending ego, although the focus is on the immediate effects of a disturbing situation the staff person has experienced. The supervisor helps the staff person to express feelings and then to make appropriate discriminations between the reality and fantasy elements of the event (Horowitz, 1979). Consultation is a strategy of helping in which the supervisor arranges a meeting between staff persons and an outside professional colleague who provides information and recommendations for problem solving, offers material related to interpersonal relations, or otherwise provides the opportunity for new learning.

In some situations supervisors may have to engage in crisis intervention. However, if they feel inadequately prepared to handle a crisis intervention—because of the acute nature of the person's problems or because of the supervisor's lack of training—they may help the staff person by referral to a qualified mental health professional (e.g., psychologist, certified social worker, or psychiatrist).

It is beyond the scope of this text to describe and explain the processes of crisis intervention. However, it may be useful to briefly outline some of the common strategies involved.

Listening

Many people take for granted that listening is a part of crisis intervention because it is fundamental to interpersonal relations and communication. However, when supervisors are intervening in a crisis, time may be limited. Therefore, they need to be fully attentive in order to process vital information and maintain the appropriate focus on the problem being presented. When staff members bring problems of a highly emotional nature to supervisors, the supervisors should adopt as their first course of action the encouragement of open verbalization of feelings. If supervisors are to respond in helpful ways, they need to have a clear understanding of what is being communicated about the staff person's relationship with the work environment. Supervisors must resist the impulse to make quick determinations of the nature of the problem, for if they cut off the individual and intervene too soon, they may cause the person additional frustration and distress. To the extent that they are attending and actively listening to the person, supervisors should maintain a perspective on the problem and be able to prevent or minimize the individual's digressions. Both the supervisor and the staff member who comes through the "open door" must keep the problem in focus.

Tapping Interpersonal Resources

Stress-related problems brought before supervisors or managers by staff members are problems that usually involve other people. Therefore, the supervisor needs to use the input of others, as well as their influence and support, if the individual's problem is to be successfully managed. If supervisors are aware of the social system and the patterns of relationships among their staff, they can tap into that system and elicit the aid of others who may be close to the troubled staff member. Anyone who is a significant other in the troubled person's life may also be affected by the individual's problem. If that is the case, then it is sometimes helpful to involve that person in the problem-solving intervention.

Referrals

Staff members may present difficulties that a supervisor is not equipped to handle. They may require more intensive therapeutic interventions or they may need information that the supervisor does not possess. In either case, supervisors should make an appropriate referral so that the person's needs can be met. Resource persons may be available within the health care organization, and, if they are, the supervisor should use those resources. In certain cases, however, this course of action may be contraindicated. For example, a nurse who is experiencing burnout may be trying to cope with the stress of the job by excessive drinking, a problem which has come to the attention of the supervisor. Although the nurse's performance does not warrant termination, the problem may justify referral for alcoholism counseling, information, or education. The supervisor may decide that referral for in-house services through the alcoholism treatment program is not in the nurse's best interest. In this case the supervisor should refer the nurse to another program for appropriate services.

Advocacy

The stress experienced by many health professionals is a direct function of organizational stressors. When staff members experience stress that is related to conditions within the organization or to failures of the administration to meet the staff's legitimate needs, supervisors must take an advocacy role on behalf of their staff. They may need to personally intervene and represent the interests of their staff to the administration. This advocacy role can be a powerful one, in that supervisors can demonstrate their support and respect for staff by acting on the staff's behalf. The staff members feel that someone is listening to what they are saying and that at least one person is trying to do something about their legitimate problems. The advocacy role is one of clear action. It entails much more than merely voicing support to the staff. In fact, supervisors who communicate understanding to their staff, agree with staff that working conditions are deplorable, and then do nothing about the problem are ineffective. Supervisors are the link between the staff and the administration. If that link is weak, then staff members have a continual reminder of their relative powerlessness in the organization.

Confrontation

In certain situations staff members may play a significant role in creating and maintaining the stressful circumstances that have led them to complain of a problem to the supervisor. Their behavior may be self-defeating, they may be overly defensive, and they may be unwilling to view stress situations from perspectives different from their own. For example, consider the radiological technician who puts in 3 to 4 hours of overtime each day, drinks heavily after leaving work, and then has trouble getting to work on time in the morning. If the technician cannot understand the reason for feeling so much tension, it may be necessary for the supervisor to point out the discrepancies in what the technician is doing. Or think of the licensed vocational nurse who persists in taking long work breaks and then complains of maltreatment when pressured to return to work within a specified period. Finally, consider the registered nurse who never says no to any request and yet complains that "everyone wants something from me, but no one cares about what I want."

A supervisor may need to help staff members see that they play a part in creating some of their own problems. The supervisor should not refrain from commenting on a staff member's maladaptive, self-defeating behavior. Ultimately it is in the best interest of staff members who are presenting problems for the supervisor to point out the eventual consequences of their persistent maladaptive patterns. If staff persons cannot see that they play an active role in some of their problems, and if the supervisor can see how they do, the supervisor has an obligation to let them know how the supervisor sees the situation.

Imparting information

Sometimes the problems brought before supervisors by staff members exist because those staff members lack information and, therefore, cannot deal with a situation adaptively. A prime example is new graduate nurses who believe that they should be able to handle any kind of situation. Supervisors can help to reduce a great deal of stress by giving practical information that explodes that myth. An even better example is nurses who conclude that because they are not able to meet the expectations of a person in their position, they must leave the nursing profession and go into a different occupation. In both instances individuals are acting on distorted information. When this happens, supervisors can be extremely helpful by providing factual, reality-based information. They can also support that information by referring the staff member to another person or providing documentation of their observations to an authoritative source.

Exploring coping resources

When staff members present problems to a supervisor, the supervisor must help them look at all available options and resources for coping. The fact that the problems are even presented to the supervisor suggests that the individual has been unsuccessful in responding to the situation. The supervisor and staff person should then examine the apparently unsuccessful coping efforts and explore the possible reasons why those coping strategies have failed. In so doing, the supervisor may help the individual to see that some coping resources have been overlooked or that certain coping strategies can be modified into successful ones. In addition, the supervisor can help the staff person explore coping methods used successfully in the past. Those methods might hold some promise of success for coping with the present situation.

When supervisors are unable to help a staff member generate viable coping strategies, they should encourage the individual to consider new alternatives. If supervisors see that some of these alternatives are possible adaptive approaches to solving the problem, they should reinforce these approaches for the person.

Suggestions and guidance

Although there are legitimate arguments against offering advice and making recommendations, sometimes advice is exactly what a troubled staff person needs from a supervisor. Provided that supervisors are clearly familiar with the problem being presented, and provided that supervisors are familiar with the individual presenting the problem (as well as the general circumstances surrounding the problem), they may be justified in giving advice.

However, the supervisor should be aware that some staff persons will take advice and run with it, thinking they have the ultimate solution to their problems when in fact they may not. Others will not listen to any advice that the supervisor may offer. Still others will accept the advice, follow it, and fail. Given the numerous possible outcomes of giving advice, supervisors should be extremely cautious in providing solutions to problems.

As a general rule, supervisors should consider some important questions: What will be the consequences of providing bad advice? What will be the consequences of giving good advice? Will the individual become dependent on the supervisor for solutions? Does the supervisor know enough about the person, the problem, and the situation to give advice? Is advice giving the only recourse?

CONTROL OF REWARDS

Supervisors and administrators in complex health care organizations are usually inefficient in distributing rewards such as praise, recognition, encouragement, appreciation, and, in some cases, even attention. Yet each of these rewards is very important to health care practitioners. In fact, Pines and Aronson (1981) found that in some organizations employees were better equipped to handle great work stress when these kinds of rewards were available to them. When there is a noticeable lack of such rewards, health professionals often experience increased stress and burnout. In general, burnout is closely associated with working in a job that is perceived as offering few intrinsic and extrinsic rewards. Supervisors must realize that they are in direct control of organizational rewards that can serve as powerful buffers against stress and burnout. Understanding the needs of health professionals for rewards and the effects those rewards can have when delivered by the supervisor can open avenues for supervisors to exert an influence in the organization-wide effort to reduce the problem of burnout among staff. This section examines the function of rewards in the context of the learning theory concept of *positive reinforcement*. Principles of reinforcement are outlined, different kinds of rewards are identified, and the administration of contingent rewards to staff members is described.

Principles of Reinforcement

The idea that rewards have an influence on how people behave has a history as long as the human race. The first major theoretical treatment given to this concept, and one that pervades contemporary psychology, was by Edward L. Thorndike (1911). Thorndike proposed the *law of effect: Behavior that is followed by satisfaction (reward) is more likely to recur, and behavior that is followed by discomfort (punishment) is less likely to recur.* Few psychologists today would challenge the validity of this law—at least the first part of it. There is some disagreement over the precise effects of punishment on behavior. However, it is noteworthy that the emphasis of the law of effect is on the impact of the *consequences* of behavior. This law stresses that the kind of consequences (rewarding or punishing) that follow behavior have a determinant effect on the subsequent occurrence of that behavior when similar situations arise. Contemporary psychologists use the term *reinforcement* in connection with those rewarding behavioral consequences that have the effect of increasing the probability of future occurrence of a behavior. Although rigorous definitions would preclude the interchange, the term *reinforcement* is used in this discussion as being synonymous with *reward*.

Reinforcements are external to individuals in that they are environmental events that follow behavior. Thus, reinforcement is not the same as motivation, which is considered an internal phenomenon. This distinction is an important one because, for example, it is much easier for supervisors to devise ways of having positive influences on a person when they focus on external reinforcers, which they often can control, rather than the internal motivational states of an individual, which they have neither access to nor equal power to influence. Clearly the distinction is more than an academic one, for the focus in reinforcement is on things that the supervisor *can* control.

Positive and negative reinforcement

Reinforcement *strengthens* a given behavior, and this result applies whether the reinforcement is positive or negative. *Positive* reinforcement involves the *presentation* of something pleasant—a desirable consequence that has the effect of increasing the likelihood that a behavior will recur. *Negative reinforcement,* on the other hand, is often incorrectly equated with punishment. Like positive reinforcement, negative reinforcement has the effect of increasing the probability that a given behavior will recur—except that it involves the *termination* or *removal* of something *unpleasant.* Complimenting a nurse for a quick and timely response to a "code blue" is an example of positive reinforcement. Such a consequence (praise) should increase the likelihood of similar responses in the future. When a worker leaves an unpleasant work environment at the end of the day, that action is negatively reinforcing because the worker is terminating or escaping from an uncomfortable situation. Similarly, when a person turns down the volume on a loud radio, that behavior is negatively reinforcing because it terminates something noxious. The likelihood that the first individual will leave the work environment when able to do so and the likelihood that the second one will turn down a loud radio on subsequent occasions are both increased because these actions brought about desired results.

Since negative reinforcement is much more complicated than positive reinforcement, several examples may be helpful. Workers try to look busy when a supervisor comes around if they anticipate that they will be reprimanded for not being busy. Being busy is negatively reinforced if it keeps them from being reprimanded. Consequently, it may become a habitual mode of responding when a supervisor is expected to arrive. People pay their bills, not because paying them is rewarding and fun, but because it keeps unpleasant consequences from happening. Ducking into the lavatory when you see a friend whom you owe money coming down the hall is a way of avoiding possible unpleasant consequences. Refraining from questioning a doctor's orders is maintained by negative reinforcement because a nurse is able to prevent unwanted consequences. Often when an individual's behavior is under the control of negative reinforcement, the individual acts in prescribed ways in order to avoid punishment of some kind. Health professionals conform to hospital policies to *avoid* being punished. Supervisors follow orders from the administration to *avoid* being punished from above. Administrators try to have a balanced budget to *avoid* losing their jobs. Many of the things health professionals do on their jobs are under the control of negative reinforcement and are, therefore, aimed at avoidance. A challenge for supervisors and top administrators is to somehow turn things around so that personnel are influenced more by positive outcomes than by escaping from or avoiding unpleasant ones.

Naturally, one would expect to see even more avoidance and escape behavior from those health professionals who have strong negative perceptions of their work environment. People who are experiencing burnout are included in this category.

Primary and secondary reinforcement

Primary reinforcers are innately satisfying to people. They are unconditional rewards that become more and more potent as people are deprived of them for longer periods of time. Examples include food and water, shelter and clothing, even medications and relief from pain. Supervisors do not have to be concerned about using these kinds of rewards in their role. However, *secondary reinforcers* do deserve their attention.

Secondary reinforcers are rewarding; people have learned to value them because of their association with primary reinforcers. Money, for example, is hardly a primary reinforcer. No one comes into the world with a thirst for it. *Money* is a secondary reinforcer because it is associated with the primary reinforcers that it can buy. Other important secondary reinforcers that supervisors can offer are *attention, praise,* and *tokens.* Attention involves nonverbal posturing, orientation toward another person, eye contact, and verbal responses—all of which are reinforcing to people. Praise is communicating approval of another person or that person's behavior. Some theorists argue that praise is so highly reinforcing that it is the prime force behind much of human behavior. Tokens—in the form of salaries, raises, promotions, bonuses, vacations, privileges, continuing education, training, office trappings, equipment, and supplies—are some of the most frequently used secondary reinforcers. With these examples of secondary reinforcement in mind, supervisors should consider the stressful effects on workers who are deprived of adequate wages, are not given adequate attention, do not receive praise or recognition, and are not afforded an adequate amount of tokens. When these reinforcers are withheld from workers, the quality of their work experience is low and their behavior comes under the control of negative reinforcement, as they try to avoid and escape the unpleasantness of their jobs.

Instrinsic and extrinsic reinforcement

It is sometimes difficult to distinguish intrinsic from extrinsic reinforcers because of their various definitions. As conceptualized here, *intrinsic rewards* are *internally generated response consequences.* They may take the form of pride in one's work, a sense of accomplishment, fulfillment, competency, and success. This concept of intrinsic reinforcement comes very close to the concept of motivation. *Extrinsic reinforcers are externally generated;* that is, they are generated by someone else. The primary and secondary reinforcers discussed before are extrinsic since they come from outside the individual.

Reinforcement contingencies

The concept of *contingency* ties together the idea that behavior is a function of its consequences. Essentially, a contingency is a special kind of condition, an if-then relationship between behavior and its consequences. Reinforcement is said to be contingent on behavior when reinforcement is delivered if—and only if—the desired behavior occurs. *If* a specified response is made, *then* certain consequences follow. For example, if someone says "hello" to John first, then he will reciprocate—but only if this contingency exists (only if the other person says "hello" first).

In the course of their training, health professionals learn numerous behavioral contingencies. They learn to expect that if they do their jobs, then patients will get better. If they work hard, then they will be rewarded. If they apply what they have learned in their professional training, then they will be successful practitioners. Soon after entering the profession, however, new graduates often learn that the contingencies of reinforcement do not necessarily hold up in actual practice. They learn different contingencies. They learn that if they do what they are told, then they can stay out of trouble. If they conform to organizational values, then they will have a much easier time at work. If they lower their expectations, then they will reduce their potential for burnout. In addition, they learn that *if they detach themselves emotionally from patients, then they can relieve stress; if they dehumanize their patients, then they can tolerate the suffering they see; and if they leave the profession, then they can eliminate the pain they feel.*

One of the most important tasks for supervisors is to rearrange such contingencies as best they can. Often the best they can do is to make the health professional's job performance a target behavior to work with. They can then undertake a systematic attempt to make meaningful extrinsic rewards contingent on the work performance of staff members. Staff members can be regularly and consistently praised for what they do, they can be complimented for numerous things, and they can be formally recognized and informally rewarded in countless ways. If burnout is seen as a problem that involves a chronic lack of positive reinforcement and a chronic overexposure to unpleasant working conditions, then it should be apparent that supervisors are in a prime position to have a positive impact on their staff. Of course, the responsibility for combating burnout is not theirs alone. But supervisors must recognize those things that they *can do*. What they *can do* is control some conditions to which staff are exposed. They can also use their own behavior as a source of reward for their staff.

Guidelines for Applying Contingent Consequences

The general key to success in using contingencies of reinforcement is *consistency* and *systematization*. Supervisors must be consistent and systematic in the contingent delivery of rewards as well as discipline. There are some practical guidelines to keep in mind when supervisors develop, plan, and carry out an efficient reward system based on contingencies.

Differential rewards

Health professionals are no different from other persons in the labor force in terms of their desire for fairness and equity. They want their "just rewards" for what they do in their jobs. But their desire for fairness and equity does not mean that they want to be rewarded the same as everyone else. People want fairness, but they also want differentiation. They want to be rewarded in accordance with their perceived individual worth, not in accordance with the perceived collective worth of the organizational work force.

Through a process of social or performance comparison, workers evaluate their own performance against that of others in the organization. They also compare the rewards they receive with the rewards they see their colleagues receiving. By comparing their performance and rewards in this way, they can gauge their relative worth to the organization, and they can make some inferences about the extent to which they are being fairly compensated for their contributions. There is a hitch to this process when an organization has a policy of rewarding all people the same, or when supervisors dispense the same rewards across the board. Rewarding all people the same tends to encourage average performance. Those who perform at a high level see that others who perform at a low level are rewarded the same as they are. Consequently, they conclude that there is no need to work so hard because they can receive the same reward for doing less. Besides, their relative importance to the organization is now clear: No one seems to notice or care that they are working harder. In the technical sense, the behavior of these persons is being extinguished. Conversely, those low-level performers are being rewarded for their performance. They see that they receive the same kind and amount of rewards for their efforts as high-level performers earn for theirs. They learn that hard work does not pay off. So they are encouraged to remain where they are.

The lesson for supervisors is that *people must be rewarded differently.* Do not ignore either the high-level or the low-level worker, for the rewards they receive must be commensurate with what they do.

Supervisors should also keep in mind that if they fail to respond to the performance of workers, this *inaction may have reinforcing consequences* for those workers. As indicated before, when workers receive adequate rewards for low-level performance, they may come to believe that what they are doing is acceptable.

In other instances *inaction may have punishing consequences—* when workers see that their hard work is not appreciated. The supervisor is, therefore, in a critical position of making sure that people receive the appropriate kinds of feedback for what they do on the job. The supervisor must be able to discriminate between individuals in terms of how they perform, or else one consequence may be the reinforcement of a health professional's sense of insignificance and impotence.

Clarifying contingencies

By clarifying the performance-reward contingency for the individual worker, the supervisor is helping workers to recognize a built-in feedback system regarding their work behavior. In other words, health professionals who know precisely what rewards to expect in connection with particular task performances are persons who can assess their own level of work performance. Individuals also learn that they do not have to ingratiate themselves to demonstrate loyalty to the supervisor in order to get rewarded on the job. The challenge for the supervisor is to be consistent in delivering agreed-upon rewards, or the specified performance criteria will no longer serve to influence the workers' performance.

Feedback on errors

Rewards should be freely administered contingent upon the health professional's work performance. However, if they are to be withheld for any reason, the professional needs to know why. If people are not informed of the reasons why rewards are being withheld, they may come to believe that they are being punished for something they did in the past, or they may think that they did something they were not aware of—something that the supervisor must believe warrants the withholding of rewards. The result is that the workers' performance of specific tasks may deteriorate in terms of efficiency since good performance is not being rewarded.

When these guidelines are followed closely by the supervisor, the most important message communicated to workers is that the workers are in control of the consequences that follow their work behavior. They learn that if they do A, then B will follow, and if they do not, then C will follow. This approach can go a long way toward giving workers a sense that the rewards they receive in the work setting are not arbitrary and are not determined by chance or the supervisor's whim.

Discipline

Many observations can be offered about the matter of formalized punishment within organizations (i.e., discipline). One of the most important things for supervisors to remember is that they should *praise in public and punish in private*. Being reprimanded in front of one's colleagues is a humiliating and stressful experience for most people. This practice deals a telling blow to the self-esteem of the individual being punished, and it is also an unpleasant experience for those who must watch what is happening. Much hostility can be generated by the supervisor as a result of the indiscriminate use of public reprimand. The person being punished grows angry and is motivated to retaliate in some way. One way that person can retaliate against the supervisor is by being passive-aggressive and doing something that reflects negatively on the supervisor. The rest of the staff has also been punished indirectly, so they may become less cooperative and communicative with the supervisor who punished "one of their own."

Fairness

Supervisors must be fair in administering rewards. If staff persons are performing their job in an exemplary fashion, they should receive the recognition and praise that is rightly theirs. If, on the other hand, they are not performing their job adequately, they also need to know about it. People should not be overrewarded for their efforts, nor should they be ignored for the same. Overrewarding may lead them to feel guilty, while underrewarding may make them feel unappreciated and angry with the system. The lesser of the two evils appears to be overrewarding staff members. When staff persons are consistently underrewarded for their work, their work performance levels are lowered and their efficiency extinguished. Eventually these individuals may look for other jobs that promise a more equitable system of rewards.

Using Schedules of Reinforcement

A major premise of the contingent reward system is that extrinsic rewards produce positive changes in both the attitudes of workers and their work behavior. A legitimate question that supervisors might ask is precisely how and when to deliver rewards such as praise, compliments, recognition, and other forms of performance-related feedback. It is already clear that rewards that follow performance closely in time are more potent reinforcers than those that are delayed. However, it is still necessary to examine the various ways in which contingent rewards can be arranged or scheduled. A *schedule of reinforcement* is a relatively formal definition of the relation of a reward to time or number of responses made. When staff persons are rewarded after each occurrence of a specific behavior, the rewards are said to be administered on a *continuous* schedule of reinforcement. Because desired behaviors are rewarded after each occurrence, the strength and frequency of those behaviors tend to increase rapidly. However, when the reward is withheld, the behavior stops quickly. So supervisors will probably not want to use continuous reinforcement for very long, both for practical management reasons and because of the potential for rapid extinction of the work-related behavior upon removal of the reward. It is more practical and more efficient to use a schedule of *partial* or *intermittent* rewards. Schedules of partial reinforcement are those in which rewards are not delivered after every occurrence of the desired behavior. There are four basic types of partial reinforcement schedules:

1. Fixed ratio
2. Fixed interval
3. Variable ratio
4. Variable interval

Fixed ratio schedules provide for the delivery of rewards only when a fixed number of responses are made. Sales quota systems are fixed ratio schedules of reinforcement, as are piece-rate systems in factories. A specified number of product outputs must be made before the rewards are given.

Fixed interval schedules are in effect when rewards are administered only after a specified period of time has elapsed since prior rewards were given. Paychecks are given every week or two weeks, contingent upon individuals performing the jobs they were hired to do. This kind of reward system is not a good one for supervisors to use in delivering praise to staff members. For example, suppose that staff members know that the supervisor comes to the nursing station only three times each day—at 8:00 A.M., 1:00 P.M., and 3:00 P.M. Also imagine that the supervisor is usually gracious to staff members and doles out praise lavishly at each visit, especially at 3:00 P.M., when everyone is preparing for a shift change. The fixed interval schedule by which this supervisor delivers praise and recognition will probably influence staff nurses to work hardest at those times when visits are expected. After the supervisor leaves, their performance effort may decrease and increase again only as the next expected arrival time approaches.

Variable ratio schedules allow for the delivery of rewards only after a number of desired responses have been made, with the number of behaviors varying. On a variable ratio schedule, for example, nurses are praised after they perform two specified tasks, then after five specified tasks, then after three specified tasks, then again after two tasks. Rewards are given on a schedule that varies around an average of one compliment for every three tasks performed. The best example of the variable ratio schedule is gambling behavior, in which individuals come to expect monetary payoffs, but they cannot be sure when they will occur.

Variable interval schedules provide for rewards after various intervals of time have elapsed since the last reward. For instance, if no one knows the exact times to expect the supervisor at the nursing station, staff members may maintain a high level of performance throughout the day since they do not know when the supervisor's praise and recognition are to be delivered.

Hamner and Organ (1978) emphasized that each of these reward schedules can be used for different purposes. As these authors suggested, wages can be administered on a fixed interval schedule, promotions and salary increments on a variable interval schedule, and *praise and recognition on a fixed ratio schedule.* Using a combination of different schedules of reinforcement is a highly efficient means for enhancing the quality of work life and contributing to greater job satisfaction among workers.

Because supervisors are not in direct control of the monetary resources of the health care organization, they must capitalize on other potent rewards to create a more satisfying and less stressful work environment for staff. There may be many forces in the organization beyond the control of supervisors, but *praise and recognition are rewards that they control directly.*

RESOLVING INTERPERSONAL CONFLICT

Supervisors can help to reduce some of the stress generated through interpersonal conflicts that staff members may have with one another. The kinds of conflict supervisors can help to resolve are usually limited to their own work group. Within that group, conflict generally falls into one of three categories (Hamner and Organ, 1978):

- Role conflict
- Issue conflict
- Interaction conflict

Role conflict exists when there are discrepancies between the expectations that a person holds about two or more positions that person occupies or when various expectations associated with one position are incompatible with one another. The expanding and sometimes poorly defined nursing role may create role conflict for individual nurses exposed to the pressure of diverse expectations held by patients, physicians, and administrators. At times nurses may be expected to perform functions not in their job description and not compatible with the nurses' own perception of their job. A supervisor may require them to perform a certain range of duties, a physician may order a set of incompatible patient care actions, and patients themselves may express a need for the nurse to be more than a medical caregiver. When there are incongruities among the various expectations nurses themselves hold about two or more positions that they occupy, they also experience role conflict. For example, the expectations of being objective, cool, and unaffected health professionals may come into conflict with the expectations individuals associate with their positions as parent, spouse, and church member. In general, the kinds of pressures that create role conflicts are exerted by other people within an organizational structure. Often these people are superiors and subordinates or other professionals who have a job-dependent relationship with the individual.

It is important to point out that supervisors frequently suffer from role conflict because they are the people "in the middle." One set of expectations centers around the supervisor's position as a management person, a role in which the supervisor is to share and display the values and attitudes of the administration. An opposing view is that the supervisor, having risen from within the ranks, is still part of the work group and, therefore, should hold and support the values and attitudes of that group. A third set of expectations may be that supervisors should have their own set of values and attitudes, since they are the link between management and the work force (Luthans, 1977). Naturally, problems arise for supervisors when they cannot decide which set of expectations to endorse.

Issue conflict occurs when two or more members of a work group disagree about the solution to a problem (Hamner and Organ, 1978). Each individual's perspective on the problem is different. The conflict may center on different perceptions of the facts involved, different ideas about the proper goals to be achieved, different suggestions about the methods for accomplishing the goals, or even individual differences in values concerning the problem, the method, or the goals. Part of the reality shock syndrome (Kramer, 1974) involves issue conflict. In this syndrome new graduates cannot accept the realities of the health care system since they are clinging desperately to the ideal values they acquired in training. Experienced nurses who attempt to provide practical information to a new graduate are often rejected because they seem to be suggesting values that are incongruent with those learned during training.

Interaction conflict exists when two or more individuals are polarized in their views of one another and are intolerant of one another's behavior. Sometimes this conflict is called a *personality clash.* Two interacting persons tend to dislike each other, feel hostility toward each other, and experience tension during their encounters with each other. The perceptions they have of each other are incompatible with the perceptions they have of themselves. For instance, John views Louis as incompetent and Louis considers John incompetent, but neither one sees himself as being incompetent. John dislikes Louis and Louis dislikes John, but neither dislikes himself.

Strategies for Conflict Resolution

One of the best formats for resolving interpersonal conflict is the social support system, through which individuals have an opportunity to disclose themselves safely and, at the same time, come to better understand their colleagues. However, there are other useful strategies for conflict resolution: lose-lose methods, win-lose methods, and the win-win method.

Lose-lose strategies

Lose-lose methods of conflict resolution are so named because neither person really accomplishes what he wants, or each person gets only part of what he wants (Filley, 1975). In effect, both parties lose. A common lose-lose method is that of *compromise* or *capitulation.* Compromise is a strategy that permits neither person to accomplish what he wants, even if the parties reach some sort of settlement and make public the fact that they have compromised. Another stragegy is to *pay off* the other person with some sort of compensation for agreeing to lose. In health care organizations this strategy may take the form of paying someone to take over tasks that one does not want to do. A third lose-lose strategy is to use an outside *mediator* or *arbitrator* to settle the conflict. In this method individuals avoid confronting each other and submit to having a neutral third party decide the outcome of the conflict. If the conflict is resolved in favor of one of the parties involved, then the situation becomes a win-lose situation. But most arbitrators seek a common ground and arrive at some form of compromising settlement for the two in conflict. The situation then becomes a lose-lose strategy because the outcome is seldom satisfactory for either side. A fourth lose-lose strategy involves *resorting to rules* and invoking policies or regulations to solve the conflict. Neither person confronts the issue; instead both resort to chance factors to determine the outcome.

Lose-lose strategies of conflict resolution focus on the means for solving the problem, while losing sight of the ultimate goals and purposes of resolving the conflict. Neither person encourages agreement on a definition of the problem because neither person is truly interested in how the other sees the situation. Both persons are committed to solving their problems according to the ways they see fit.

Win-lose strategies

Supervisors who attempt to resolve a conflict with a subordinate by falling back on their own authority and power are using a *win-lose* method. Similarly, supervisors choose a win-lose strategy when they use threats to control the behavior of a subordinate; they apply pressure to conform. Supervisors, or other persons, employ a win-lose strategy of resolving conflict when they resist taking action on a request. When an outcome is dependent on their actions, and when the particular outcome is not what they want, these persons can control the situation and eliminate the conflict simply by remaining passive. Win-lose methods also include the *majority rule* to resolve conflict. Majority rule is a win-lose method because there are always people in the minority who lose out. Conversely, when *minority rule* is invoked—as in the case of a small group of administrators making decisions that have a negative impact on a majority of workers—the majority loses. Or a person in a power position may "railroad" an issue through a meeting by soliciting supporters and then intimidating the rest of the group, who represent the majority (Filley, 1975).

Filley, House, and Kerr (1976) identified some of the characteristics of a win-lose situation:

- There is a clear we-they distinction between the parties.
- There is an atmosphere of victory and defeat, in which the persons involved direct their energies toward each other.
- Persons in conflict see the issue only from their own perspectives.
- Conflicts became personalized and highly judgmental.
- There is no planned sequence of problem-solving activities to work through the conflict.
- The parties look at the issue in terms of the short run.

The most significant problem with win-lose strategies is that someone must lose. Because most people do not like to lose, and since some people experience such losses as blows to their self-esteem, losers may become hostile and vindictive, seeking to regain lost self-esteem by winning a victory another time.

Win-win strategies

Win-win strategies focus on the ultimate outcome or the goals of conflict resolution. Such methods are the most desirable for supervisors to promote among staff since energies are directed toward solving the problem instead of beating the other person (Luthans, 1977). When win-win methods are employed, both persons achieve outcomes they want. Filley (1975) described the following two basic forms of win-win methods.

Consensus is a strategy of decision making in which a final solution is reached that is acceptable to everyone. Individuals focus on the problem and not one another, they accept conflict rather than avoid it, they seek facts that will move them closer to resolution, and they keep the interests of the group in mind.

Filley identified *integrative decision making* (IDM) as another win-win strategy. Whereas consensus is used as a means for solving problems when a variety of solutions are available, IDM involves sequencing the decision-making process through a series of steps. According to Filley, such methods are especially useful in situations where parties in conflict are polarized around a few solution strategies. The emphasis of IDM is on pooling the goals and values of interacting parties after the parties have become polarized.

Both consensus and IDM are *problem-solving* strategies of conflict resolution. Problem-solving activities of groups or individuals encourage participants to express their needs, beliefs, and positions on an issue. The aim of each person is to satisfy individual as well as group interests. The supervisor who is seeking ways of resolving conflicts with or among staff may find problem-solving approaches to be extremely helpful. Engaging people in problem solving to work out their differences encourages them to focus on goals and not on who has the best ideas or suggestions for accomplishing them. Problem solving also encourages staff members to be open and honest about their thoughts and feelings; at the same time it gives them a sense that they have something to say about what happens. It fosters a sense of power and control over forces that might otherwise be perceived as highly threatening. Problem-solving approaches to conflict resolution are clearly superior to those methods that ensure that at least someone—if not everyone involved —loses.

Summary

Conflict is a naturally occurring interpersonal phenomenon, and it is not without merit and advantage. It can facilitate effective decision making and lead to satisfying outcomes for all persons involved. When supervisors are called upon to resolve conflicts, they must first accept the fact that conflict exists and then recognize that it may offer benefits for the parties involved. Supervisors should then be open to conflict and establish means that allow it to surface without leading to interpersonal hostility and destructiveness. Supervisors must be aware of the dynamics of conflict and the strategies available for managing it. They should use strategies that permit the attainment of outcomes that are satisfactory to all persons concerned (Hamner and Organ, 1978). When conflict is resolved, a significant source of stress has been eliminated, and thus the potential for burnout has been reduced.

SUPPORT SYSTEMS

Earlier in the text the concept of social support was introduced as an interpersonal mechanism for coping with stress and burnout. Support systems consist of people upon whom an individual can rely for emotional or informational assistance during times of need. The people who comprise an individual's support system typically share a certain number of interests and values, and, therefore, they represent sources of reinforcement during noncritical periods as well. Most important, feelings can be shared with these people at any time, without fear of ridicule or rejection. People in the support system "stick together through thick and thin." During the "thin" times, people who support an individual provide whatever resources they have in order to help the person maintain well-being. Most people have at least one support group, and often that group is the person's family. Such groups can also be found in the work setting, for example, in the informal cliques that individuals belong to. However, formal support groups may be necessary for persons working under high-stress conditions. Supervisors are in an excellent position to develop a formalized support system within their staff. Indeed, they should ensure that some type of support group exists, for it may be one of the most effective mediating buffers between the health professionals and their work environment.

While it is inherently wise for health care organizations to promote the development of cohesive and supportive work groups, the concept is much more than a practical idea. Maslach and Pines (1979), for example, found that burnout among health professionals was lower in those situations where individuals had effective support systems at work.

Scully (1981) argued for the use of staff support groups as a means of helping nurses help themselves cope with stress and burnout. She suggested that such groups can deal with professional issues related to the nursing role and also provide a forum for stress and burnout management. In addition, Scully noted that staff groups can teach and explore methods of conflict resolution, offering nurses the opportunity to disagree constructively, "to examine and understand their own response to criticism, and to focus on issues rather than on personalities when in conflict with others" (p. 49). Various formats can be used to promote staff cohesiveness and support, but *it is critical that the group not be viewed as a therapy group.* That is, staff persons should not perceive the group as a vehicle being used to correct their personalities by forcing a focus on personal problem areas.

According to Pines and Aronson (1981), support groups can provide effective prevention against burnout when they fulfill six vital functions.

1. Individuals comprising the support system must *actively listen* to one another, without being quick to offer advice.

2. The support system should communicate an *appreciation* for the individual's technical abilities on the job.

3. Interactions with colleagues who know as much or more about a particular job can provide constructive *technical challenges* for individuals by encouraging critical thinking, creativity, and higher goal setting.

4. The effective support system provides *emotional support* and communicates that the individual is appreciated for who he is, not for his position or accomplishments.

5. An effective support system offers an *emotional challenge* by constructively confronting individuals about their behavior, when that behavior is self-defeating, incongruent, or inappropriate.

6. The support group *shares perceptions of social reality* and thus enables individuals to make more accurate appraisals of events taking place around them.

Although individuals alone may be unable to serve each of these functions, a group usually can. This is one of the advantages of the support *group*: It can provide a broader range of total support than a single individual can offer another.

Stressing the importance of these functions, Pines and Aronson (1981) stated, "To the extent that social support functions are not completely covered, burnout can occur. To the extent that hardly any of them are covered, burnout is almost inevitable in a stressful situation" (p. 130).

Supervisors need to find ways of developing effective support groups within the conditions and constraints of their staff and organization. In assessing the need for formal support groups, supervisors need to determine the extent to which the six support functions noted before are being served in the organization. If people are not paying attention or listening to one another, if they do not often show recognition of one another's technical abilities, if they ridicule and criticize one another instead of challenging one another in constructive ways, if their mutual emotional support is a contingent one, if they rarely challenge unacceptable or self-defeating behavior, and if staff persons rarely share their views of events in the organization—then the existing social system of the staff is dysfunctional. In such a case it should be clear to the supervisor that a support system is needed.

By building low-stress relationships a staff can develop a team concept, a we-feeling that characterizes cohesiveness. Cohen and Ross (1982) described a strategy for enhancing unit cohesiveness between shifts at a hospital. Through a systematic process of coordinating intrashift and intershift meetings, staff members were brought into contact with one another in order to accomplish defined goals. Understanding of the problems and responsibilities of one another's roles was reportedly enhanced and renewed esprit de corps was reported among unit members within and across shifts. Ostensibly there was a reduction in the amount of stress generated by formerly poor communication and cooperation among staff members. In terms of interpersonal reactions, Cohen and Ross found that supervisors came to develop a better appreciation for the demands of day-to-day patient care activities, while staff members gained a greater appreciation for the role of the nursing supervisor and administration.

Health professionals can be their own strongest source of support in a service-delivery organization. But the pivotal person is the supervisor. Supervisors are in a position to facilitate the strengthening of peer support when they undertake to build a viable support group within the organizational structure. Certainly, anyone among the staff could take the initiative on such a project. However, if supervisors want to be an important part of the "solution," they should take a leadership role in helping the organization to become a more supportive work environment.

SUMMARY

If supervisors and managers in allied health seek to have a positive impact on the problem of burnout among staff personnel, they must

- Recognize stressors in the work environment
- Recognize signs and symptoms of stress and burnout among staff
- Commit themselves to doing something about the problem
- *Act* on their commitment

This chapter outlines some general approaches that supervisors and managers can follow in combating burnout in the health care setting. By implementing a true open-door policy, a policy of being available and accessible to staff, supervisors can intervene through direct interactions with individual workers. They can mediate the stress experienced by staff personnel by engaging in active listening, debriefing, or consultation. They may also use direct crisis intervention with troubled health care providers. Various strategies employed by supervisors may have a direct impact on the burnout problem. These strategies include the efficient management of rewards such as praise, recognition, encouragement, appreciation, and attention. Basic principles and concepts of reinforcement are presented as well as practical guidelines for managing contingencies of reinforcement and reward. As a mediator of interpersonal conflict, the supervisor can intervene and help individuals to reduce tension and antagonism they may be experiencing in relation to one another on the job. The chapter also discusses the notion of conflict and highlights different strategies for conflict resolution. Finally, the supervisor's role in helping to promote support systems is considered, and suggestions are made as to how such supports might be established.

REFERENCES

Baldwin, A., & Bailey, J.T. Work site interventions for stress reduction. *Journal of Nursing Education,* 1980, *19*(6), 48–53.

Cohen, M., & Ross, M. Team building: A strategy for unit cohesiveness. *Journal of Nursing Administration,* January 1982, pp. 29–34.

Filley, A.C. *Interpersonal conflict resolution.* Glenview, Ill.: Scott-Foresman, 1975.

Filley, A.C., House, R.J., & Kerr, S. *Managerial process and organizational behavior* (2nd ed.). Glenview, Ill.: Scott-Foresman, 1976.

Hamner, W.C., & Organ, D.W. *Organizational behavior: An applied psychological approach.* Dallas: Business Publications, 1978.

Horowitz, M. Psychological response to stressful life events. Paper presented at conference on Adaptation to Stressful Life Events, San Francisco, November 3–4, 1979.

Kramer, M. *Reality shock: Why nurses leave nursing.* St. Louis: C.V. Mosby, 1974.

Kramer, M., & Schmalenberg, C. *Path to biculturalism.* Wakefield, Mass.: Contemporary Publishing, 1977.

Luthans, F. *Organizational behavior* (2nd ed.). New York: McGraw-Hill, 1977.

Maslach, C., & Pines, A. Burnout: The loss of human caring. In A. Pines & C. Maslach (Eds.), *Experiencing social psychology.* New York: Random House, 1979.

Pines, A., & Aronson, E. *Burnout: From tedium to personal growth.* New York: Free Press, 1981.

Scully, R. Staff support groups: Helping nurses to help themselves. *Journal of Nursing Administration,* March 1981, pp. 48–51.

Thorndike, E.L. *Animal intelligence.* New York: Macmillan, 1911.

Veninga, R.L., & Spradley, J.P. *The work stress connection: How to cope with job burnout.* Boston: Little, Brown, 1981.

CHAPTER 9

Organizational strategies for managing burnout

Organizational administrators are often ready to support programs designed to combat burnout when those programs are aimed at teaching workers skills for coping with their work. When this is the only kind of change program they support, however, the implicit message is that burnout is the individual's problem and the individual is, therefore, responsible for the solution. Thus, many administrators seem to endorse the moral model (see Chapter 6). An underlying assumption is that if workers do not like the way things are, they should recognize that they are responsible for learning how to cope with the situation and should start doing something about it, rather than sitting around complaining. If they do not take advantage of opportunities to learn skills for coping with the stresses of their work, then they should accept the way things are.

When health care organizations promote only those programs that teach workers skills for coping with their jobs, the organizations themselves are trying to cope with a problem by resorting to palliative strategies. They are attempting to find "relief" from "symptoms" presented by individuals. They are taking no direct action to change the environmental conditions that are contributing to the problem. However, unless the environment is changed in some way, the problem will continue. It makes little sense to simply bolster the defenses of workers in order to render them more capable of tolerating environmental conditions that go unattended. Administrators should take heed that the burnout problem cannot be controlled merely by changing workers; modifying the work environment is another necessary step.

Burnout is inherently a problem of reduced job satisfaction and performance efficiency. It is a morale problem, and demoralized health professionals are persons whose satisfaction with their jobs has been severely undermined. Their ability to fulfill their personal needs through their work has been reduced. When job satisfaction is low, individuals hold negative attitudes toward their jobs. The complex assemblage of thoughts and feelings that makes up these attitudes has an important influence on what individuals *do* on their jobs, and what they actually do on their jobs in turn affects their level of satisfaction. Furthermore, the extent to which persons are satisfied with their jobs also has an effect on overall satisfaction. Burned-out, demoralized health professionals often carry their dissatisfaction into their personal lives, and anyone who has ever been around persons who are very dissatisfied with their jobs knows how stressful that situation can be.

In the work area, it is commonly assumed that job satisfaction influences work performance, that satisfied workers are better workers than dissatisfied workers. Although there is intuitive appeal to this notion, the research findings generally fail to support it (Lawler and Porter, 1967; Sheridan and Slocum, 1975; Strauss, 1968; Organ, 1977). Satisfied workers do not *always* perform better than dissatisfied workers. However, satisfied workers do tend to have better attendance records than dissatisfied workers, and they are less likely to quit their jobs. Furthermore, job dissatisfaction is a major reason why workers join, support, and become active in unions (Hamner and Smith, 1978; Schriesheim, 1978). Therefore, in terms of the administrator's bottom-line considerations, job satisfaction can have a significant impact. Apart from reducing the organizational costs of job dissatisfaction, there are humanitarian reasons for trying to improve workers' job satisfaction. One is that job satisfaction can influence how persons feel about their lives as a whole (London, Crandall, and Steals, 1977).

Burned-out health professionals are dissatisfied, demoralized helpers, and, as Cherniss (1980) suggested, demoralized healers do not heal—at least not as effectively as those who are enthusiastic and dedicated. It is helpful, therefore, to think of burnout as a problem that involves increased job dissatisfaction. When viewed in this way, it is possible to highlight some general categories that determine job satisfaction and then focus on those areas of organizational change that are in need of improvement. This chapter examines the quality of work life as a function of the individual's appraisals of the organizational climate, job tasks, and organizational reward systems. It is within these three areas that programs for change must be directed if burnout is to be addressed at the organizational level. As a preface to the problem of improving the quality of work life, the following section suggests some of the means organizational psychologists have developed for measuring job dissatisfaction. Administrators need to be able to assess the level of dissatisfaction among health professionals as a first step toward a systematic attempt to combat burnout.

ASSESSING JOB SATISFACTION

The various methods of assessing job satisfaction among people working in the health care setting include the following:

- Interviews
- Observations
- Questionnaires
- Existing documents
- Indirect questioning

The most obvious and direct way of learning how satisfied health professionals are with their jobs is to ask them. Formal *interviews* can be used on a regular basis to discuss the job with the worker. Informal interviews can be conducted in the form of casual conversations. Exit interviews also can be used to gather job-related information from people who either voluntarily terminated their employment or were terminated involuntarily. While the chief advantage of interviews is that they provide the opportunity to obtain detailed information through guided inquiries, the main disadvantage is that they may not be economical in terms of time and cost. More importantly, interviews may lead the interviewees toward desired responses, or the respondents themselves may bias their responses to avoid saying anything that they think will have negative repercussions. Finally, the kind of information obtained through interviews is subjective in nature and, therefore, not quantifiable.

Observations of people at work can be useful. This approach affords the opportunity to obtain a sample of workers' actual behavior on the job. However, one problem with observations is that they too may be biased by the observer, who may perceive the worker's behavior selectively. Since the observations must be interpreted, the subjective element enters into observation in the same way that subjectivity colors interview data. Another problem is that when workers know they are being observed, they may not act in ways that are representative of their normal behavior (when they are not being monitored). Therefore, the behavior sample obtained by the observer may be a reactive measure—biased by the workers' knowledge that they are being watched. Finally, the initial decision about who is to be observed is a critical one that may "stack the deck" from the very beginning.

Questionnaires are a useful means of assessing job satisfaction. They can be administered to a large group of people at the same time, they can usually be machine scored, and respondents are likely to give honest answers if they are certain that their identities will not be revealed. Constructing an adequate questionnaire is a complex and time-consuming process that is best left to someone knowledgeable in test and measurement theory. However, a number of ready-made questionnaires are available. The advantage of using them is that they have been field-tested and they provide normative data for comparison with other groups. One questionnaire that has been widely used in job satisfaction research is the Job Description Index, developed by Smith, Kendall, and Hulin (1969). This instrument assesses five aspects of satisfaction:

1. The work itself
2. Pay
3. Promotion
4. Supervision
5. Co-workers

Most of the other instruments used to measure job satisfaction are attitude scales (Landy and Trumbo, 1980).

Administrators who are interested in assessing burnout in their health care organizations can obtain useful information by using an appropriate scale to measure the amount of stress or behavioral change associated with major *life events*. Several such scales exist, although not all are equivalent in terms of the reliability and validity of the data obtained. The Social Readjustment Rating Scale (Holmes and Rahe, 1967) is an instrument devised to obtain estimates of the average degree of life change and readjustment that individuals attribute to life change events. The authors of this scale later developed the Recent Life Changes Questionnaire (Schedule of Recent Experience, or SRE), which is a promising clinical and research tool (Miller, 1981). Volicer (1973) developed the Hospital Stress Rating Scale (HSRS), which was designed for studying the psychosocial stress experienced by hospitalized patients. The Psychiatric Epidemiological Research Interview-Life Events Scale (PERI-LES), developed by Dohrenwend, Krasnoff, Askenasy, and Dohrenwend (1978), and the Universal and Group-Specific Life Changes Scale (UGSLCS), designed by Hough (1980), are two other promising instruments. However, Graffam (1970) developed a measuring instrument specifically for nursing stress, the Schedule of Nurse Response to Patient Complaints of Distress. This is one of the most appropriate tools for assessing the stress experienced by nurses at work.

Existing documents can be used to draw inferences about job satisfaction and burnout. Personnel files represent the major source of information here. Administrators should recognize that information concerning absenteeism, tardiness, critical incidents, turnover, and grievances are usually good indicators of job satisfaction. Soliciting information indirectly—through inquiries about such matters as accidents, patient complaints, or damaged equipment—is also helpful.

IMPROVING THE QUALITY OF WORK EXPERIENCE

There are several avenues of change open to organizations committed to improving the quality of the work experience for workers. Most of the innovative programs for change currently being used have been classified into three categories by Hamner and Organ (1978). *Climate* or *organizational* development programs are based on the assumption that positive changes in the overall organizational climate and in the attitudes of personnel can enhance worker satisfaction and performance. *Task structure* or *job enrichment* programs are founded on the premise that job satisfaction and performance will increase when job tasks are intrinsically rewarding and challenging for workers. *Positive reinforcement* programs operate on the premise that job satisfaction and performance are enhanced when the consequences of performing job tasks are extrinsically rewarding. Any program in these three categories is grounded in the premise that some form of positive change in the organization can lead to an improvement of workers' job satisfaction and performance (Hamner and Organ, 1978). Such a program also includes the implicit assumption that the overall quality of the work experience will be inherently rewarding when such changes are instituted. Thus, these programs are ultimately concerned with altering the intrinsic and extrinsic rewards associated with working. Consequently, although organizational programs for change may focus on different aspects of the work experience and involve different kinds of change strategies, they are not entirely independent approaches.

Burnout, as an organizational problem that involves reduced job satisfaction and suboptimum performance, can be approached by instituting change through any or all of the means included in the aforementioned categories. In determining the kind of program necessary to manage the burnout problem in an organization, administrators must assess the workers' perceptions of three factors:

1. The work environment
2. The tasks they perform
3. The reward structure within the organization

When workers' perceptions of these three components of the job are favorable, job satisfaction is high. When perceptions of one or more of them are negative, job satisfaction is low. The following sections examine the three categories of change programs in relation to workers' perceptions of the organization, job tasks, and contingent rewards.

It should be noted first, however, that there is another kind of program often used by organizations as a built-in mechanism for enhancing job satisfaction. This approach includes *flex-time* and *four-day workweeks*. These programs are not included in the following discussion because, as Hamner and Organ (1978) pointed out, they are designed to give workers more time away from the work environment and do not include an attempt to change the work environment itself. Although such programs may be appealing to many health professionals as a means of temporarily escaping the stresses of their work, the stresses are still there to greet them as soon as they return.

Job Enrichment Programs

Job enrichment programs are based on the assumption that jobs should include opportunities for personal achievement, recognition, growth, responsibility, and advancement. Through such programs, jobs are enriched to the extent that they satisfy the individual worker's needs in these areas. The content of the job—tasks, duties, functions—is changed so that it includes certain characteristics identified by Herzberg (1974):

- Direct feedback—workers receive timely, noncritical, and direct information concerning their performance.

- New learning—workers are provided the opportunity to feel that they are growing psychologically.

- Unique experience—workers can feel that aspects of their job are different from the jobs of others in similar positions.

- Scheduling—workers have opportunities to schedule their own work.

- Control over resources—workers are allowed to manage their own budgets, either individually or in groups.

- Personal accountability—workers are encouraged to monitor their own work output and efficiency to some degree.

Several other researchers (Hackman and Oldham, 1976; Hackman, 1977) have identified certain "core job dimensions" that determine the extent to which individuals experience their work as meaningful and satisfying. These dimensions include the following:

- Degree to which the job requires workers to perform a *variety of activities that challenge their skills* and abilities

- Degree to which the job requires completion of an *outcome that can be identified*

- Degree to which the job is *significant* in terms of having a substantial effect on the lives of other people, the organization, or the world

- Degree to which the job gives the person *autonomy*

- Degree to which workers obtain *feedback* concerning the effectiveness of their efforts

With these points in mind, let us consider what aspects of the jobs of health professionals could be enriched through a program designed to curb the effects of job dissatisfaction and burnout. With

the focus on specific aspects of job tasks, administrators could look
at practitioners' perceptions of the following:

- Discrepancies between accountability and authority
- Extent to which the job provides sufficient variety and challenge
- Extent to which the health professional's role is clearly defined
- Extent to which the health professional's role conflicts with the pur-
  ported roles of others of different status or position
- Opportunities for continued training and professional development
- Adequacy of supplies, equipment, and work space
- Amount of actual freedom and independence the health professional
  has on the job
- Extent to which the health professional is receiving substantial and
  useful feedback concerning the performance of job tasks

Clearly, the first step in determining the appropriateness of a job
enrichment program is to ascertain how workers are perceiving and
appraising their task assignments (Is the job itself something that
needs to be changed? If so, what aspects of the job are causing the
most difficulty?).

Earlier in the text various aspects of the work of health professionals were identified as contributing to stress and burnout. These
should serve as useful guides for developing strategies to make
positive changes in the job assignments of staff. For example, work
overload was identified as one important source of stress and burnout. As the number of persons the health professional serves
increases, so also does information overload. Pines and Maslach
(1978) found that the larger the ratio of patients to staff in mental
health settings, the more dissatisfied staff members became with
their work and the more they tried to separate from it. It is reasonable to expect that the same attitude would apply in health care. As
the nursing shortage continues to make understaffing a problem that
imposes large ratios of patients to nurses, for example, work overload
will continue to take its toll on those nurses. In job enrichment programs ways *must* be found to reduce the ratio of patients to staff.
Unfortunately, the staffing problem is much broader in scope, so
reducing ratios may have to be preceded by strong efforts to make
nursing more rewarding in general.

Enabling health professionals to have some say in the tasks they
perform is one approach to job enrichment. This approach could

involve making it possible for nurses, for instance, to be relieved of the stress of caring for terminally ill patients if and when the nurses express a desire for rotation to a different unit. Nurses could also be allowed to "float" more frequently, a procedure that would give them periodic breaks from high-stress duties. Floating also provides variety, which may be missing in their jobs. Conferences and workshops for continuing education may help to reduce burnout (Pines and Aronson, 1981) because they offer health professionals the opportunity to develop new skills or to simply get away for awhile. Although it is frequently difficult for health professionals to gain a sense of completion in their work (since often they cannot see continued changes in patients discharged from treatment), there are ways of compensating for this task-related stressor. Standards of performance can be emphasized and used as measurable criteria for health professionals to use in assessing their efforts, and supervisors can provide frequent feedback to help enhance staff members' feelings of competence and success. These are but a few of the job enrichment activities that can be instituted as a means of altering the stressful effects of the work environment. Whatever activities are employed, however, job enrichment must not become a gimmick that has no meaningful connection to the broader organizational philosophy. It must be grounded in a comprehensive philosophy of human resources management and, therefore, coincide with other coordinated changes and policies. Furthermore, given the nature of stress and burnout, job enrichment programs are not sufficient efforts for change when used as the sole approach to managing these problems. Such programs should represent *part* of a coordinated organizational change process that includes organizational development activities and positive reinforcement programs as well.

Organizational Development Programs

The approach of organizational development aims at changing properties of the organizational environment or climate that are believed to be major influences on the workers' overall satisfaction and performance. The properties focused on include the following (Hamner and Organ, 1978):

- Size and structure of the organization
- Leadership patterns
- Interpersonal relationships and communication patterns

- Goal direction
- System complexity

As an educational strategy, the emphasis of organizational development is on changing the *culture* of an organization (Margulies and Raia, 1978). Changing the culture of an organization involves changing the values and attitudes of individuals within the organization and thereby altering the structure of interpersonal relationships. An attempt is made to create a climate of warmth and support for each individual.

According to Schein (1970), a healthy organizational climate is one that

- Processes and communicates information reliably and validly
- Has the internal flexibility and creativity to make changes demanded by the information obtained
- Includes integration and commitment to the goals of the organization
- Provides internal support and freedom from threat

Organizational development programs are used to help organizations attain such a climate. The objectives that facilitate the attainment of this kind of climate are to

- Increase the level of support and trust among individuals
- Increase open confrontation of organizational problems
- Increase openness and genuineness in interpersonal communications
- Increase personal enthusiasm and self-control

An organizational development program may be indicated when workers' perceptions of the organization are negative. In particular, negative appraisals of leadership styles, perceived lack of cohesiveness within the organization, the absence of clear goals, and no internal support systems are among the most significant factors that suggest the need for an improved organizational climate. In health care the overall climate of the institution is perceived negatively when there is a rigid power structure. Many nurses appraise their work climates negatively because of a male-physician-dominated hierarchy of power and authority. Being at the bottom of the pecking order is to be in a relatively powerless position that feeds into job dissatisfaction, stress, and burnout. Furthermore, perceiving that the organization is concerned with only that aspect of one's total self that contributes to the purpose of the organization is inherently stressful. In an environment that lacks the capacity for providing support, individuals feel isolated and alone, and they typically do not like the organization they work for.

One of the main activities of the organizational development approach is called *team building*. When support systems are developed (such as those discussed in Chapter 8), an attempt is being made to change the work environment by promoting the kind of cohesiveness within work groups that is often the focus of team building. Team building aims at improving communications in work groups. To the extent that communication is enhanced through such methods, interpersonal conflict can be reduced to manageable levels, and people can be freed from much of the stress generated by conflict and faulty communication. Because burnout is a response to the stress of repeated emotional contact *with people*, any program that can enhance the quality of interpersonal relationships should have a positive impact on the well-being of health professionals. Therefore, it would seem that a program directed toward improving the overall climate of the work situation, by promoting better interpersonal understanding, should be a principal strategy of the administrator who is committed to combating burnout.

Positive Reinforcement Programs

Principles of operant conditioning and reinforcement were discussed in Chapter 8. Programs for change that follow this approach are supported by the premise that job satisfaction and performance are enhanced when the consequences of performing one's job are rewarding. Thus, a positive reinforcement program calls for a maximum use of positive behavioral consequences and a minimum of punishment (Hamner and Organ, 1978). The program's focus is external to the individual, in that an attempt is made to modify the consequences of the individual's job performance in ways that increase the probability of receiving extrinsic rewards. The mechanics of a working positive reinforcement program have already been discussed, but there are other related issues that are important to recognize.

Money as positive reinforcement

Hamner and Organ (1978) noted several shortcomings associated with a reliance on positive reinforcement programs that were built primarily on merit pay, or pay for performance. These shortcomings are reviewed here, lest the administrator conclude that a potential solution to the discrepant reward structure of the health care system is simply a matter of rearranging salaries or paying out more money, contingent on performance.

Hamner and Organ argued that workers do not necessarily *perceive their pay as being related to job performance.* Unless this contingency is perceived accurately, monetary incentives may not enhance motivation or job satisfaction at all. In addition, merit pay systems may have disadvantages when workers view *evaluations of their work performance as biased.* The system may also suffer because of the inability of supervisors to discriminate between good and bad work performance. Consequently, with merit pay increases contingent on performance evaluations, workers may do their jobs very well and still not receive the merit increase—if the subjective judgment of their immediate supervisor is the sole measure of what constitutes performance efficiency. A related problem is that the workers come to realize that they are dependent upon the supervisor for merit rewards. In order to obtain the desired merit pay, workers may then develop their own strategy of ingratiating themselves to the supervisor in order to be better liked, while not necessarily improving their work performance. Another problem is that workers *may not view rewards as rewards,* if (1) inequities among the staff exist in relation to their salaries, (2) the pay increase is kept secret, thereby suggesting to the employee that management does not want others to know the employee is being rewarded, or (3) if receipt of the monetary reward is contingent upon competing with others and being forced into a win-lose situation. In merit systems managers or supervisors may be *more concerned about the worker's satisfaction with the pay than about the worker's job performance.* A merit system will not have its intended effect when administrators see money as the primary motivator, while ignoring the job itself. Redesigning and enriching jobs may be more rewarding for workers than any monetary reward system developed independently. People are positively reinforced by more than monetary rewards for performance, and administrators must not lose sight of this fact.

Positive work conditions

Modifying the aversive conditions of the workplace can have strong positively reinforcing effects for workers. Reducing noise, building more spacious work areas, providing reliable equipment, and

stimuli such as pictures, flowers, plants, or
)wer the level of stress experienced by some
; can also contribute to more satisfactory work
.cing bureaucratic interference with the per-
f workers, simplifying paperwork, untangling
.nels, and eliminating unnecessary work pro-
cedures (Pines and Aronson, 1981). People spend approximately one-
third of their lives working, and if the conditions under which they
spend that time are unpleasant, they become stressed by factors that
could be controlled.

Promotions

If promotions are based on competency, if the procedures and
criteria for awarding promotions are standardized and public, and if
performance evaluations are perceived as fair—then promotions can
serve as significant reinforcers. However, if any one of these conditions is not met, promotions may not function as rewards. Were it not
for union agreements, many organizations would opt for promotions
based on competence and not seniority. Yet seniority is a usual
criterion for promotion in many organizations, and it is often seen by
workers as not being contingent on performance. When promotions
are made by a secret ballot or similar process rather than through a
formalized procedure that everyone understands, those promotions
are typically viewed as noncontingent. When promotions are based
on evaluations that workers see as unfair, the performance-reward
contingency is not linked, and people will not see their work performance as necessarily offering the promise of an eventual promo-
tional reward.

Extrinsic rewards such as pay, positive work conditions, and
promotions are performance-related consequences of great
importance to the level of satisfaction that workers have with their
jobs. Therefore, such rewards must be treated seriously and systematically by administrators seeking to enhance job satisfaction and
ward off the effects of stress and burnout.

Summary

When viewed exclusively from the perspective of learning theory,
burnout can be considered as a response to a chronic lack of positive
reinforcement and a chronic overexposure to aversive environmental
stimuli. When an individual's behavior is under the contol of

threatening stimuli, that person's actions will be aimed at escap...
from or avoiding those stimuli whenever possible. Individuals wh...
are experiencing burnout may develop a pattern of responding to the
work environment that represents a pervasive attempt at warding off
threatening situations. Nurses receive little, if any, positive reinforcement for their work—minimum recognition, expressions of appreciation, just wages, earned promotions, and tangible evidence of making
a positive impact on a patient's well-being. They may be at the lower
end of a pecking order—with administrators and physicians at the
top—and, therefore, subject to the unequal distribution of rights,
power, and authority. The rewards they expected to be built into the
job may not be apparent as they once defined them. Patients do not
always get better, so nurses must somehow construct a system of
extrinsic rewards. But given the nurses' position and the conditions
under which they work, an effective system of self-administered
extrinsic or intrinsic rewards may not be operable. Such rewards may
simply lack the potency to keep them going.

When nurses look around them and see that they are powerless
over so many patient-care outcomes and powerless within the
organizational structure, they are, in effect, unable to control the contingent consequences of their job. They are also unable to control the
contingent consequences of their professional status if they happen
to work in an organization that does not communicate an attitude of
respect for them as professionals. People rarely burn out in a positive
work environment, where administrators assume a professional
advocacy role and demonstrate a genuine respect for the training,
standards, and ethics of *all* the health professionals working there.
When an attitude of respect and caring permeates the organization,
administrators and practitioners are not thrown into adversary
relationships that are stressful for all parties involved.

Administrators can demonstrate an openness and respect for
practitioners in many ways, one of which is simply to have an
operable open-door policy. By making themselves available to any
staff person, administrators show by their actions that they are
receptive to and interested in the people and issues before them.
Administrators may be distracted from important tasks by someone
who comes to the door and interrupts, but they also receive the most
valuable information they can possibly get about the organization. If
administrators truly want to know about stress and burnout, or
about any personnel issue in their organization, they will tap into the
"front line" and hear what those persons have to say. The open-door
policy is often rejected by administrators who claim they cannot get

anything done if they permit constant interruptions. This may or may not be a rationalization, but certainly one question emerges: If they turn away from people and concentrate on paperwork, are they not demonstrating their priorities?

Administrators can learn to become somewhat democratic in their leadership styles. A totally autocratic style of leadership contributes to staff feelings of powerlessness in the organization. Administrators should, when appropriate, encourage staff participation in decision making, especially about policies that will ultimately affect the staff. When staff members as a group become involved in decision making, their sense of powerlessness as individuals can be compensated for by their power as a group.

The philosophy of administrators must focus on whether line staff are delivering the product the organization is supposed to deliver. If people are burning out, they are probably not delivering a quality product. Thus, responsibility of administrators is to facilitate change within the organization—change that is positive for service providers and that ultimately contributes to a reduction in burnout and an improvement in the quality of care given to patients. After assessing the problem situation, administrators have three general options for facilitating change:

1. To revitalize the organizational climate

2. To revitalize the jobs people perform

3. To develop a meaningful system for delivering contingent rewards

In most organizations where burnout is a critical problem, all three options need to be pursued in one way or another.

SOCIALIZING THE NEOPHYTE HEALTH PROFESSIONAL

As indicated earlier in the text, health professionals often burnout within two years after beginning their job. In many cases the people who burn out during that time period are neophyte professionals—recent graduates. In nursing, for example, turnover among new graduates is a serious problem. Kramer (1974) hypothesized that new nurses experience "reality shock" when they find themselves in a work situation that they thought they were prepared for—after several years of training—and suddenly discover that they are not. Reality shock may be a special aspect of the burnout experience for health professionals. Fortunately, Kramer (1974) and Kramer and Schmalenberg (1977) proposed some productive strategies for resolving the conflict created by reality shock. They suggested that health professionals can be trained to achieve competence in the new work subculture, while retaining values from the old school subculture. Kramer and Schmalenberg advocated that health professionals become *bicultural*. This section examines the process of biculturalism as described in Kramer's program of *anticipatory socialization* (1974). As an introduction to that topic, the following discussion addresses the general background of professional socialization experience.

Professional Training and Socialization

Socialization is the process by which individuals learn the values, attitudes, beliefs, and standards of behavior of a particular culture or subculture of which they are becoming members. When individuals are socialized into the helping professions, they learn formal and informal values, beliefs, attitudes, standards of practice, modes of interaction, and styles of communication specific to their chosen profession. They are trained to think and act in certain ways that are consistent with the ways of their profession. They are indoctrinated into a whole philosophy of professional being. In health care, socialization processes teach trainees various ideals that are soon challenged upon entry into practice.

Training often depersonalizes health care by focusing on the mechanical or technical aspects of the job, while de-emphasizing its interpersonal aspects. In general, it also fails to provide instruction in stress management, or it communicates the idea that stress is something that is managed easily and, therefore, not a relevant topic for study. Health professionals are trained to be objective and "professional"; the implicit message is that emotions must be controlled at all costs and not allowed expression. Inevitably, however, the objective, cool, and calm trainee encounters a crisis soon after beginning the job—perhaps on the first day of work. The experience of a patient's death is extremely distressing for most beginning health professionals, yet their training taught them that they would "handle it" or "get over it." When they do not handle it or get over it quickly, many new professionals feel inadequate. After all, they are supposed to be calm and cool. Afraid or unable to reveal these feelings, they become anxious because the stress of controlling powerful emotions is threatening to shake their whole sense of self.

One consequence of dealing with threatening emotions is to seek even more objectivity and detachment. Another option is to leave the profession. For health professionals to respond adaptively to conflicts between their old values and the demand for competence in their new work culture, they need to learn how to cope at an early point in their careers—if their new professional role is to become a career at all. Their socialization experiences need to be modified to include an initial exposure to stressors that lead to burnout *before* these health professionals have an authentic experience that may be emotionally devastating. Kramer's anticipatory socialization program (1974) is one method of countering the effects of reality shock and potential burnout.

The classic program developed by Kramer consists of three parts:

1. A series of six seminars in which new graduates share their thoughts and feelings about their current professional experience

2. Five modules that explore the concepts of reality shock, testing, feedback, values, and conflict resolution

3. Several day-long workshops on conflict resolution that include the new graduates and their supervisors

The program enables new health professionals—usually nurses—to resolve, in their own minds, the discrepancy between what they learned in training and what they are faced with in the real world of practice. Their own values are clarified, as are those of others in the organization, and methods for resolving conflicts between them are learned (Hollefreund, Mooney, Moore, and Jersan, 1981). The various phases of the program encompass skill and mastery of routine, social integration, outrage, and conflict resolution.

Skill and mastery of routine

Shortly after enthusiasm about the new job begins to wane, many of the realities of the helping role begin to manifest themselves to the new graduates. They struggle to learn all of the things they must know to do their job, and they strive to get the routines down, get themselves organized, and get on with becoming competent practitioners. At the same time they also begin to learn about their lack of skills and information. Although they are mastering some skills, they are growing painfully aware of how many other skills they have yet to learn. They then feel a need to modify any personal goals they brought with them from training. For instance, they may have seen their skills as a means of ending or relieving a patient's suffering. But they learn that others view the performance of tasks as ends in themselves ("You do your job," or "You do what you can, that's all you can do.") For the new graduate, that is often not enough.

Social integration

As time passes, new graduates become concerned with the image they are projecting to others. They are aware that they are being evaluated by others, but they sense that they have some leeway to act like inexperienced health professionals for a while. However, they know that they cannot get away with being neophytes for long; they are expected to catch on and carry their own weight. As they try to appear more competent, they usually begin doing more things on their own, and they become less approachable by others who may offer suggestions and advice. At this point they have a conflict to resolve. They must determine whether they want to appear independent or approachable. Usually new health professionals opt for appearing independent and competent. When they do so, however, integration into the social system of other professionals is temporarily blocked—because they are then less approachable.

Outrage

Eventually health professionals become frustrated and angry that they cannot practice as they were taught because the health care organization functions differently from the way they expected. They may resent the fact that they were inadequately prepared for the realities of health care. They may be outraged that the system operates in such a contrary fashion and equally outraged that what they learned in training is not operative in actual practice. This outrage causes a distortion in the way they perceive their circumstances, and the turmoil they experience contributes to a general depletion of energy. At this point, they may begin to experience burnout. If health professionals cope successfully with this phase of their new career, they do so partly by altering their appraisal of the situation to include the belief that this phase is something they must move through and not allow to discourage them.

Conflict resolution

One way for health professionals to resolve the problem of conflicting value systems is by clinging to the values they internalized during training but acting in accordance with the values of the organization. In other words, they can capitulate. Although they "sell out" behaviorally, they may persist in verbalizing their true values. They hold on to their true values while acting in an incompatible way on the job. This intrapersonal conflict creates additional stress. At this point health professionals also begin identifying more with patients than with the organization. Consequently, they resist getting more involved in the organization by avoiding new learning of job tasks. This conflict is great enough for some individuals to leave the profession altogether in order to resolve it.

Those who remain somehow convince themselves that the organizational values are defensible. Once they are convinced, the conflict is resolved and tension and stress are reduced. At this point they may become more attached to the organization and ready to reject their former values in order to stay comfortably connected. Others may resolve the conflict by dissociating themselves from both sets of values and making a complete occupational change.

In-Service Anticipatory Socialization

Kramer's socialization program (1974) is aimed at helping new graduates anticipate job conflicts and stress through socialization. In using a socialization program, health care organizations are advised by Kramer to do the following:

- Introduce all new graduates to the socialization cycle and the underlying theoretical perspective of the approach.
- Help new graduates to establish identifiable and concise goals for themselves.
- Facilitate the new graduates' awareness of and sensitivity to unforeseen experiences and distorted perceptions that are likely to occur during the phase of outrage, and present ways of helping them manage their feelings of powerlessness and victimization.
- Enhance the quality of the role performance of the socialization agent (i.e., cultivate and use role models who can demonstrate adaptive conflict-resolution skills).
- Promote the development of skills for reactive compromise, and promote the notion that adjustment does not mean that new graduates must necessarily give up their prior values.

Socialization programs can be conducted in the educational departments of health care organizations, as part of in-service training. Such programs offer the opportunity for new graduates to experience reality shock through safe in-service training sessions. The effect is to foster a smoother transition from training to practice and to enhance the new graduate's ability to adapt to the constraints of the new job. As Kramer maintained, reality shock must be dealt with as individuals undergo role transformation, coming from idealistic learning environments to the realities of health care organizations. Because the two cultures hold conflicting values, new graduates must be helped to become *bicultural*. If they are not helped with this transition, they may ultimately reject both value systems and leave the profession because the stress associated with such conflicts is seen as too high a price to pay. The organization that institutes a reality shock program is one that demonstrates a clear commitment to its personnel.

Promoting Realistic Expectancies

As noted earlier, the most enthusiastic and idealistic health professionals are usually the most vulnerable to burnout. It is clear, therefore, that training programs must begin focusing more on the realities of helping and health care. Students in human service or health care programs must be helped to set realistic expectations for themselves, for their work environments, for those they work with, and for those they serve. They need to understand that there are no simple solutions to problems, at least not as simple as academic preparation would suggest. They need to learn that clear and immediate successful outcomes of their efforts will not always be apparent to them. They need to realize that not all patients want to get better and that not all patients will get better. They need to learn which things they have no control over and which they do. They need to understand that their efforts at helping those in need will not always be appreciated, even by those who are helped. They need to recognize that their professional roles, as defined in training, do not necessarily bear a perfect correspondence to their eventual roles as practitioners. They need to learn that the service-delivery context is one in which they may not be able to find many of the rewards they anticipate, that they may not receive the continued training and support they expect, and that there are limits to the amount of power and status that will be afforded them.

Farber and Heifetz (1982) noted that graduate training programs that prepare students for the practice of psychotherapy show a traditional reluctance to confront the potentially dysfunctional or distressing aspects of therapeutic work. The authors argued that in order to mitigate the possibility that these professionals will become vulnerable to high rates of burnout, graduate programs must attend more to the limitations and stresses of the psychotherapeutic role. The same recommendation seems applicable for those trained in the health care professions. In psychotherapy, for example, dissatisfaction has been found to stem from a perceived lack of therapeutic success and burnout to be influenced by nonreciprocated attentiveness, giving, and responsibility demanded by the therapeutic relationship (Farber and Heifetz, 1982). It seems that therapists expect that their efforts will pay off, when in fact they may not pay off in the manner expected. The same probably holds for health care professionals.

In regard to the perceived lack of therapeutic success, there is something worth noting. Professionals in counseling and psychotherapy—and this includes many nurses today—probably need to measure client progress differently from the way they learned in graduate training. My colleague in private practice, Robert Warwick, Ph.D., is a former administrator of a community mental health center. Through his experience as an administrator and as a practicing psychologist, he has modified his own conceptualization of client progress. In Dr. Warwick's opinion, the fact that psychotherapy clients do not always get better warrants the promotion of more realistic expectations among therapists. In particular, he advises that the expectation should be that *"people will not get any worse."* Dr. Warwick suggests that practitioners should think in terms of what would have happened to people if those people had *not* come into treatment at *that* particular time. He further believes that burnout begins when therapists see their intervention as a drop in the bucket—even though that intervention may have made a difference in whether or not a client committed suicide. Indeed, these are realistic perspectives that exemplify the kind of emphasis that must become an integral part of professional training. Although health care tasks are different, and although patients' problems are predominantly biological, health care professionals can benefit from a similar perspective: Normally people do not get any worse from the medical treatment and nursing services they receive. Many will not improve, and, inevitably, many will die, but few will get worse because health professionals have helped them.

MARGINAL EFFORTS TO CHANGE

In their search for feasible solutions to personnel problems, administrators may fall into the trap of grasping for whatever sounds good at the time. Sometimes this trap involves an attraction to the surface appeal of the latest fad in training programs. Equally appealing as a palliative treatment for the distressful symptoms emanating from within the organization are innovative "time off from work" options. And, of course, there is always the choice of bringing in a high-powered consultant to diagnose problems that the administrator cannot see and then hiring one or more trouble-shooting "saviours" to come in, shake things up, and generate some new spirit in the organization. Unfortunately, each of these options may be marginally effective in the long run.

Workshops

There seems to be a pervasive but naive assumption that the solution to any problem in an organization is to run a workshop. Given the thousands of workshops and seminars being conducted in this country each year, it would be interesting to learn how many of them are generated by the actual needs of professional persons for continuing education and how many are offered because of someone's hunch that "it might be just what we need." Notwithstanding the requirements of many health professionals for continuing education, it is a safe bet that one-half of the workshops they are sent to are unnecessary. Often organizations have budgeted monies for training and staff development, and these monies need to be spent. So when someone in the organization looks lethargic and burned out, that individual may be a likely candidate for some "band-aid" workshop treatment: "Let's give her some time off to attend a weekend workshop somewhere." As long as there is official documentation that the person attended the workshop, the administration may not be at all concerned about whether it was worthwhile. However, the administration may be quite concerned that the worker realize that they have spent a considerable sum of money to send her to a workshop because they "care about the staff."

The "workshop high" is a phenomenon known very well to professional educators and to many participants of such programs. It involves a short-lived boost in morale and spirit, a feeling of optimism, and a transient sense that things are going to be much better because the workshop has "shown the light." A few weeks, or sometimes even a few days, after the workshop, however, the individual no longer has that high level of energy and enthusiasm. One of the most common responses given by people who are asked how they liked a workshop can be summarized this way: "It is nice to get away for awhile, and I met some interesting people. The person who conducted the workshop was really good." In most instances the workshops leave a general impression on participants, but the information they acquired often does not have the intended results.

My own personal experience has been similar to that of many people who attend a workshop and then go back to the organization with fresh ideas that are clearly beneficial for everyone—only to find that no one really cares about what you learned. Several years ago, for example, I was sent 2,000 miles across the country to learn all I could, during a one-day session, about university-based peer counseling programs. When I returned with a briefcase full of documents and notes, tape recordings of interviews, and my own general impressions, no one was the least bit interested in this information. I later learned that one reason for the lack of administrative interest was that monies proposed for counseling services had been diverted into the athletic fund.

Workshop highs fade back into disillusionment. In fact, the backlash effects of workshop highs can be devastating for demoralized health professionals who attend workshops on burnout and fail to come away with more than a transient good feeling. To them, such workshops seem like a panacea, offering the promise of formula solutions for recapturing peace of mind. On the other hand, some demoralized health professionals may have few expectations for positive outcomes from workshops on burnout. As a balance, such workshops should promote realistic expectations and help facilitate relevant and achievable goals for participants. A nominal or token workshop on burnout can do more harm than good; and unless it is carefully planned and conducted by professionals familiar with the problem, the outcomes sought by administrators will not be attained. Workshops on burnout need to be more than a "good idea," and they must be viewed in proper perspective.

When carefully planned and conducted by competent and reputable professionals, workshops on burnout can be highly valuable contexts for new learning. Participants in such workshops are afforded the opportunity to learn how others are affected by job stress and burnout. They can learn innovative ways of managing stress and burnout. Often this new learning occurs not only through formal presentations and written documents but also through the kinds of interpersonal exchanges that encourage the sharing of information among participants themselves. A carefully planned and conducted workshop on burnout is a context wherein people may examine and discuss everything known about the problem. Didactic presentations are typically combined with experiential learning, so as to provide the opportunity for participants to become more aware of the stresses in their own work settings. A clear advantage of such workshops is that they give participants a time out from day-to-day job stress and a chance to work with other people who are in similar situations. Together they can engage in cooperative problem solving and move toward viable solutions to the stressors that may threaten to engulf them.

Time Off from Work

Time off from work is often used as part of an organizational reward system. There are many creative and effective ways of using this incentive, all of which are designed to ensure that individuals have sufficient time away from work to balance their professional lives with their personal lives. Flexible scheduling, compensatory time, personal days, and exchanging on-call availability for mornings or afternoons away from work are a few examples of potentially useful time-off options.

When used without other interventions that affect the total organizational environment, time-off options tend to represent reinforcements for staying away from aversive job circumstances. When time away from work is used as a major work incentive, it may not have its intended effects—if the overall quality of the work experience is not addressed by the administration. People who come to live for their vacations and their free days are people with a high degree of motivation to escape a work situation that is failing to provide the intrinsic and extrinsic rewards they seek.

Edelwich and Brodsky (1980) proposed some guidelines for time-off programs in a model hospital setting. First, they suggested that when time off from work is used as a reward, *time off should be made up*. For example, when a person is on call for a weekend, there may be no calls or several calls. Yet even though the number of hours actually put in on the weekend will vary, that person *is* available and *does* put in extra time during off-duty hours. Therefore, the organization is getting something in return for granting the worker subsequent time off. As Edelwich and Brodsky pointed out, the program can be justified on budgetary grounds because the time off is contingent. Second, the authors noted that the time-off policy must be *applied consistently and equitably to all eligible workers.* It should not be a privilege afforded to only a few departments or selected staff personnel. Third, the time-off program should be an integrated *part of a coordinated program* for managing burnout on various levels. Again, this means that time off should not be the sole means that administrators use to combat stress and burnout. Fourth, the time-off program must be *conducted openly and honestly.* There should be nothing to hide, and time off should not be granted surreptitiously, through private arrangements between workers and their supervisors. Favors should not be traded in secret between these persons, with the worker trading the favor of being on call for that of having some extra time off.

Hiring Saviours

Sometimes administrators seek change through the hiring of highly skilled outsiders who are supposed to come into the organization and "make things happen" where others before them have failed. When these persons enter the organization, no one knows what to expect from them. Rumors fly and many begin to wonder if major personnel changes are to follow. In some cases the "saviour" makes an initial positive impact on staff, and a renewed sense of hope and enthusiasm glimmers before them. But things often return to normal after the grand illusion fades. One person who is hired and "planted" in a selected department cannot "make things happen" in an organization that is stress-infested to its core. When administrators become dissatisfied with the new person's inability to clean up the organization, that person may be removed and a new person may be hired to clean up the mess left by the exiting one. All the while staff members are left behind with another reason to feel burned out (Edelwich and Brodsky, 1980).

CONDITIONS OF CHANGE

Organizations, like individuals, do not awaken one morning with the inspiration that today is a good day to change. Change occurs in response to *need.* In organizations change occurs when conditions demand new adaptive responses that will ensure the continuity, survival, and service or product capabilities of the system. The problems that organizations experience when change is demanded are similar to those faced by individuals who are forced to adapt to new circumstances: They typically resort to habitual modes of responding. What has worked in the past is tried in the present. When successful, habits become stronger and the likelihood of using them again in similar circumstances is increased. When unsuccessful, however, old ways of handling demands must be replaced. Again, just like individuals, organizations may have a hard time replacing customary modes of responding.

To the extent that newer, more adaptive responses to organizational problems fail or are not tried, needs go unsatisfied and worker satisfaction may decrease. When the problem of burnout is vibrating throughout every health care organization in the country, old methods cannot be relied on. Health care organizations must have the adaptability and flexibility to respond as needed to the problem of burnout. As Douglass and Bevis (1979) argued, "Failure of a nursing care delivery system to meet the needs of its practitioners, clients, and/or employers ensures changes in or the death of the system" (p. 229). The system will change anyway, for better or for worse. To ensure changes for the better, administrators must use organizational crises such as burnout as vehicles for change and growth. Most health care organizations are experiencing crises, and they are, therefore, at a point of choice: They can move forward and grow, or they can regress. At the crisis point, however, change is reactive because problems have accrued to the boiling point. Whether reactive or proactive and preventive, organizational change should occur against certain conditions.

Douglass and Bevis (1979) suggested that administrators in health care organizations, in collaboration with others, can establish certain conditions that are conducive to planned change. First, key organizational people must support and participate in the change process. The idea of planned change must be backed by a total group effort, not just a select few administrators. This procedure entails relinquishing some power to the group, an action that also promotes trust and collaboration within the organization. Second, the processes of change must be compatible with the philosophy and goals of the change. When that philosophy and the identified goals are in the interests of staff and employees, planned change cannot involve dishonesty, subterfuge, double-dealing, or other kinds of exploitative manipulations. Third, participation in change should be voluntary, and since opposition to change is also voluntary, differences of values and opinion must become open conflict for constructive resolution. The group involved in the change process must work out its issue conflicts without pressure from higher authorities. Fourth, everyone to be affected by the change should be oriented to the fact that change is occurring in one organizational unit, so that the change does not disrupt other organizational units. Everyone who has a need to know about the changes should be informed of the changes that are taking place. Change should not be imposed abruptly and without warning. Often planned changes are blocked by certain individuals (or departments) who were not consulted or alerted about what to expect. If planned changes in the organization are attempted as a means of responding to the burnout crisis, these considerations are important for those involved.

SUMMARY

This chapter examines the quality of work life as a function of the individual's appraisals of the organizational climate, job tasks, and organizational reward systems. If burnout is to be addressed at the organizational level, programs for change must be focused within one or more of these three areas. Before any program is implemented, however, administrators must assess the relative degree of *job satisfaction* among staff. Methods of assessing job satisfaction are discussed in terms of their relative advantages and disadvantages. The following are three major categories of organizational programs for change:

1. *Job enrichment* programs are based on the premise that job satisfaction and performance will increase when job tasks are intrinsically rewarding and challenging for workers.

2. *Organizational development* programs are based on the assumption that positive changes in the overall organizational climate and attitudes of personnel can enhance worker satisfaction and performance.

3. *Positive reinforcement* programs work on the premise that job satisfaction and performance are enhanced when the consequences of performing job tasks are extrinsically rewarding.

The issue of *professional socialization* is then examined and suggestions are offered for improving the socialization experience for entry-level health professionals. *Marginal change efforts* are identified in terms of their frequently palliative effects on stress and burnout. The last section of the chapter addresses the issue of the *need* for change in organizations and the challenge health care systems face when confronted with hard evidence that something needs to be changed if we are to protect our most valuable organizational assets—human beings.

REFERENCES

Cherniss, C. *Staff burnout: Job stress in the human services.* Beverly Hills, Calif.: Sage Publications, 1980.

Dohrenwend, B.S., Krasnoff, L., Askenasy, A.R., & Dohrenwend, B.P. Exemplification of a method for scaling life events: The Peri Life Events Scale. *Journal of Health and Social Behavior,* 1978, *19,* 205-229.

Douglass, L.M., & Bevis, E.O. *Nursing management and leadership in action* (3rd ed.). St. Louis: C.V. Mosby, 1979.

Edelwich, J., & Brodsky, A. *Burnout: Stages of disillusionment in the helping profession.* New York: Human Sciences Press, 1980.

Farber, B.A., & Heifetz, L.J. The process and dimensions of burnout in psychotherapeutics. *Professional Psychology,* 1982, *13*(2), 293-301.

Graffam, S.R. Nurse response to the patient in distress: Development of an instrument. *Nursing Research,* 1970, *19,* 331-336.

Hackman, J.R. A new strategy for job enrichment. In H.K. Downey, D. Hellreigel, & J. Slocum, Jr. (Eds.), *Organizational behavior.* St. Paul: West Publishing, 1977.

Hackman, J.R., & Oldham, G. Motivation through the design of work: Test of a theory. *Organizational Behavior and Human Performance,* 1976, *16*(2), 250-279.

Hamner, W.C., & Organ, D.W. Organizational behavior: An applied psychological approach. Dallas: Business Publication Inc., 1978.

Hamner, W.C., & Smith, F. Work attitudes as predictors of unionization activity. *Journal of Applied Psychology,* 1978, *63*(4), 415-421.

Herzberg, F. The wise old Turk. *Harvard Business Review,* September-October 1974, pp. 70-80.

Hollefreund, B., Mooney, V.M., Moore, S., & Jersan, J. Implementing a reality shock program. *Journal of Nursing Administration,* 1981, *11*(1), 16-20.

Holmes, T.H., & Rahe, R.H. Social Readjustment Rating Scale. *Journal of Psychosomatic Research,* 1967, *11,* 213-218.

Hough, R.L. *Universal and group-specific life changes scale* (Life Changes and Illness Research Project). Unpublished manuscript, University of California, Los Angeles, 1980.

Kramer, M. *Reality shock: Why nurses leave nursing.* St. Louis: C.V. Mosby, 1974.

Kramer, M., & Schmalenberg, C. *Path to biculturalism.* Wakefield, Mass.: Contemporary Publishing, 1977.

Landy, F.J., & Trumbo, D.A. *Psychology of work behavior.* Homewood, Ill.: Dorsey Press, 1980.

Lawler, E., & Porter, L. The effect of performance on job satisfaction. *Industrial Relations,* 1967, *7,* 20–28.

London, M., Crandall, R., & Steals, G. The contribution of job and leisure satisfaction to quality of life. *Journal of Applied Psychology,* 1977, *62*(3), 328–334.

Margulies, N., & Raia, A.P. *Conceptual foundations of organizational development.* New York: McGraw-Hill, 1978.

Miller, T.W. Life events scaling: Clinical methodological issues. *Nursing Research,* 1981, *30*(5), 316–320.

Organ, D. A reappraisal and reinterpretation of the Satisfaction Causes Performance Hypothesis. *Academy of Management Review,* 1977, *2*(1), 46–53.

Pines, A., & Aronson, E. *Burnout: From tedium to personal growth.* New York: Free Press, 1981.

Pines, A., & Maslach, C. Characteristics of staff burnout in mental health settings. *Hospital Community Psychiatry,* 1978, *29*(4), 233–237.

Schein, E.H. *Organizational psychology* (2nd ed.). Englewood Cliffs, N.J.: Prentice-Hall, 1970.

Schriesheim, C. Job satisfaction attitudes toward unions, and voting in a union representation election. *Journal of Applied Psychology,* 1978, *63*(5), 548–552.

Sheridan, J.E., & Slocum, J.W. The direction of the causal relationship between job satisfaction and work performance. *Organizational Behavior and Human Performance,* 1975, *14*(2), 159–172.

Smith, P.C., Kendall, L.M., & Hulin, C.L. *The measurement of satisfaction in work and retirement.* Chicago: Rand-McNally, 1969.

Strauss, G. Human relations—1968 style. *Industrial Relations,* 1968, *7,* 264.

Volicer, B.J. Perceived stress level of events associated with the experience of hospitalization: Development of a measurement tool. *Nursing Research,* 1973, *22,* 491–497.

CHAPTER 10

Postscript: Practical suggestions

In Chapters 7, 8, and 9, various intervention strategies were out-lined at three different levels: front-line professionals, supervisors, and health care administrators. No sure-fire solutions were proposed, simply because there are no universally effective interventions at any level. There are, however, overall strategies and orientations that can facilitate the discovery of interventions appropriate to the unique circumstances of individuals, supervisors, and organizations as a whole.

This chapter is grounded on the premise that the first step toward managing the problem of burnout is to recognize that it exists. Awareness is the basis for intervention. Individuals must be able to identify stress-related problems if they are to do anything about them. Supervisors must know that a definable problem exists before they can take any kind of action. Administrators must do the same if they are to make any constructive changes in the health care environment. The focus of this chapter, however, is on the front-line health professional. Some suggestions are offered for assessing the stressful aspects of the job and for moving toward increased control over controllable stressors through assessment, problem solving, mutual support, professional help, and rational restructuring. The material presented here does not attempt to include the numerous other approaches to managing burnout. For example, relaxation techniques are not discussed; nor is the importance of diet and exercise. The decision to exclude these valuable stress-management tools from the present discussion is based on avoiding duplication since these approaches are covered thoroughly in the vast majority of publications on stress.

ASSESSMENT OF WORK STRESS

As indicated earlier, one of the first steps in managing job burnout is to become aware of the problem. However, many health professionals may be suffering the symptoms of burnout, yet they may be completely unaware that they are responding to stressors in the work environment. To manage the problem of burnout, it is essential that individuals take steps to identify the problem before they take any sort of action. Veninga and Spradley (1981) suggested that individuals need to take a systematic stress inventory of major stressors from family life, environmental demands, and work life. In spite of the interactional effects of each of these categories of stressors, it is vital that the health professional take a principal focus on the stresses associated with the job.

As a guide for identifying job stresses, the boxed material that follows provides a general outline of the kinds of factors that may be included in an assessment of work stress. You may find the outline somewhat restricted in that it may not include some specific stressors to which *you* are exposed in *your* work as a health professional. If that is the case, the outline will have served a useful purpose, because your responses should help to enhance your overall recognition of the problem. You may have already developed a habit of identifying the stressors of your work, so there may be various items you would add to the inventory. If so, you can use the guide as a rough draft of the kind of assessment format you would prefer to use. It may be helpful to modify this format as a way of developing your own system for identifying work stresses. At the same time it may serve as a framework for discussing, within your professional peer group, a system for analyzing the relative effects of work stressors.

The items on this list characterize the kinds of stressors you are exposed to in your work as a health professional. Check those features of the job that you see as stress conditions to which you are exposed. For each category there are blank spaces for you to add stressors that are not listed.

Assessment of Work Stress, continued

	PERSONAL AND GENERAL CONCERNS
_____	Staff is inadequately trained.
_____	Insufficient time for orientation.
_____	Conflict between professional values and organizational values.
_____	Personal tendency toward compulsivity.
_____	Expectations incongruent with reality of the job.
_____	Personal problems carrying over into job.
_____	Job problems have contributed to personal problems.
_____	Too much contact with people.
_____	_____
_____	_____
_____	_____

CONTROL OF STRESSORS

In Chapter 6 the concept of *locus of control* was discussed in terms of the extent to which individuals believe that they control the outcomes of their actions. Persons whose orientation is toward an *external* locus of control tend to see events as largely chance-determined and believe that they do not have much control over what happens to them. Conversely, persons with beliefs grounded in an *internal* locus of control perceive themselves as having a certain degree of control over what happens to them. Extreme internal or extreme external orientations may contribute to the amount of stress an individual experiences. What seems desirable for most people is a balance between internal and external beliefs. An appropriate balance promotes moderate expectancies in both directions and may keep individuals from feeling either totally helpless or totally self-sufficient. A moderate set of beliefs with both internal and external loci of control enables individuals to recognize those stressors that they can control and those that they cannot control. The following boxed material provides a stimulus to begin examining those stressors that are within your control and those that are beyond your control. If burnout is to be managed, it is essential to recognize the factors that are manageable and the ones that are not.

There is no score for this assessment. However, if you wish, you can total all the factors "within control" and weigh them against the sum of the factors "beyond control" in your work environment. Regardless of how they compare, managing burnout requires that you begin by trying to get control over those stressors that you know you can change. As you experience success in controlling stressors, you may wish to repeat this survey to determine if there are manageable stressors that formerly seemed unmanageable.

The following items are stressors that you may consider either beyond or within your control. Place a *B* next to those stressors that you believe are *beyond* your control. Place a *W* next to those that you think are *within* your control. Give each item careful consideration in order to avoid premature conclusions. If some factors are judged to be partially within and partially beyond your control, place both letters next to the respective items.

Stressors Beyond and Within Control

1.	_____	Maintaining current employment.
2.	_____	Salary.
3.	_____	Shift.
4.	_____	Rotation.
5.	_____	Standards of professional practice.
6.	_____	Continuing education.
7.	_____	Work area.
8.	_____	Place of employment.
9.	_____	Other people's expectations of professional role.
10.	_____	Own expectations of professional role.
11.	_____	Days off from work.
12.	_____	Promotions.
13.	_____	Peer acceptance.
14.	_____	Peer recognition.
15.	_____	Understaffing or overstaffing.
16.	_____	Inadequately trained personnel.
17.	_____	Deficiencies in personal knowledge and skills.
18.	_____	Policy and procedure changes.
19.	_____	Unit cohesiveness.
20.	_____	Supervisory recognition.

Stressors Beyond and Within Control, continued

21.	_____	Overtime worked.
22.	_____	Cooperation between shifts.
23.	_____	Cooperation within shift.
24.	_____	Cooperation of patients.
25.	_____	Cooperation of physicians.
26.	_____	Respect of others for your role and position.
27.	_____	Self-respect for role and position.
28.	_____	Self-recognition.
29.	_____	Anxiety.
30.	_____	Noise on unit.
31.	_____	Functioning of equipment.
32.	_____	Alcohol consumed.
33.	_____	Work breaks.
34.	_____	Values promoted by organization.
35.	_____	Number of contacts with patients.
36.	_____	Duration of contacts with patients.
37.	_____	Quality of contacts with patients.
38.	_____	Conflict with one or more staff members.
39.	_____	Accountability.
40.	_____	Patient care emergencies.
41.	_____	Patient deaths.
42.	_____	Responsible decision making.
43.	_____	Lack of supplies.
44.	_____	Opportunities for advancement.
45.	_____	Daily routine.
46.	_____	Paper work.
47.	_____	Professional autonomy.
48.	_____	Personal compulsivity.
49.	_____	Extent of authority.
50.	_____	Staff morale.
51.	_____	Burnout.

PROBLEM SOLVING

One way of looking at burnout is to conceptualize it in terms of ineffective behavior that leads to adverse physical, mental, and emotional consequences. The ineffectiveness of this behavior is in relation to coping with problem situations. Individuals are coping ineffectively when they have not generated, selected, or used potentially adaptive responses to problem situations. One way to enhance individuals' behavioral effectiveness is to improve their problem-solving skills. Indeed, if health professionals are to become more personally effective in managing their feelings and behavior in relation to the stresses of their work, then it is fundamental that they become efficient at problem solving. Fortunately, since a large portion of their work entails problem solving, most health professionals are well equipped to meet the challenges of their work. What is needed is a transfer of learning to demand situations that are personally relevant, so that existing problem-solving skills are applied to the task of selecting and implementing the most effective responses to stressful situations.

Five Stages

In spite of individual differences in the way people solve problems, there does appear to be an identifiable set of cognitive operations that are involved in effective problem solving. Goldfried and Davison (1976) outlined five stages of problem solving, noting that there is a general consensus among theorists and researchers about the processes involved in solving problems.

General orientation

An individual's orientation or attitude toward a stress situation can have a significant effect on the response to that situation. An effective problem-solving orientation is one in which the individual sees a problem situation as a normal part of life, as one that can be managed, and in which the person resists first impulses to action. An important variable is the individual's belief that it is possible to cope with the situation, even if a solution is not immediately apparent. To the extent that this expectation is present, there is a greater likelihood that the individual will, in fact, find the appropriate solution (Bloom and Broder, 1950). In addition, it appears that when one holds an internal locus of control orientation (see Chapter 6), the expectation of being able to control one's environment facilitates efforts at actively coping with the problem when it arises (Rotter, 1966).

In the course of most events, persons encounter challenges and demands and respond to them habitually and almost automatically, without giving them much thought. If their responses do not bring about the intended results, then, without much deliberation, they attempt something else. When all their efforts have failed to eliminate the demands of the situation, then they begin to see that they may have a problem on their hands. They suspect the problem when they begin to feel frustrated or anxious, or even angry. Thus, their emotions tip them off to the fact that they are facing a dilemma. To the extent that individuals are able to acknowledge their emotional responsiveness, they are able to recognize that a problem is before them. From the perspective of Lazarus's (1966) transactional model (see Chapter 2), problem recognition involves a "yes" answer to the question, Am I in trouble? This response represents an accurate perception of the situation. However, in response to the second question, What can I do about it?, individuals feel confident that they have the resources to work out the problem. Finally, in effective problem solving it is important that individuals not act on impulse. At the stage of orienting themselves to the problem situation, they must take some time to think before acting.

Problem definition and formulation

At the second stage of problem solving, individuals must formulate the problem *concretely*. They must define the problem in terms of the actions that are demanded by the situation. Once individuals define the problem operationally—in terms of behavioral demands—and classify all aspects of the problem, they are ready to begin generating alternatives (Goldfried and Davision, 1976).

Generating alternatives

Determining the options available for solving the problem is the pivotal process in problem solving. The task at this stage is to generate as many possible solutions as one can—through something akin to a brainstorming session. This means that individuals not censor their ideas, that they entertain as many options as happen to come to mind, and that they think about potential solutions that others may suggest. At this stage individuals may either generate general strategies or come up with some specific courses of action. If they entertain a selected few general options, they may then proceed to the decision-making phase and later come back to the stage of generating alternatives to determine the most appropriate acts to follow. That is, they can move from general alternatives to selecting one alternative and back again to choosing specific tactics from general alternatives.

Decision making

If the individual comes up with only one solution for the problem, no real decision making takes place about what course of action to follow. Having only one option seriously limits the range of effective actions that can be taken. At the decision-making stage the individual must make some predictions about the probable consequences of taking one course of action versus another and then select the tactic that brings about the most desirable results. One difficulty that individuals may face at this stage is that they get caught in going back and forth, entertaining one solution, then another, and never getting to a point where they feel confident that they can take action. They vacillate and struggle with their ambivalence. For most people, the possibility of getting lost in obsessive arguments and counterarguments is slight. But some individuals get stuck at this stage and cannot go further because they cannot commit themselves to any course of action.

Verification

Miller, Galanter, and Pribram (1960) proposed a "test-operate-test-exit" (TOTE) framework for conceptualizing individuals' plans in relation to their actions. The TOTE framework suggests that one's problem solving is guided by the extent to which the consequences of one's actions are congruent or incongruent with a particular standard. For instance, after engaging in considerable mental effort, if individuals "test" the progress they have made and decide it is congruent with a standard of acceptability, then they "exit" from those activities. If they determine that they have not made sufficient progress, as measured by a match against the standard, they continue to "operate" until the standard is reached.

As Goldfried and Davison (1976) described it, one must deal with a problem situation by carrying out a chosen course of action, note the consequences of one's actions, and then match the actual outcome with the expected outcome. When the match is acceptable, the problem-solving process can be terminated. When the match is unsatisfactory, one must continue to "operate" through the latter four stages until a satisfactory match is achieved. Then the problem-solving process can be terminated.

Specific Approaches

Individual health professionals may find it useful to follow an orderly problem-solving sequence when there seems to be no way in which habitual modes of responding to stress are effective. The following discussion focuses on the five stages of problem solving and suggests some approaches to improving skills at each stage.

Orientation

It may be helpful to draw upon the rational restructuring strategies outlined in Chapter 7 and use them as guides for assessing expectations concerning one's ability to cope with various situations. This may help you to orient yourself to the fact that coping *is* possible when problem situations present themselves. Problem-solving strategies can be practiced by selecting general problems that occur in the normal course of daily events and then orienting oneself to the fact that they can be resolved with thought and restraint and patience.

Definition

Here it is helpful to think about stress-related problems as specific situations rather than in abstract terms. At this stage you should identify typical antecedent conditions (those that precede a stress-related emotion), thoughts and feelings while in the stressful situation, and the usual consequences of your actions in those situations. What leads up to the problem? What do you usually think? How do you feel? How do you act? What are the usual consequences? In this way it is possible to make a functional analysis of the problem-solving situation and define the problem in concise, concrete terms. At this point you may also specify your goals in situations of this kind.

Alternatives

During this phase you can brainstorm options to deal with the situation. After generating various ideas about *what* to do, you should then move toward a specification of *how* you are going to do it. In other words, you should move from the general to the particular. Once the most apparent response alternatives are specified, you are ready to decide on the best course of action to pursue.

Decision making

This stage involves predictions about which alternatives and courses of action are the most appropriate. Therefore, it is helpful to consider the possible consequences of following each of the likely options generated: What will probably happen if I do A? What will happen if I do B? (and so on for each alternative). It is important to remember that only gross judgments are made at this stage since it is not possible to make highly accurate predictions of outcome at this point. After weighing the costs and payoffs of each option, you should make a selection, based on the cost-benefit estimates that point toward options holding the highest payoffs and the least costs.

Verification

Once you have decided on the best course of action, you should pursue that course and then verify the effectiveness of the response. You must note the consequences of your actions and determine how satisfied you are with the outcome. If you are satisfied with the outcome, then the process is ended. If you are not satisfied with the consequences, you may need to return to phase two and proceed from a redefinition of the problem, the generation of different alternatives, or the selection of a different (but already-considered) strategy.

Summary

Problem solving is a rational, logical process of generating and selecting a variety of potentially useful courses of action in response to stressful situations. When followed systematically and carefully, problem solving can increase the probability of finding the most effective solution to a given problem. Effective problem solving is another means for enhancing one's overall effectiveness and sense of personal competency. Although everyone uses some sequence of problem-solving activities for situations that cannot be resolved through habitual responses, people may fail to respond adaptively if the essential elements of the foregoing general stages are missing.

Outline for Problem Solving

As a general outline for problem solving, the five stages described here could be placed within a structured format for sequencing activities toward problem resolution. Silverstein (1977) proposed a method for generating alternatives and choosing from among them. Some of the steps he proposed can be integrated with the aforementioned stages to provide a procedural guide for problem solving.

Identify the problem

As a necessary first step in problem solving, you should specify the nature of the problem. Write down a work-related problem that is important to resolve. As suggested earlier, define the problem as concretely as possible. In this phase you may find it useful to think in these terms: *Who* does *what*, to *whom* (if another person is involved), how, under what *circumstances*, and with what *effect*? For example, a staff nurse defined a problem she wanted to resolve as follows: "My supervisor tries to intimidate staff members." This problem definition states who is involved and something about the flow of behavior (the supervisor does something to staff members). What is unknown is the behavioral description of "intimidation" and the circumstances under which it is manifested. In addition, the consequences of this set of behaviors are unknown. Defining a problem as globally and ambiguously as this nurse has may preclude effective problem solving. There is no specific target behavior or action, no clear consequences to be changed, and no circumstances or context in which to focus problem solving.

In this example the nurse is implying that the supervisor in some way tries to force staff members to comply with the supervisor's desires or expectations either by punishing or by holding some threat over them. The supervisor probably displays such behavior in certain situations more than in others. A concrete problem definition would require the nurse to identify the problem in terms such as these:

During our *staff meetings* (circumstances), my supervisor (problem source) deters all of us from expressing our real thoughts and feelings about work (consequences) by responding sarcastically to our complaints or by stating, "That's the way things are, and people ought to be thankful they have a job these days."

This concrete description makes it clear that it is the supervisor's verbal responses to staff during staff meetings that are in need of change.

Brainstorm

Once the problem is defined concretely or operationally, the next step is to brainstorm and write down as many possible solutions as you can think of. It may be useful to place each alternative in a distinct category associated with its respective probability of occurrence. For example, categories could be set up in the following way:

MOST PROBABLE

In the most probable category you could write your prediction of what probably will happen. For the example of supervisory intimidation, a most probable course for the nurse might be, "We'll all continue sitting there, keeping our thoughts and feelings to ourselves, without calling her attention to what we see her doing to us in staff meetings."

MOST PREFERRED

In the most preferred category you could write out the best possible outcome you can imagine. For instance, the nurse might let her mind go and write, "Either she'll be fired and we'll get a more understanding supervisor, or she'll come in one day and be a totally different person—encouraging us, rewarding us for speaking our piece, and then following up with some positive actions to change things."

MODERATE PROBABILITY

As a moderate probability you might specify an alternative that has an equal chance of success or failure. The nurse might see the following as an option with a 50-50 chance of success: "I'll confront the supervisor during the staff meeting, and maybe others will support me."

LOW PROBABILITY

Under the category of low probability you could list some courses of action that probably would not work, perhaps because they have been tried before and failed. For example, the nurse might see confrontation as having a low probability because she has tried to point things out to the supervisor in the past, but no one backed her up during the staff meeting.

LEAST PREFERRED

The worst possible outcome could be listed here as least preferred. For instance, the nurse might indicate, "I'll confront my supervisor during the staff meeting, and she will become angry with me and either retaliate immediately or she'll keep watching me, harassing me, and putting on more pressure." For this nurse the least preferred outcome may be the same as the most probable one: "We'll all continue sitting there, keeping our thoughts and feelings to ourselves, and nothing will change."

Decide

After listing all potential solutions, you must weigh the positive and negative consequences of each. Important questions need to be answered at this point: Is it worth the risk? What will happen if I don't do anything? Will I lose my job? Is it all right to lose my job, if that is a possible outcome? Will I eventually have to leave anyway, if the problem becomes absolutely intolerable?

At this stage a potential barrier to effective problem solving is to become carried away with what-if thinking. Consider the consequences, but avoid getting trapped into inaction because of obsessive wondering about potential outcomes. An important commitment at this stage is to make a firm decision. You must *decide to decide.*

Once you have made your decision, carry out the chosen alternative within a definite period of time. Do not keep putting off your intervention. All too often problem solving stalls at this point, as evidenced by the often-heart comment, "I decided a long time ago that one of these days I'm going to . . ." But "one of these days" does not come. (For a summary of the problem-solving format described here, see the following box.)

Problem-Solving Guide

IDENTIFY THE PROBLEM

   A. Problem Source? What Happens?

   B. Who Is Affected? How?

   C. What Circumstances?

   D. Consequences?

BRAINSTORM

   A. Most Probable

   B. Most Preferred

   C. Moderate Probability

Problem-Solving Guide, continued

BRAINSTORM (continued)

   D. Low Probability

   E. Least Preferred

DECIDE

  Positive Consequences

  Negative Consequences

  Positive Consequences (Benefits) vs. Negative Consequences (Costs)

  Chosen Alternative

MUTUAL HELPING

One source of stress for health professionals may be the behavior of their colleagues in the work environment. Sometimes the behavior of one professional becomes intertwined with that of another professional in a mutually self-defeating spiral. In such cases one person may not be able to change unless the other one does. Neither person is able to effect personal changes because neither one is acting toward the other in ways that permit those changes. For example, if one staff member sees another staff member as obnoxious, the first person may act in ways that tend to elicit obnoxious behavior from the second person. Or one staff member may be critical of another staff member, who, in turn, responds with criticism of the first person. In both examples the individuals involved are acting in nonrewarding ways toward each other. They are failing to reinforce the kinds of behaviors they want to see from the other person. Their tendencies are to respond in kind toward the other, "an eye for an eye." The more infrequent the desired behaviors, the more the persons involved respond out of frustration and antagonism.

One way out of this stressful downward spiral is for the parties involved to identify the behaviors they would like to see the other display. In other words, they reach an agreement about what to do and what not to do in relation to each other. This amounts to making a contract—a mutual agreement to help each other out of a stressful relationship. The key is for each person to identify what he wants so that each one increases his chances of receiving the behavioral reinforcements he wants from the other. An agreement of this kind makes it possible for each person to receive something of value from the other, through reciprocal rewards.

PROFESSIONAL HELP

Mental health workers are involved in a "catch-22" situation because of the unrealistic expectations of persons outside the helping professions. One set of assumptions holds that these professionals are supposed to be immune from the kinds of problems that affect everyone else. A set of contradictory assumptions holds that these professionals are predisposed to emotional difficulties by virtue of presumed inadequacies and vulnerabilities that guided them into their profession in the first place. Of course, the logic behind these expectations is as irrational as that which holds that health care professionals should be immune from physical illnesses or, on the other hand, prone to them by virtue of the physical anomalies and systemic vulnerabilities underlying their entry into health care practice. The same kind of logic has been attached to the health professional's response to stress. The "catch-22" for health professionals is that (1) because they come into contact with so much suffering, they should not be affected by it; and (2) if they are not affected by the suffering they see, they are cold and uncaring and something is wrong with them. There are, indeed, great and unrealistic expectations associated with the health professional's role. And sometimes health professionals accept those expectations. To the extent that they take on such unrealistic expectations, the professionals' view of themselves as paragons of strength may prevent them from seeking help in resolving problems that they have failed to work through by themselves. In fact, some health professionals are the last ones to seek help for themselves.

Most health professionals have a remarkable ability to cope with the stresses and anxieties of their work. Being essentially no different from other human beings, however, there are times when they do need the help of other people to think things through and find solutions to problems. In cases of burnout, some dimensions of the problem may cause so much psychological distress and take on such complexity that the help of a professional therapist is needed. Health professionals need to view this form of assistance as yet another coping option.

Getting professional help for problems related to burnout does not mean that the health professional turns over those problems to a trained therapist. The therapist is not like a watchmaker who takes a broken timepiece, repairs its damaged mechanisms, and then returns it in perfect working condition. Counseling and psychotherapy do not work that way. Counselors and therapists do not solve your problems for you. They help *you* to find effective and appropriate solutions. Their goal is to help you regain the balance and control that is missing in your life. Professional help offers no escape from the measure of personal responsibility that is rightly yours.

Believing that counseling and psychotherapy will enable you to assign responsibility for solving your problems to someone else is the opposite extreme of believing that you are capable of solving your problems entirely on your own. For some people burnout may impose demands that exceed their personal resources. No matter how hard they try, they are not able to stand alone in solving the problems. The tragedy for some of these persons is their perception that there is nothing they can do about the problems that are causing them so much distress. Seeking professional help as an option for coping with stress-related problems is a coping effort in itself. It is a direct-action mode of coping in some instances and a palliative or indirect mode of coping in other cases. It is hardly a sign of weakness for the health professional to seek professional help. In some cases it may be a sign of foolishness to claim self-sufficiency in dealing with chronic stress. Knowing when and how to get professional help is as much a part of managing burnout as changing peer relationships to build a support system at work.

RATIONAL RELABELING

Given that one's perceptions and appraisals of situations are principal determinants of one's experience of stress, it follows that irrational beliefs upon which appraisals are made may significantly impair the accuracy of those judgments and, consequently, influence an increase or decrease in the experience of stress. Furthermore, it is clear that various distressing emotions and behaviors are mediated by unrealistic expectations of oneself and others. Therefore, managing burnout may require the individual to restructure irrational beliefs and expectations in order to break through habitual maladaptive ways of thinking and of perceiving the world.

According to Ellis (1962), many people learn a set of ideas or attitudes that are irrational. These ideas or attitudes are irrational because they are not likely to be supported by objective information.

Commonly held irrational beliefs, according to Ellis, include the following 11 statements:

1. It is a necessity for an adult person to be loved or approved by virtually every significant other in the adult's community.

2. One should be thoroughly competent, adequate, and achieving in all possible respects if one is to consider oneself worthwhile.

3. Certain people are bad, wicked, or villainous and they should be severely blamed or punished for their villiany.

4. It is awful and catastrophic when things are not the way one would like or expect them to be.

5. Human unhappiness is externally caused and people have little or no ability to control their unhappiness.

6. If something is or may be dangerous or fearsome, one should be terribly concerned about it and dwell on possibilities of its occurrence.

7. It is easier to avoid than to face certain life difficulties and responsibilities.

8. One should be dependent on others and one needs someone stronger than oneself on whom to rely.

9. One's past history is an all-important determinant of one's present behavior and because something once strongly affected one's life, it should indefinitely have a similar effect.

10. One should become quite upset over other people's problems and disturbances.

11. There is invariably a right, precise, and perfect solution to human problems and it is catastrophic if this correct solution is not found.

From Ellis's perspective, the extent to which an individual labels situations in accordance with one or more of these irrational beliefs will significantly affect emotions and maladaptive behavior. It must be noted that Ellis does not assume that people consciously repeat these statements to themselves while in those situations. Rather it is assumed that these irrational beliefs have been internalized to the point of being habitual criteria against which many situations are evaluated automatically and without conscious deliberation. Because people often do not tell themselves anything while in stressful situations, it may not become apparent until after the situation has passed that they are reacting *as if* they supported unrealistic beliefs about the situation that occurred. In addition, individuals may approach stressful situations *as if* they were telling themselves that it would be catastrophic if they did not act appropriately.

What people tell themselves about a situation or about their feelings or behavior may distort their appraisals and contribute to an increase in the stress they experience. What follows are samples of irrational self-statements that health professionals use in various situations. These statements represent sources of self-induced stress, which, *if restructured*, could effect a reduction in the signs of burnout.

Examples of Irrational Beliefs

The following irrational beliefs are examples of the kinds of misguided assumptions that correspond to Ellis's 11 irrational statements. Each example is numbered (1 to 11) to indicate that correspondence.

1. The health professional must be appreciated and approved of by virtually every patient receiving direct care.

2. Health professionals must be thoroughly competent and effect positive changes in every patient served, or else they are not effective providers.

3. Health professionals who do not seem to care what happens to their patients are bad and wicked, and they should be blamed and punished for their badness.

4. It is catastrophic whenever anything does not work out as planned in the health care environment.

5. The unhappiness and distress associated with burnout are caused by factors that health professionals have no control over, and there is nothing they can do to change their level of distress.

6. Patient care is a fearsome responsibility, and the health professional should be terribly concerned about it and dwell on it at all times.

7. It is easier to avoid the sources of stress in the health care environment than it is to face the challenges of changing them.

8. It is necessary to always rely on others who are more skilled and knowledgeable and not try to make independent decisions at any time.

9. Because of my past mistakes and blunders on the job, I will never feel or be perceived by others as competent and effective.

10. Health professionals should be upset when they encounter human suffering and distress.

11. For the management of stress-related work problems, there is invariably a right, precise, and perfect solution, and it is catastrophic if this solution is not found.

It is possible to categorize many of the thoughts that health professionals have about their professions, their jobs, and themselves that contribute to the problem of burnout. Forney, Wallace-Schutzman, and Wigger (1982), for example, found that it was possible to distinguish between career development professionals whose thinking prevented them from burning out and those whose thinking contributed to the problem. Furthermore, they reported that those individuals who subscribed to the greatest number of irrational beliefs tended to be the ones who were burning out. If it is true that individuals have a greater likelihood of experiencing burnout by unthinkingly accepting certain illogical premises, then it should be possible to affect the course of burnout by persuading individuals to short-circuit burnout by relabeling their thoughts. However, the first step toward rational restructuring is to recognize that certain premises underlying cognitive appraisals are illogical premises from which irrational conclusions are drawn. For the purpose of this discussion, it is this first step that is significant. It may be helpful to take a few moments and think about a stressful experience you have recently encountered. Give some thought to how you appraised that situation at the time and how you appraise it now. Do you think that part of your emotional response at the time could have been influenced by some implicit assumptions you hold about the significance of such situations?

It may also be useful to consider the reasonableness of the expectations you have of yourself in your professional role. A great deal of self-induced stress is generated by people who place unrealistic and unreasonably high expectations on themselves. The criteria by which they judge themselves are not only rigid, but also sometimes irrational. These criteria may have a connection to one or more of the beliefs outlined by Ellis.

From personal experience I can attest to the values of rethinking and altering the premises of certain beliefs. Several years ago I thought it was imperative that I arrive at the airport at least an hour and a half to two hours before my flight was to depart. After all, I thought, it would be disastrous if I were to miss a flight. So whenever I was to fly, I hurried around and put tremendous pressure on myself to get to the airport with plenty of time to spare. Not until I checked my baggage could I begin to relax. Then one day while I was waiting two hours for a departing flight, a thought occurred to me: "This is stupid! Why am I sitting here waiting? So what if I missed my plane? What is the worst thing that could happen?" I asked myself if I would be slain for such a villanous deed, such an irresponsible act.

Would someone burn my house down? Would I lose my job? Of course not. The answer was "no" in all cases. So, I thought, what would I do if I missed a flight? Clearly, *I would get another flight*! I am not sure that I have completely handled this situation since my current attitude toward flying is such that I leave virtually no time to sit around waiting. But, at the same time, I do not worry about it either! Sure, I want to be on time for my departures, but if I am not, then I will just get another flight.

There is no escaping the fact of stress in health care. In fact, some authorities maintain that burnout is an unavoidable problem in human services and health care practice. However, both stress and burnout can be managed by any individual who has the personal and environmental resources to begin taking control over those stress factors that are changeable. There are no universal solutions, no formula approaches to managing stress or burnout. Solutions must ultimately come from individual human beings who are closer to their own circumstances than anyone else is. Yet solutions must also come from persons in health care organizations who are in positions to manage the stressors to which others are exposed. Management of stress and burnout are individual and organizational responsibilities. With this fact in mind, Edelwich and Brodsky (1980) commented, "One cannot smooth out the surf, but one can ride the waves—*if one sees them coming*" (p. 39; italics added).

SUMMARY

The first step toward managing the problem of burnout is to recognize its presence among health care providers. The foregoing discussion focuses on some possible means for developing an increased awareness of job burnout, its causes, and additional ways of controlling its effects. An *assessment of work stress* is outlined as a useful approach for increasing awareness of the signs, symptoms, and antecedents of the stresses associated with health care delivery. The chapter includes an assessment of manageable and unmanageable *job stressors* and presents a guided format to stimulate a process of identifying controllable and uncontrollable stressors. Since the management of stress and burnout involves a lot of problem solving, five stages of the *problem-solving process* are outlined. There are also some general procedural guides for enhancing one's effectiveness in solving problems contributing to stress and burnout. *Professional help* is one stress management option that may be of considerable value in helping individuals find more effective ways of handling the stresses of their jobs and their lives. *Rational relabeling* is another useful approach for restructuring irrational beliefs and expectations that may be imposing unnecessary stress on individuals as they attempt to meet the demands of their professional roles.

REFERENCES

Bloom, B.S., & Broder, L.J. *Problem solving processes of college students.* Chicago: University of Chicago Press, 1950.

Edelwich, U., & Brodsky, A. *Burnout: Stages of disillusionment in the helping professions.* New York: Human Sciences Press, 1980.

Ellis, A. *Reason and emotion in psychotherapy.* New York: Lyle Stuart, 1962.

Forney, D.S., Wallace-Schutzman, N., & Wiggers, T.T. Burnout among career development professionals: Preliminary findings and implications. *Personnel and Guidance Journal,* 1982, *60*(7), 435–439.

Goldfried, M.R., & Davison, G.C. *Clinical behavior therapy.* New York: Holt, Rinehart, & Winston, 1976.

Lazarus, R.S. *Psychological stress and the coping process.* New York: McGraw-Hill, 1966.

Miller, G.A., Galanter, E., & Pribram, K.H. *Plans and the structure of behavior.* New York: Holt, Rinehart, & Winston, 1960.

Rotter, J.B. Generalized expectancies for internal versus external control of reinforcement. *Psychological Monographs,* 1966, *80*(1, Whole No. 609).

Silverstein, L.M. *Consider the alternative.* Minneapolis: CompCare Publications, 1977.

INDEX

A

Absenteeism, burnout and, 77

Accountability overload, burnout and, 91

Achievement, orientation toward, in compulsive individual, 106–107

Action encouragements as direct-action coping strategy, 139

Activity level in burnout, 69–70

Adaptation energy in stress response, 25–26

Administrative approaches to burnout, 147–172

  control of rewards in, 154–164; *see also* Reinforcement(s); Rewards

  crisis intervention in, 150–154; *see also* Crisis intervention

  interpersonal conflict resolution in, 164–169; *see also* Interpersonal conflict

  open-door policy in, 149–154

  reactive support in, 149–154

  support systems in, 169–172

Adrenal cortex in stress response, 22

Adrenal corticoids in stress response, 22

Adrenal medulla in stress response, 23–25

Adrenalin, secretion of, emergency, in response to stress, 20, 23

Adrenocorticotrophic hormone (ACTH) in stress response, 22

Advice, offering of, in crisis intervention, 154

Advocacy in crisis intervention, 152

Alarm in general adaptation syndrome, 21

Alcohol, abuse of

  in burnout, 13, 75–76

  as palliative coping strategy, 128–129

Altruistic values, burnout and, 11

Anger, open expression of, in burnout, 74

Anticipatory socialization program of Kramer, 190

  conflict resolution in, 193

  in-service, 193–194

  outrage in, 192

  parts of, 191–193

  skill and mastery of routine in, 191–192

  social integration in, 192

Anxiety

  in burnout, 61–63

  problem solving and, 52–53

Apathy

  in burnout, 59–60

  detachment and, 60

  empathy and, 60

Appraisal, cognitive, in transactional model of psychological stress,

H

I